PERUVIAN TRADITIONS

OXFORD

PERUVIAN TRADITIONS

By
RICARDO PALMA

Translated from the Spanish by
HELEN LANE

EDITED WITH AN INTRODUCTION AND CHRONOLOGY BY
CHRISTOPHER CONWAY

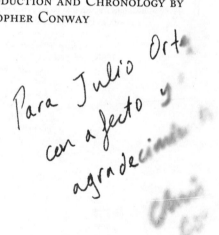

*Para Julio Orta
con afecto y
agradecimiento*

OXFORD
UNIVERSITY PRESS
2004

OXFORD
UNIVERSITY PRESS

Oxford   New York

Auckland   Bangkok   Buenos Aires   Cape Town   Chennai
Dar es Salaam   Delhi   Hong Kong   Istanbul   Karachi   Kolkata
Kuala Lumpur   Madrid   Melbourne   Mexico City   Mumbai   Nairobi
São Paulo   Shanghai   Taipei   Tokyo   Toronto

Copyright © 2004 by Oxford University Press, Inc.

Published by Oxford University Press, Inc.
198 Madison Avenue, New York, New York 10016

www.oup.com

Oxford is a registered trademark of Oxford University Press

Library of Congress Cataloging-in-Publication Data
Palma, Ricardo, 1833–1919.
[Tradiciones peruanas. English]
Peruvian traditions / by Ricardo Palma ; translated from the Spanish by Helen Lane;
edited with an introduction and chronology by Christopher Conway.
p.   cm.
Includes bibliographical references.
ISBN 0-19-515908-X ISBN 0-19-515909-8 (pbk.)
1. Legends—Peru.
2. Peru—History.
I. Lane, Helen R.
II. Conway, Christopher.
III. Title.
F3409.P173213   2004
398.2'0985—dc21   2003050876

1 3 5 7 9 8 6 4 2

Printed in the United States of America
on acid-free paper

Contents

Series Editor's
General Introduction

The Library of Latin America series makes available in translation major nineteenth-century authors whose work has been neglected in the English-speaking world. The titles for the translation from the Spanish and Portuguese were suggested by an editorial committee that included Jean Franco (general editor responsible for works in Spanish), Richard Graham (series editor responsible for works in Portuguese), Tulio Halperín Donghi (at the University of California, Berkeley), Iván Jaksić (at the University of Notre Dame), Naomi Lindstrom (at the University of Texas at Austin), Francine Masiello (at the University of California, Berkeley), and Eduardo Lozano of the Library at the University of Pittsburgh. The late Antonio Cornejo Polar of the University of California, Berkeley, was also one of the founding members of the committee. The translations have been funded thanks to the generosity of the Lampadia Foundation and the Andrew W. Mellon Foundation.

During the period of national formation between 1810 and into the early years of the twentieth century, the new nations of Latin America fashioned their identities, drew up constitutions, engaged in bitter struggles over territory, and debated questions of education, government, ethnicity, and culture. This was a unique period unlike the process of nation formation in Europe and one that should be more familiar than it is to students of comparative politics, history, and literature.

The image of the nation was envisioned by the lettered classes—a minority in countries in which indigenous, mestizo, black, or mulatto peasants and slaves predominated—although there were also alternative nationalisms at the grassroots level. The cultural elite were well educated in European thought and letters, but as statesman, journalists, poets, and academics, they confronted the problem of the racial and linguistic heterogeneity of the continent and the difficulties of integrating the population into a modern nation-state. Some of the writers whose works will be translated in the Library of Latin America series played leading roles in politics. Fray Servando Teresa de Mier, a friar who translated Rousseau's *The Social Contract* and was one of the most colorful characters of the independence period, was faced with imprisonment and expulsion from Mexico for his heterodox beliefs; on his return, after independence, he was elected to the congress. Domingo Faustino Sarmiento, exiled from his native Argentina under the dictatorship of Rosas, wrote *Facundo: Civilización y barbarie*, a stinging denunciation of that government. He returned after Rosas's overthrow and was elected president in 1868. Andrés Bello was born in Venezuela, lived in London where he published poetry during the independence period, settled in Chile where he founded the university, wrote his grammar of the Spanish language, and drew up the country's legal code.

These post-independence intelligentsia were not simply dreaming castles in the air, but vitally contributed to the founding of nations and the shaping of culture. The advantage of hindsight may make us aware of problems they themselves did not foresee, but this should not affect our assessment of their truly astonishing energies and achievements. Although there is a recent translation of Sarmiento's celebrated *Facundo*, there is no translation of his memoirs, *Recuerdos de provincia*. The predominance of memoirs in the Library of Latin America Series is no accident—many of these offer entertaining insights into a vast and complex continent.

Nor have we neglected the novel. The series includes new translations of the outstanding Brazilian writer Machado de Assis's work, including *Dom Casmurro* and *The Posthumous Memoirs of Brás Cubas*. There is no reason why other novels and writers who are not so well known outside Latin America—the Peruvian novelist Clorinda Matto de Turner's *Aves sin nido*, Nataniel Aguirre's *Juan de la Rosa*, José de Alencar's *Iracema*, Juana Manuela Gorriti's short stories—should not be read with as much interest as the political novels of Anthony Trollope.

A series on nineteenth-century Latin America cannot, however, be limited to literary genres such as the novel, the poem, and the short story. The literature of independent Latin America was eclectic and strongly influenced by the periodical press newly liberated from scrutiny by colonial authorities and the Inquisition. Newspapers were miscellanies of fiction, essays, poems, and translations from all manner of European writing. The novels written on the eve of Mexican Independence by José Joaquín Fernández de Lizardi, included disquisitions on secular education and law, and denunciations of the evils of gaming and idleness. Other works, such as a well-known poem by Andrés Bello, "Ode to Tropical Agriculture," and novels such as *Amalia* by José Marmol and the Bolivian Nataniel Aguirre's *Juan de la Rosa*, were openly partisan. By the end of the century, sophisticated scholars were beginning to address the history of their countries, as did João Capistrano de Abreu in his *Capítulos história colonial*.

It is often in memoirs such as those by Fray Servando Teresa de Mier or Sarmiento that we find the descriptions of everyday life that in Europe were incorporated into the realist novel. Latin American literature at this time was seen largely as a pedagogical tool, a "light" alternative to speeches, sermons, and philosophical tracts—though, in fact, especially in the early part of the century, even the readership for novels was quite small because of the high rate of illiteracy. Nevertheless the vigorous orally transmitted culture of the gaucho and the urban underclasses became the linguistic repertoire of some of the most interesting nineteenth-century writers—most notably José Hernández, author of the "gauchesque" poem "Martin Fierro," which enjoyed an unparalleled popularity. But for many writers the task was not to appropriate popular language but to civilize, and their literary works were strongly influenced by the high style of political oratory.

The editorial committee has not attempted to limit its selection to the better-known writers such as Machado de Assis; it has also selected many works that have never appeared in translation or writers whose works have not been translated recently. The series now makes these works available to the English-speaking public.

Because of the preferences of funding organizations, the series initially focuses on writing from Brazil, the Southern Cone, the Andean region, and Mexico. Each of our editions will have an introduction that places the work in its appropriate context and includes explanatory notes.

We owe special thanks to the late Robert Glynn of the Lampadia Foundation, whose initiative gave the project a jump-start, and to Richard Ekman and his successors at the Andrew W. Mellon Foundation, which also generously supported the project. We also thank the Rockefeller Foundation for funding the 1996 symposium, "Culture and Nation in Iberoamerica," organized by the editorial board of the Library of Latin America. The support of Edward Barry of Oxford University Press was crucial in the founding years of the project, as has been the advice and help of Ellen Chodosh and Elda Rotor of Oxford University Press. The John Carter Brown Library at Brown University in Providence, Rhode Island, has been serving since 1998 as the grant administrator of the project.

—Jean Franco
Richard Graham

Translator's Note

Translating Ricardo Palma's *Peruvian Traditions* has been a challenging experience. There is the usual problem of being faithful to a nineteenth-century style, and other hurdles as well. I was duly forewarned of them by the Spanish Larousse encyclopedia, which alerted me to the "archaisms, Peruvianisms, and proverbs" that are a hallmark of Palma's style, and by a book by Palma titled *Two Thousand Seven Hundred Expressions Missing in the Dictionary* (1906).

Confronted by these rather daunting obstacles as I began my translation, I worked with my editor Christopher Conway to comb through specialized dictionaries and other reference books for answers to lexical mysteries that I had been unable to solve unaided. Despite many successes, there were still problematic words and phrases. I acknowledge with gratitude the indispensable contributions to this volume by Professors Julio Ortega, José Amor y Vázquez and Luis Millones Figueroa, whose detailed input resolved my remaining doubts. Thanks are also due to Jerelyn Johnson, for helping prepare the originals for translation.

—Helen Lane

Chronology of Ricardo Palma

1833   Birth of Ricardo Palma.

1849   Palma enters the Convictorio de San Carlos, Lima's most important school.

1851–1852   Palma writes "Consolation" and stages three of his plays: *Rodil, La hermana del verdugo,* and *La muerte o la libertad.*

1853–1855   Publication of patriotic miscellany, *Corona patriótica* (1853), early traditions, and a collection of poetry, *Poesías* (1855). Palma on active duty in the Peruvian navy.

1858   Editor of the newspaper *El Liberal* (1858).

1860   Participates in failed coup against President Castilla.

1861–1863   Exile in Chile, where he publishes traditions in the *Revista del Pacífico* and the *Revista de Sudamérica.* Upon his return to Peru, Palma publishes his *Anales de la Inquisición de Lima* (1863), a precursor to his *Peruvian Traditions.*

1864   Travels in Europe.

1865–1866   Returns to Peru and supports the overthrow of President Pezet because of his conciliatory approach toward Spain over the Chincha Island crisis. Palma at the Battle of Callao, where the Spanish fleet is defeated by Peruvian forces.

1868   Personal secretary of President Balta and senator for the state of Loreto.

1872   Death of Balta and rise of the *Civilistas* under President Manuel Pardo. Palma retires from political life. The first volume of the *Peruvian Traditions* appears, the "first series."

1874–1880   More volumes of the *Peruvian Traditions,* series two (1874), three (1875), and four (1877). Palma marries Cristina San Román (1876). Publication of the controversial study *Monteagudo y Sánchez Carrión* (1877); because of the criticism over this monograph, he pledges not to write about politics again.

1880–1883   The War of the Pacific. Chilean occupation of Lima. Palma's home and personal library are destroyed, and the National Library in Lima is ransacked. Palma protests and is jailed briefly by Chilean authorities.

1883–1884   The *Peruvian Traditions,* sixth series (1883). Palma accepts the post of Director of the National Library and rebuilds its collection.

1886–1887   Translates Heinrich Heine from the French (1886) and publishes memoir *La bohemia de mi tiempo* (1887).

1888   Manuel González Prada gives a speech at the Politeama Theatre in which he criticizes the genre of the tradition.

1889–1892   *Ropa vieja* (1889) and *Ropa apolillada* (1891) published (later rechristened as series seven and eight of the *Peruvian Traditions,* respectively). Palma travels to Spain and urges the Royal Academy to accept Latin American regionalisms into its dictionary.

1893–1894   The first Spanish edition of the *Peruvian Traditions* (three volumes) is a resounding success.

1896   Publication of *Neologismos y americanismos,* reflecting Palma's continuing interest in reforming the dictionary of the Royal Academy of Spain.

1899–1910   Publication of *Tradiciones y artículos históricos* (1899, later series nine of the *Traditions*) and *Mis últimas tradiciones peruanas y Cachivachería* (1906) and *Apéndice a mis últimas tradiciones peruanas* (1910), both of which contain Palma's final traditions.

1912   Palma resigns from the National Library. Manuel González Prada is named its new director.

1919   Death of Ricardo Palma.

Introduction

In January of 1881 the Chilean army occupied Lima after a string of naval and land victories over Peru's poor defenses. To the horror of its inhabitants, Chilean regulars vandalized parts of the city, cutting down trees, destroying monuments and fountains, and pillaging all valuables from the medical school, including the wooden benches in the lecture halls. Worst of all, the National Library was taken over by occupying forces and transformed into an army barracks. The library held some 50,000 books and 8,000 rarities, including colonial accounts of the *Autos de Fé* that had taken place in Lima, an edition of Plato dated 1491, and the Mozarab Missal of Toledo of 1500.[1] Almost the entire contents of the library, including portraits of historical personages such as Pizarro and the Spanish Viceroys, were destroyed or dispersed by Chilean soldiers, who shipped some valuables to Chile and sold many of the books to innkeepers in Lima for use as wrapping paper.

The assistant director of the library was Ricardo Palma, a celebrated man of letters who had retired from political life in 1872 to pursue research and writing. When Chilean forces advanced on Lima, they set fire to his house, destroying his personal library and several unpublished manuscripts. Displaced with his wife and children in Lima, Palma deplored the destruction of the National Library and drafted a letter of protest for the director of the library, Manuel de Odriozola, to sign. "To seize upon the libraries, archives, cabinets of physical and anatomic objects, works of art, scientific apparatus and instruments, and all that is necessary for intellectual progress," he wrote, "is to invest war with a barbarous character foreign to the lights of the age, to the usages of honorable belligerents, and to the universally recognized principles of right."[2] When the protest was sent to diplomatic representatives of the United States, and smuggled out to Ayacucho, where the Peruvian government-in-exile published it, the Chileans briefly imprisoned Palma and Odriozola for undermining their authority.

After the signing of the Treaty of Ancón in 1883, which ended the Chilean occupation of Peru, a minister in the Peruvian administration of President Miguel Iglesias summoned Palma and requested that he become director of the National Library and to supervise its reconstruction. Flabbergasted by the enormity of what was being proposed, and the paucity of resources at his disposal, Palma responded: "Do you propose that I become a mendicant librarian?" "That's right," replied the minister, "ask for alms for the good of your homeland."[3] Palma agreed and began a letter-writing campaign imploring friends, acquaintances, and public institutions around the world to help rebuild the library. Numerous governments and cultural institutions, commercial firms, and distinguished writers agreed to assist Palma by donating books. Meanwhile, the "mendicant librarian" and his assistants scoured Lima and recovered thousands of books from the original collection. Less than a year after beginning his task with a tenth of the original contents of the library intact, Palma reopened the library on July, 28 1884, with a catalog that was almost 30,000 strong.

The restoration and growth of the National Library under Palma's tenure, which lasted until 1912, was a monumental achievement, but also one full of resonance within the arc of his career as one of the most popular writers of his time on the Latin American continent. For Palma, the cultural terrain of his unstable country was not dissimilar to the gutted library of Lima: the manifold stories of the republic's past, as woven into custom, tall tales, and popular speech, needed to be preserved for posterity. Beginning at mid-century, before the disastrous war with Chile, Palma experimented with a new way of combining history and fiction: the tradition. What began as a romantic exercise in historical fiction, full of the emotional and expressive cliches of that style, evolved into a polished combination of historical fact and invention expressed in the vernacular speech of the inhabitants of Lima.[4] In the process, Palma succeeded in capturing the comic sensibility of the city's *criollo*, whose penchant for irony and satire is well known in Peruvian culture and literary history.[5] Unlike a significant segment of the nationalist intelligentsia of the continent, which enshrined the civilizing authority of the printed word over orality in the name of "progress," Palma recovered the humorous inventiveness of popular speech for building and maintaining a national historical memory. His traditions were published in the principal newspapers of Latin America, in Peruvian and Spanish editions, and translated in the North American and British press.[6] Readers delighted in his irreverent approach to portraying characters and events from Peru's colonial past, as in the case of a fifteenth-century Spanish captain whose embraces could kill, the rivalry between a bell ringer and a viceroy in the seventeenth century, and the prodigious miracles of a saint who could bring a dog, cat, and mouse to eat from the same plate. "To save literary jewels and historical events from forgetfulness" Palma wrote about his work as a *tradicionista* (author of traditions), "is to perform a useful service to the cause of America."[7] Thus, the epistolary crusade to restore the National Library was a task well suited to Palma, whose traditions were predicated on an all-consuming passion for old manuscripts and books, and on the repositories of historical memory that existed in popular culture. By the end of the century, thanks to Palma's popularity, the tradition spread across the continent in a variety of forms, as imitators revisited oral traditions and old manuscripts for their own historical fictions.[8]

Ricardo Palma and Nineteenth-Century Peru

The milieu of Ricardo Palma's childhood and adolescence prepared him well for the role of chronicler of the past. The son of a local merchant of Lima, Palma was born on February 7, 1833, and named Manuel Palma (he began using Ricardo at age 15). At the time, Lima was a city more colonial than republican in appearance and custom; everywhere the young Palma turned, he was faced with buildings, characters, and stories that echoed the republic's recent colonial past. "Nothing changed in my homeland" Palma wrote about the first half of the nineteenth century, "except the form of address: 'his excellency *señor* viceroy' was substituted with 'his excellency *señor* president."[9] In the Lima of his childhood, Palma came into contact with notable characters of the City of Kings[10] during its *ancien regime*: Pancho Sales, an old black basket-weaver who had once been an executioner employed by viceroys, and who continued to uncover his head when he spoke of "our master the king"; María Abascal, a beautiful woman named after Viceroy Abascal (and rumored to have been his illegitimate daughter) who became the mistress of the patriot hero Bernardo Monteagudo during the Wars of Independence; and Juanita Breña, also known as Juana la Marimacho, a butcher in the central plaza who had once been one of the viceregal capital's most famous bullfighters.[11] Moreover, Palma's fond memories of the stories he heard in his childhood would shape the colloquial intonations of the traditions he wrote later in life. In several of his writings, he refers to elderly ladies (sometimes Aunt Catita, other times Granny) who entertained him and other neighborhood children with "a thousand and one rumors, stories, histories, legends, and miracles, in which the viceroyalty, religion, and superstition combined into the most captivating image of the past that a child could have."[12]

Palma once wrote that in his adolescence he was a militant romantic, "one of those poets who would light his cigarette with a star from the night sky."[13] His ubiquity in bohemian, romantic circles capped his rise from a modest home and small schools to the city's most important educational institution. It also paralleled the strengthening of the Peruvian state at midcentury under General Ramón Castilla (president 1844–1851 and 1854–1862), whose rise to power coincided with the beginning of a large influx of money into state coffers through the guano trade. During Castilla's first term in office, the 16-year-old Palma ascended to center stage in the social and cultural life of Lima by entering the Convictorio de San Carlos, the city's most prestigious educational institution. Founded in the eighteenth century and ruled by European models of instruction, the patrician school was often at the center of the city's political life: The president and his magistrates would attend and participate in the school's examinations, and invite distinguished students to the presidential palace and other public functions.[14] In this privileged setting, Palma made friendships and alliances that would last a lifetime, and that partially explain some of his later political activities.

Between 1848 and 1860, Palma and his friends gathered to discuss literature, published their writing in newspapers, and staged their extravagant plays on exotic and Peruvian themes. One of their defining characteristics was their irreverence and satirical bent, which was made manifest in their witty critiques of politicians and literary figures. A popular sonnet of the day that Palma cites as a representative example of their biting discourse ends this way: "If a Brutus saved Rome, why in hell can't so many brutes save this country?"[15] In this period, Palma published his first poems in the newspaper *El Comercio,* founded a satirical newspaper with his friends, authored three plays that he later disowned (*La Hermana del Verdugo, La Muerte o la Libertad,* and *Rodil*), and wrote a romantic story, "Consolation," that he later chose to include in his last collection of traditions. In 1853, the 20-year-old Palma joined the navy, in which he served for six years, all the while remaining current with Lima's literary scene and publishing poetry and prose. The Castilla regime had become unsteady and Palma was about to enter into the center of revolutionary and political currents that would shape his life for over a decade and ultimately lead to a deep disenchantment with politics. "Where two Peruvians come together there is civil war," he once wrote to his Mexican friend Vicente Riva Palacio, "and where three or more gather there is anarchy."[16]

Since Palma found himself deeply involved in the political life of his country between 1860 and 1872, a brief introduction to Peruvian history is in order. Like other Latin American nations in the nineteenth century, Peru began its republican life under the damaging influence of economic depression and a succession of military caudillos and civil wars. In the decades that followed independence, Peru was less a nation than a aggregate of regional interests centered around the power of the *estancieros* (the owners of large landed estates) and their military protectors, the caudillos, who in turn were networked under the authority of a caudillo president.[17] The absence of a ruling class capable of taking the reins of power after independence resulted in the preeminence of the military as arbiter of the presidency and national politics until the last quarter of the nineteenth century. Between the end of Simón Bolívar's dictatorship in 1825 and when General Ramón Castilla came to power in 1845, Peru endured over a dozen different shifts in presidential control, most of them violent, and an occupation by Bolivia that was finally ended with the military intervention of Chile.

The pacification imposed by General Ramón Castilla beginning in 1845 enabled some modernization in political administration, education, and culture. The nation's first budget was presented to the congress in 1845, a state accounting agency and statistics bureau was established, national measures were taken to improve education, the railroad arrived, and a Bureau of Public Works went to work in Lima, paving streets, building promenades, and erecting monuments.[18] Most importantly however, the state began to take advantage of the rich deposits of guano on the islands off the coast of Peru. The great demand for this fertilizing agent in Europe inaugurated a 40-year period in which the national economy was predicated entirely on this product. Despite the large amounts of capital that guano introduced into Peru, the use of a consignment system that worked through foreign firms for the sale of the product was inefficient and wasteful.[19] Worst of all, the false confidence created by guano resulted in expenditures that were larger than the income it generated, and ultimately weakened the economy.[20]

In 1856, a liberal congress enacted a constitution that sparked a revolt by conservatives appalled by its emphatic anticlericalism; Castilla decided it was best to temper the law of the land and dissolved the congress so that a more conservative body could draft a moderate constitution. The abrogation of the Constitution of 1856 in favor of the Constitution of 1860 energized many of the more liberal elements in Peru against Castilla. Although Ricardo Palma had socialized with President Castilla and benefitted from the state's protection for many years as a navy officer, he was drawn to the liberal reaction through the influence of General José Gálvez, an alumnus of the Convictorio of San Carlos.[21] In Gálvez's plot to overthrow Castilla, Palma was to serve as a liaison with conspirators in the port city of Callao. When the coup failed, Palma and others, including Gálvez, were forced to flee to Chile, where they lived in exile for three years.

In Valparaíso, Chile, Palma wrote articles for the local press and befriended notable Chilean writers, such as José Victorino Lastarria, Alberto Blest Gana, and Benjamin Vicuña Mackenna.[22] In his journalistic writings of this period, Palma criticized the Peruvian state's version of the coup of 1860, and passionately rallied Latin Americans against future Spanish incursions in the continent.[23] On the literary front, the tradition had begun to mature. Between 1859 and 1861, Palma's early traditions had appeared in print in Lima (for example "Palla Huarcuna"), and continued appearing in Chile during his exile. Palma was steadily moving away from the conventions of romanticism and finding the style that would define the tradition as a distinctive form. Moreover, Palma's work on a compendium of tales about the

Spanish Inquisition in Lima, *Anales de la Inquisición de Lima* (1863), encouraged him to further cultivate the cross-pollination of history and fiction that the emerging tradition embodied. When the new Peruvian president declared amnesty in 1863, Palma returned, but not before a peculiar incident in which, upon hearing a passionate critique of the tyranny of Castilla in a Chilean theatre, he rose to publicly defend his former foe. Palma's idolization of Gálvez and his defense and eventual reconciliation with Castilla underline how his liberalism was linked to the cult of personality surrounding caudillismo: in a political system where power was only adjudicated by the military, liberals and conservatives channeled their aspirations through the men who could militarily bring them to power.[24]

After returning to Peru, Palma traveled to Europe, where he visited Paris and London. The trip was cut short because Peru and Spain were on the verge of war. President Juan Antonio Pezet's conciliatory dealings with Spain, which had assaulted Peruvian sovereignty by taking control of the Chincha Islands, provoked popular unrest and energized several caudillos, including Palma's old mentor José Gálvez to overthrow the president. Colonel Mariano Prado took the presidency, and with Gálvez as defense minister, led the country in a successful war against Spain. Palma was stationed in the port city of Callao with Gálvez during the short war, and almost perished in the Spanish cannon fusilade that killed his political mentor. Once victory over Spain was attained, Peru found itself divided again over the issue of the Constitution of 1860, which was replaced with a more liberal charter in 1867. This time, Palma sided with the conservative reaction, which deposed Prado and put Colonel José Balta in the presidency. The 35-year-old Palma now moved to the center of political life during Balta's troubled tenure, serving as the president's personal secretary and as senator for the state of Loreto.

Balta's presidency was largely ineffectual and characterized by corruption and wastefulness. One sector of Lima's political and economic elite had begun to seriously question the centrality of the military in politics, opposing Balta and militarism in general. They represented the interests of the plutocracy that had attained economic affluence through guano, whether as merchants, financiers, or landowners, and sought a larger role in managing guano profits and the national economy.[25] They called themselves the *Civilistas*, and their presidential candidate and principal ideologue, Manuel Pardo, would win the presidency in 1872. During Balta's presidency, Palma's parliamentary speeches underline how far from *Civilista* ideology he truly was. Most notably, when a prospective monument to José Gálvez was criticized for representing the hero as an individual, Palma defended his old mentor and the inclusion of individuated allegories in national monuments.[26] When some senators, preoccupied by the lack of funds in state coffers, raised financial objections to proposals to provide recompense in the form of gold medals to the veterans of the Battle of Callao where the Spanish fleet was repelled, Palma was intransigent: "I do not understand how, in speaking of prizes and rewards, our lips pronounce the word economy."[27] The rejection of the word "economy" is revealing here, for it underlines Palma's distrust of the classically liberal, and antimilitarist tenets of emergent *Civilista* ideology, which spurned Balta's extravagant expenditures.[28] In 1872, when President Balta was assassinated in a failed coup, Palma's political career came to an end.

During the *Civilista* presidency of Manuel Pardo (1872–1876), and the return of Mariano Ignacio Prado to the presidency (1876–1879), Palma remained publicly silent on political affairs; he had decided to sideline himself permanently from politics.[29] Instead, he focused his energies on his varied literary projects, primarily the publication of several volumes of traditions. In 1876, the 43-year-old Palma, who once referred to himself as the "eternal bachelor," married Cristina San Román and started a large family.[30] A year later, he found himself embroiled in a controversy that strengthened his resolve to remain politically inconspicous. Palma published a historical monograph that suggested that Bolívar had ordered the assasination of the Peruvian patriot Bernardo Monteagudo, unleashing passionate protests and stinging criticism by Bolivarians across the continent. Palma withdrew into his role of *tradicionista,* telling Vicuña Mackenna "I have learned the lesson not to write any more about contemporary history."[31] Although he would continue to write about Bolívar and other republican and post-independence figures in his traditions, their stories would be anecdotal, like those of the colonial characters that dominate most of the *Peruvian Traditions.*

The Chilean invasion and occupation of Peru during the War of the Pacific (1879–1884) enabled Palma to fashion himself as the savior of the National Library in the years following the war. He was a personal friend of General Miguel Iglesias, who negotiated the Treaty of Ancón, and under whose authority he became director of the library. When General Cáceres overthrew Iglesias in 1885, Palma felt himself alienated by the new president's administration, although he was careful not to criticize the leader directly in his correspondence.[32] Fearful of another revolution, he confided to his friend Vicente Riva Palacio that he did not trust liberals or conservatives to save the country.[33] With the election of President Morales Bermúdez in 1889, Palma's reticent political views become even harder to trace. Peru was now heading toward a period of relative stability that historians have called the "Aristocratic Republic" (1895–1919), in which a series of alliances and counteralliances between political parties steered the country away from constant turmoil and toward modernization. One of Palma's roles in this period was that of consummate bureaucrat, whose post in the National Library both protected and marginalized him from politics. Always on hand for ceremonial ocassions, Palma sought to be as politically circumspect as possible throughout the years, while trying to secure financial resources for the maintenance of the library.

Palma's close relationship with President Nicolás de Piérola, who came to power in 1895, provides some indication of the writer's sympathies toward the end of the century. Piérola had been Balta's finance minister and was the most passionate and conspiratorial anti-*Civilista* on the Peruvian political scene.[34] According to Peter Flindell Klarén, Piérola "believed that Catholicism and a firm authoritarian hand at the head of a centralist state were the key political ingredients necessary to hold together a geographically disparate, heterogeneous and highly class-based society."[35] Palma always considered himself a liberal, but his distrust of the capitalist roots of *Civilismo* (that explains his identification with Piérola) and his rejection of the Jacobinism of the younger generation of liberals underscore his conservatism.[36] The aging author and librarian greeted the new century as a political anachronism, a throwback to the liberal caudillismo of the first half of the century. In the words of José Carlos Mariátegui: "The *criollo* or, rather, demos of Lima was neither consistent nor original. From time to time he was aroused by the clarion call of some budding caudillo; but once the spasm had passed, he fell once again into voluptuous somnolence. All his impatience and rebelliousness were converted into a joke, an impertinent remark, or an epigram, which found their literary expression in the biting satire of *Tradiciones*."[37] Ultimately, Palma remained an irrelevant figure in Peruvian politics by his own choosing. He repeatedly told many of his correspondents that he rejected politics in favor of his work as a librarian and the literary life.

One of the issues that dominated Palma's life continuously after the War of the Pacific was his difficult relationship with Spain and its Royal Academy over the inclusion of Latin American regionalisms in its dictionary. Palma expressed his ardent Latin Americanism by writing against Spanish imperialism during his Chilean exile and fighting in Peru's war with Spain in 1865. Later in life he continued this fight by lobbying for inclusion of Latin American regionalisms in the dictionary and by populating his traditions with Peruvian expressions. Palma was not anti-Spanish, but rather a hispanophile intent on consolidating a transatlantic community of Spanish speakers through the democratization of the dictionary of the Royal Academy.[38] For the Columbian centenary of 1892, Palma traveled to Spain and urged the Academy to accept New World regionalisms in the same manner that the peninsula's own regionalisms had been accepted and included in the dictionary. Although many words were accepted, the Academy continued to resist many of his impassioned arguments about other words. For Palma, the Academy's attitude toward the Spanish language was like that of Don Quixote with his imaginary beloved, Dulcinea of Toboso. In rejecting this idealization of linguistic purity, Palma celebrated the more mundane, changeable qualities of language and wrote: "In languages . . . [*sic*] like Maritornes."[39] Rather than diluting Castilian, or fragmenting the Spanish-speaking world, Palma believed that Latin American Spanish would enrich the mother tongue's "anemic lexicon."[40]

Despite Palma's commitment to sideline himself from politics, he became an unsuspecting target of criticism in 1886 by the representative of a new generation of intellectuals, Manuel González Prada (1848–1918). The conflict would flare up again in 1912, when Palma's disagreements with the administration of President Augusto Leguia's intrusion in library affairs led to his resignation and to the naming of González Prada as new director.[41] What is significant about González Prada is that his pointed attacks on the tradition laid the foundations for future claims among literary critics that Palma's traditions were ideologically conservative. Beginning in 1886, González Prada gave a series of speeches in which he rejected archaic writing, Spanish influence in Peruvian letters, and the timid, expressive protocols of many writers on the scene. On July 29, 1888, González Prada gave a speech at the Politeama Theatre, in which he declared: "Old men to the grave, and young men to the task at hand!"[42] A few months later, he made a thinly veiled reference to Palma by characterizing the tradition as a monstrous genre that falsified and caricatured history.[43] Other than Palma's deep disillusionment, little came of these skirmishes in 1888, but the old wounds would open again 24 years later when González Prada was named his successor as director of the National Library. Angered by the outpouring of support for Palma after his resignation, González Prada wrote a report criticizing Palma for misusing the library for personal ends, and for writing personal notes in many of its books.[44]

When Palma died in 1919, he was an icon of Peruvian letters, and one of the most popular writers in the Spanish-speaking world. In his final years, he had rejected attempts to publicly honor his service to the nation, and lived quietly, reading and dictating letters from his home. In spite of his disappointments, Palma's reputation was secure; by the twentieth century, his traditions had been recognized as a foundational document about Peru's past and a testament to the playful spirit of old Lima's *vox populi*.

Toward a Definition of Palma's Peruvian Traditions

José Miguel Oviedo writes that it is "a perilous adventure" to define the tradition: "its fabric has so many threads that one fears forgetting one of them or making an erroneous weave."[45] The problem lies in the fact that the *Peruvian Traditions* comprise a broad array of different types of narrations: historical monographs about well-known historical personages, autobiographical anecdotes or reminiscences, sensational stories about major and lesser figures, lexical inquiries, and popular superstitions. Oviedo's general, structural definition of the tradition invokes some of Palma's most popular and widely anthologized traditions, such as "The Magistrate's Ears": The tradition begins with an anecdote or setting of the scene that is interrupted by a parenthesis in which historical context is offered before continuing with the narration of the story.[46] The problem with this model is that only a few of Palma's traditions follow this structure.[47] The geneaological slipperiness of the tradition is underlined by Robert Bazin's attempt to weave a definition through a sum of other forms: romantic legend + *costumbrismo*[48] + purity of expression = tradition.[49] This definition adjudicates the particularity of the tradition to the influence of genres that are dissimilar to it, raising more questions than answers. Another definition, largely discredited among critics, is to subordinate the tradition to historiography. The 1953 edition of the complete *Peruvian Traditions*, edited by Palma's granddaughter, Edith Palma, resequenced Palma's work in chronological order, positing the traditions as an overarching history of Peru, in violation of Palma's own serialization of the traditions outside of the conventional teleologies of liberal historiography. These unsatisfactory attempts to define the tradition lend credence to Aníbal González's claim that the very notion of genre is inimical to the tradition, which resists absolute categories because of its satiric nature.[50] Rather than a uniform genre or form, the tradition may be loosely described as a type of historical miscellany that results from the combination of orality, journalistic satire, and the fictionalization of historical miscellany drawn from primary and secondary historical documents.

Despite the difficulty in defining the tradition as a genre, a general account of some of its most salient traits can help set the stage for understanding the debate over its ideological nature. We begin by repeating that the tradition can take many distinct forms: a historical monograph such as "The Protectress and the Liberatrix" lacks the fictional verve of a tale like "An Adventure of the Poet Viceroy"; a sensational story of madness and violence, such as "The Christ in Agony" is not equivalent to "The Witches of Ica," an account of popular superstitions; and the unabashed comic nature of "The Major's Calf" is not shared by stories of colonial violence like "The Demon of the Andes." The diversity of the *Peruvian Traditions* goes a long way toward explaining the difficulty in summarizing the tradition with a totalizing, singular definition. In spite of this caveat, some of the characteristics of the style, composition, and thematics of the traditions provide a more coherent view of the kind of narrative sensibility that binds them together.

The tradition is a hybrid narrative. Its nucleus is an anecdote, but historical digressions and ironic and exclamatory authorial interventions are added to the mix. Even in traditions that do not seem particularly inventive in their theme or form (such as some of the more historiographic "monographs") readers find historical discourse combined with anecdotal, autobiographical, or humorous elements. In "The Protectress and the Liberatrix," the biographies of Rosa Campusa and Manuela Sáenz are framed by autobiographical anecdotes from Palma's childhood and youth. "The Knights of the Cape" might have been a dry historical anecdote if not for Palma's artful characterizations and humorous asides, such as the passage in which a would-be political assassin skirts a puddle on his way to "bathing" himself in human blood. On another level, the prevalent combination of different discourses in the *Peruvian Traditions,* which varies in degree and in kind in different texts, also underlines how Palma empowered his documentary research with the freedom of the imagination, producing fiction through his "historical" sourcework. In "The Magistrate's Ears," for example, Palma loosely based his narrative on a brief anecdote recounted in Sebastián de Lorente's *Historia del Perú bajo la dinastía austriaca, 1542–1598* (1863). In Lorente's concise narrative, a soldier of noble descent named Aguirre receives a humiliating lashing by order of a magistrate of Potosí for failing to pay a fine. Fearing reprisal from Aguirre, the magistrate fled to Lima, only to be murdered three years later with a stab wound to the right temple. Palma changes the names, introduces the thematic nucleus of the ears of the magistrate, dramatizes events by having the dishonored nobleman insinuate his threats to the magistrate on several separate ocassions, and changes the very outcome of the original story: Instead of being murdered, the magistrate loses his ears to his attacker and dies later of humiliation.[51] Clearly, Palma was not limited by his original source, but rather used it as a frame for his own invention; like a good tailor (one of his favorite metaphors for his work as a *tradicionista*), Palma delighted in "sewing" together different types of discourse.

In the past, critics underlined the *criollismo* of the *Peruvian Traditions,* or the use of a narrative style associated with a persona common to Lima, and whose hallmark was an impish view of society. In more recent years, this rubric has been broadened or replaced by the concept of orality, suggesting that the tradition represents a challenge to the conventions of liberal print culture in nineteenth-century Latin America and its class-based hierarchies of cultural value. Julio Ortega underlines the emancipatory potential of this deployment of orality: "With the materials of Tradition, Palma's 'tradition' is a true deconstruction of what is constructed, of what is given and inculcated."[52] The use of colloquialisms, diminutives, exclamations, curse words and other elements of oral culture make monumentalist or mythic representations of historical personages impossible, challenge instrumentalist representations of the past and provide the foundation for most of the humor in the *Peruvian Traditions*.[53] For example, in "Friar Martín's Mice," Palma simultaneously questions and celebrates the famous black saint, interjecting several memorable exclamations upon reporting Friar Martin's "miracles," such as "Don't make me laugh, for I've one lip that's cracked" and the final sentences: "And . . . and . . . and . . . isn't this story all stuff and nonsense? No, of course not!" In "The Countess Who Was Summoned," Palma introduces his historical context with a sentence that disarms the notion of writerly didacticism, evoking a scene of leisure and conversation: "Reader, a cigar or a toothpick, and let us speak of colonial history." Often, the very premise of a tradition is predicated on orality, through a particular proverb or phrase that Palma seeks to explain through his tradition, thus making popular speech the *raison d'être* of his writing and not the exemplary lives of "great" men or the retelling of "great" historical events (see for example, "A Letter Sings," "Margarita's Wedding Dress," "The Judge's Three Reasons"). However, our emphasis on the orality (and ostensible populism) of the tradition as a narrative form needs to be tempered by an awareness that Palma's colloquialism was partially mediated through print culture, particularly journalism, which had adopted mundane speech and wordplay as an important tool in its satiric arsenal.[54] In his youth, Palma had been a part of a romantic coterie of writers who used journalism to skewer the social and cultural world of Lima; before beginning to write his traditions, Palma was undoubtedly familiar with the conventions of political satire, including recourse to oral forms of address.

Aníbal González notes that the thematic content of a great number of the *Peruvian Traditions* may be classified under the rubric of the *fait divers*, or the human interest story, in which strange, intranscendent, absurd, or tragic events are narrated outside of the generic confines of the standard categories of modern journalism (such as the news story about politics, economics, culture, etc.). As defined by Roland Barthes, the *fait divers* problematizes causality, situating the events it narrates in an ambivalent or aberrant context that is hard to rationally explain. "The Royalist Smells of Death to Me" is a good example of the tradition as a *fait divers*: It narrates the execution of a civilian during the

Wars of Independence, an all too common event during that conflict, within the frame of the civilian's prophetic knowledge of the future death of the colonel who has ordered his execution. Similar violent prophecies that violate rational models of causality are fulfilled in "Friars' Work!" and "The Countess Who Was Summoned." The notion of the *fait divers*, along with Palma's penchant for wordplay, underline how the *Peruvian Traditions* actively avoids the kind of historicity that is associated with modern national historiography, opting instead for lurid, ridiculous, and outlandish tidbits about personages known and unknown to "History." Even when Palma writes about well-known historical figures, he defamiliarizes them and situates their stories outside of the orbit of the mythical fictions of national or continental identity, as in the case of "The Liberator's Three Etceteras." This tradition's mention of the hygienic habits of Bolívar, and the focus on his sexual proclivities, ultimately results in a narrative that is more indebted to the notion of a humorous entertainment than to the inflated authority of liberal historiography.[55] In short, when Palma writes about foundational historical figures, he reframes them by portraying them as if they were living in the present, with all of their foibles and eccentricities intact.[56]

Finally, the sequencing of the *Peruvian Traditions* demands our attention as one of its revealing traits. Palma's traditions were first published in newspapers in Lima, Valparaiso, and Buenos Aires before being collected in volumes. When Palma began publishing collections of his traditions in book form in 1872, he called each volume of traditions a "series," but did not order each tradition chronologically within any given series. As a result, rather than a vertical telos, the *Peruvian Traditions* offers its readers a horizontal mosaic of stories about Peru's past. In "A Viceroy and an Archbishop," Palma concedes that a complete history of the era of the viceroys would be very difficult because of incomplete historical archives, "or because of the negligence of our forefathers as regards the recording of facts." If a complete national history were an edifice, Palma envisioned his traditions as something much more modest: They were the stones that might, some day in the future, be used for the construction of a more complete national structure.[57] Regardless of such statements about the lack of resources for a totalizing history, Palma's "mosaic" of the past enables his traditions to avoid positivist notions of historical development and narration, situating them instead in an oral continuum modeled by the informal transmission, from one generation to the next, of stories about the past (see for example "The Black Mass"). Rather than being a failure on Palma's part, the random serialization of the *Peruvian Traditions*, like its subject matter and humor, presents a type of historical memory that foregrounds actors, "minor" events, and narrative conventions that are excluded from more sequential and "writerly" versions of the past.

The Peruvian Traditions *and the* Critique *of Modernity*

Palma's traditions have been woven into the fabric of modern Peruvian consciousness as a particularly rich and familiar site of national memory. In fact, as Antonio Cornejo Polar has noted, Palma played a key role in "nationalizing" colonial history, integrating and disseminating it as a fact of the republic's emergent national identity. Like Walt Whitman, José Martí, and Pablo Neruda in their respective countries of origin, Palma has become an emblem of national identity. Yet, what kind of *Peruanidad* (Peruvianism) does Palma represent? Is it the uncritical and retrograde yearning for a fictional, colonial past, or the democratic and populist irony of *criollismo*? The debate over the uncertain ideological sign of the *Peruvian Traditions* began in the nineteenth century with Palma's first skirmish with Manuel González Prada. Between 1886 and 1888, González Prada gave a series of speeches later published in *Pájinas Libres* (1894), in which he called for the modernization of Peruvian letters through Positivism. In his analysis, Peruvian writers were plagued by anemic prose, false grandiloquence, archaism, senile purisms, and timidity. In particular, González Prada singled out the tradition (without naming Palma directly) as an example of the inert and reactionary literary scene: "in our prose the bad *tradition* still reigns, that monster engendered by bittersweet falsifications of history and the microscopic caricatures of the novel."[58] González Prada implied that writers like Palma were not hearing the clarion call of Positive Science and its potential for expressive, cultural, and political renewal, opting instead for convoluted and vacuous prose in which "accidents modify accidents" and incommensurate periods are combined haphazardly.[59]

González Prada's critique has had several notable heirs in the twentieth century who continue to fault Palma for his choice of subject matter and style of writing. Most forcefully, Sebastián Salazar Bondy restated the case in *Lima la horrible* (1964), arguing that in spite of his republican stripes, Palma was the most successful of all apologists of the colonial era. His traditions, Salazar Bondy argues, contributed to a colonial facade that occluded power relations between master and slave, foreigner and native, and rich and poor.[60] Salazar Bondy and other critics are essentially objecting to the phenomenon of *perricholismo* in modern Peruvian cultural history. The concept of *perricholismo* derives from the nickname of a notorious eighteenth-century actress and courtier, Micaela Villegas (1748–1819). When Villegas became the mistress of Viceroy Manuel Amat (who was 40 years her senior), details of their tempestuous relationship became the grist for conversation across Lima, serving as a kind of colonial-era soap opera. Villegas came to be known as "la Perricholi" either because an angry Amat once called her a *perra chola* (a half-breed dog), or because it was his custom to call her *pretixol* (from the Catalan word for beautiful thing).[61] *Perricholismo*, which springs from the fascination with the amorous intrigues and sumptious world of colonial-era high society and power, designates a form of reactionary nostalgia for colonial times.[62]

In spite of these critiques of the *Peruvian Traditions*, Palma found a surprising defender in the well-known Marxist theorist José Carlos Mariátegui, whose *Seven Interpretive Essays on Peruvian Reality* (1917) insightfully explored the relationship between narrative and politics in Palma's writings. Mariátegui distinguished Palma from other writers fascinated with the colonial era, and whose writings betray nostalgia for the colony: "The *Tradiciones* of Palma is politically and socially democratic; Palma interprets the common people. His ridicule, which reflects the mocking discontent of the criollo demos, undermines the prestige of the viceroyalty and its aristocracy. The satire of *Tradiciones* does not probe very deeply nor does it hit very hard. Precisely for this reason it is identified with the sugar-coated humor of the bland, sensual demos. Lima could not produce any other kind of literature and *Tradiciones* exhaust and sometimes exceed their possibilities."[63]

In spite of the fact that Palma has been co-opted by "colonialist" ideologues, Mariátegui argues that Palma's writing encodes the narrative ethos of a middle-class elite that resented the old reactionary aristocracy. Indeed, a closer look at other Peruvian chroniclers of the past underlines how Palma's traditions artfully avoided the trap of nostalgia, and enshrined a kind of populist sensibility. One of Palma's most successful followers was José Gálvez, author of the best-selling collection *Una Lima que se va* (1921), and who in 1913 had received from Palma the pen with which he had written the *Peruvian Traditions;* in a brief note that accompanied the gift of the pen, Palma encouraged the young Gálvez to use it to write "historical-sociological studies of Lima."[64] From the very title of his book ("The Lima That Is Fading"), nostalgia shapes Gálvez's writing transparently: the old customs surrounding baptism, marriage, and the *tertulias* (social gatherings) are evoked as a lost plenitude.[65] Gálvez's overtly didactic and judgemental tone is worlds away from the picaresque sensibility of Palma; in his study of the ghosts of Lima, Gálvez condemns old-time superstitions and the "detestable mania" of frightening children with lurid and fantastic stories.[66] In contrast, in "The Black Mass," Palma adopts Granny's voice and tells a witch-story to his children, exhorting them to pray "to blessed souls in Purgatory and your guardian angels to keep you safe and defend you from witches who suck the blood of children and make them scrawny."

Palma's own testimony about the meaning of the tradition, as expressed in some of the poetic prologues to his volumes of traditions and in his letters, clarifies the impulses behind his writing. First, Palma is forceful in his rejection of romanticism, which he considers a depleted aesthetic that has become hollow and false. Although Palma had been a pioneering romantic in Peru, by the 1870s he had become disenchanted with the volume and repetitive nature of romantic poetry. In his prologue-poem "Cháchara" (1875), Palma writes: "Precisely those that spill tears / on paper, are, in my view / smugglers of suffering, ridiculous / actors that mimic pain."[67] At a deeper level, Palma rejects the division of cultural production into separate, and ultimately artificial, literary and historical spheres; the hollowness of romanticism attests to the depletion of literature as a social force within this arbitrary division of expressive domains.[68] Palma professes the tradition as a nationalist renewal of literature predicated on the rejection of romantic hysterics and on the reconciliation of the discourses of literature and history: "Since no one wanted to introduce the literary sickle / into historical matters / I told myself: 'Gentlemen, without scruple, in this I surely don't sin, here you have me.' "[69] The tradition is a literary form that seeks to overcome the trivialization of literature and its separation from the constructive, nationalist didacticism of historiography. Despite the distinctiveness of the tradition as an irreverent form of counterhistoriography, Palma always conceived of his writing as a nationalist venture. "The tradition is my offering of love to the country and to letters," Palma wrote in 1872.[70]

Palma once wrote that he preferred to live in the past, a site of poetry, because the present was too prosaic.[71] He decries the loss of an experiential center under the withering march of modernity, which results in the marginalization of intellectual life and the collapse of categories of transcendental value. "Today, the life of the mind," Palma wrote in 1874, "is mercantilism: God is such and such percent and its altar is egotism."[72] In a devalued present dominated by commerce and rationalism, faith and wisdom have been lost, as well as the true measure of men. The forward-looking ideology of the present has "buried" the past, but Palma defiantly declares that "graves have their poetry."[73] His role as a *tradicionista* is that of a puppeteer who disinters the dead and brings skeletons to life again by recovering the reservoirs of historical memory in popular culture, and by disdaining the narrative and scientific sensibility of the discourses of modernity (such as modern historiography). In the process, Palma inscribes the gregarious and witty voices of the City of Kings and adopts a narrative self that is mutable and plastic in its performativity: "That which History silences I divine, I comment the suras of the Koran; if I am an eremite, I am also a libertine; if I live with Christ, I am also living with Satan."[74] The tradition, thus foregrounded against the depletions of modernity, encodes an expressive ethic that is free and emancipatory, but not one that is frivolous or escapist; Palma is clear that his writing is simply a humble offering (a "stone") to national history (a "triumphal arch" yet to be built.)[75] Each individual tradition is too small an offering to constitute monumental discourse; the tradition may provide the materials, or the incentive for a future national history, but for its irreverence, the aesthetic embodied by the tradition cuts against the grain of totalizing visions of the past, nationalist or otherwise.

In the end, the *Peruvian Traditions* speaks for itself as a critique of modernity and its formulas of narrative legitimation. In it Palma often dispenses with historical dates and names, and with the very notion that such "facts" are necessary for understanding the past. While skewering powerful colonial elites, the injustices and contradictions of the present also come under ironic fire, as a reminder that republican "progress" in Peru is often a mirage, or perhaps a mirror image of more primitive times. "Blessed be the nineteenth century, in which the principle of equality before the law is dogma, with no talk of laws or privileges" writes Palma in "Two Excommunications," before deadpanning "The fact that dogma is frequently proven false in practice is none of my business." Most of all, readers of Palma are struck by the perennial return to the richness of language itself as a template of cultural knowledge, narrative subversion, and historical memory. The past lives on in colloquial phrases, such as "Margarita's wedding dress," "a letter sings," and "the judge's three reasons," vernacular emblems that Palma reconstructs, retracing the human stories that led up to the coining of a phrase that has outlived its original context.

Palma circumscribed the *Peruvian Traditions* within a literary project similar to that of the Latin American modernists: the quest for expressive freedom and beauty in a rapidly changing terrain of economic and cultural production. As such, Palma sought to make his traditions a "poetic" alternative to the prosaic nature of rationalism and commerce, which devalued historical memory in its quest for liberal progress. Rather than a paean to the colonial era as a place in time, the *Peruvian Traditions* is a call to a historicist aesthetic capable of evoking the past on a more human scale. To attack Palma for the preponderance of traditions that deal with colonial characters, and for his emphasis on their apparently mundane foibles, is to impoverish the artistry and complexity of the *Peruvian Traditions* and to negate the humorism that lies at the heart of the tradition as a form. As Julio Ortega notes, it isn't that Palma accepts the world uncritically, but rather that he chooses to include his readers in the process of discovering the mending powers of literature and popular culture in the face of the arbitrariness of history and social hierarchies.[76] Regardless of what Palma can teach us about the past of Peru (that is very much), the enduring quality of his traditions has little to do with historiography and everything to do with the restorative powers of art. Palma himself put it best when he said: "For me, the tradition is not a light piece of work, but a true work of art."[77]

This Edition of the Peruvian Traditions

The task of choosing a sampling of Palma's traditions for English readers has been daunting for several reasons. On the one hand, the over

500 traditions that Palma published in his lifetime made narrowing the field for a single volume very difficult. Also, the large number of Spanish-language anthologies of the *Peruvian Traditions,* each with a particular flavor, do not necessarily provide a uniform list for deciding what should go in a volume such as this one. Finally, I was faced with the challenge of selecting traditions that lent themselves well to English translation. The difficulty of translating Palma cannot be overstated: The ubiquity of wordplay, colloquialism, and local speech threaten to deprive readers of English (or any language other than Spanish) from enjoying Palma's *Peruvian Traditions* at all. Some traditions are entirely predicated on puns, proverbs, or other forms of linguistic invention that cannot be translated into English without completely extinguishing their wit. For example, in "El Virrey de la adivinanza," a well-known tradition that is not contained in this volume, the punch line of the narrative comes at the end, as Viceroy Abascal is intimidated out of office when he receives three sacks: one containing salt, the second beans, and the third lime. In Spanish, these elements, "sal," "habas," and "cal," phonetically spell out the phrase "sal Abascal," which is a command form that means "leave Abascal!" In light of such challenges, I worked closely with Palma's distinguished translator, Helen Lane, to identify traditions that would not lose their spark in English, as well as difficult traditions that we felt were worth a special effort. In the end, the wit and polish that make Palma one of the most distinctive writers in modern Latin America is everywhere evident in Lane's masterful translation of the Spanish originals.

Besides selecting traditions that could be successfully translated into English, the present edition of the *Peruvian Traditions* reflects different criteria. Some of the most recognized traditions in Palma's ouevre are included, such as "Friar Gómez's Scorpion" and "An Adventure of the Poet-Viceroy" as well as attractive but lesser anthologized traditions, like "Between Garibaldi . . . and Me." Two of Palma's earliest traditions are also included, "Consolación" and "Palla-Huarcuna," in the interest of showing two early incarnations of the tradition; Palma himself was fond of these early pieces, and chose to include them in the first and tenth series, respectively. Most importantly, I have sought to share the pleasure that the *Peruvian Traditions* has given to generations of readers in the Spanish-speaking world with a new audience.

The translations in this volume are based on the Spanish Calpe edition of 1923,[78] which incorporated revisions that Palma had intended to make in his lifetime. Each tradition has been sequenced by series, not by historical period, as in the case of the 1953 Edith Palma edition of Palma's complete traditions. For the convenience of the reader unfamiliar with the finer points of Peruvian history, principal historical personages and bibliographical sources have been glossed in the footnotes, which are cross-referenced when necessary to indicate where certain events and characters reappear or are further elucidated in separate traditions. Linguistic notes belong to Helen Lane, while historical and cultural glosses are by the editor. Palma's own notes are labeled as such. For readers interested in reading the traditions by historical cluster, an appendix with such a listing has also been included. Finally, Palma frequently included fragments of poems or popular sayings in his traditions. In this edition, we have kept the rhymed couplets in the original Spanish, and provided translations in the footnotes. Otherwise, these poetic fragments appear in English in the main body of the text.

—Christopher Conway

NOTES

All translations in this introduction, excepting those from the traditions contained in this volume, are my own. Many thanks to Desiree Henderson, Helen Lane, Julio Ortega, and Matthew Wyszynski for their invaluable support during the writing of this introduction.

1. Clements R. Markham, *A History of Peru* (New York: Greenwood Press, 1968), 432.

2. Markham, 471.

3. César Miró, *Don Ricardo Palma; el patriarca de las Tradiciones* (Buenos Aires: Editorial Losada, 1953), 129.

4. An extensive study of Palma's move away from romantic historical fiction to the tradition can be found in Merlin D. Compton's *Ricardo Palma* (Boston: Twayne Publishers, 1982), 36–62.

5. The word *criollo* has multiple meanings in the Latin American context. One well-known meaning is the generic concept of a Spaniard born in the New World. In literature, *criollismo* is associated with the early-twentieth-century fiction, particularly the regionalist novel (such as José Eustasio Rivera's *La vorágine* and Rómulo Gallegos's *Doña Bárbara*). However, in the Peruvian context, *criollo* has a more local and specific meaning. In *Lima la horrible* (Mexico: Ediciones Era, 1968), Sebastián Salazar Bondy writes: "Its current meaning is . . . a native of Lima, or by extension, an inhabitant of the coast . . . who lives,

thinks, and acts according to a set of national traditions and customs. . . . Therefore when literature, Christmas, politics, or *verbigratia* are described with the adjective of *criollo* they become local or are colored by localism," 23–24. In *Genio y Figura de Ricardo Palma* (Buenos Aires: Editorial Universitaria de Buenos Aires, 1965), José Miguel Oviedo underlines the *lisura* (malice, coquetry) of the *criollo*, 150, 163. For the narrative heterodoxy of the speech of the *criollo*, see Alicia Andreu's "Una nueva aproximación al lenguaje en las *Tradiciones peruanas* de Ricardo Palma," *Revista de Estudios Hispánicos*, no. 2 (May 1989): 21–36.

6. Palma's ubiquity in the Latin American and Spanish press is well known. During his exile in Chile (1860–1863), Palma published several traditions in the *Revista de Sud América*. His following in Buenos Aires was particularly strong, as indicated by many of his Argentinian correspondents and admirers. See Angélica Palma's *Ricardo Palma* (Buenos Aires: Ediciones Condor, 1933), 87. In 1899, Palma wrote that English translations of his traditions had been well received in the United States and England. He added that the *Atheneum of London* had written a long article on his traditions. See "Epistolario," *Ricardo Palma, 1833–1933* (Lima: Sociedad de Amigos de Palma, 1934), 274.

7. Ricardo Palma, *Epistolario, vol. I* (Lima: Editorial Cultura Antártica), 57.

8. Other *tradicionistas* include Juana Manuela Gorriti (Argentina, 1818–1892), Luis Capella Toledo (Colombia, 1838–1896), Alvaro de la Iglesia y Santos (Cuba, 1859–1940), Miguel Luis Amunátegui (Chile, 1828–1888), and Artemio del Valle-Arispe (Mexico, 1888–1960). For a larger listing, discussion, and anthology of the Latin American *tradicionistas*, see Estuardo Nuñez, *Ricardo Palma escritor continental: las huellas de Palma en los tradicionistas hispanoamericanos* (Lima: Fondo Editorial, 1998).

9. Palma, *Epistolario*, 527. Palma also writes ". . . I don't have a biography. In my existence there is nothing original or curious: nothing that singles me out nor that is worth telling," 225.

10. Founded by Francisco Pizarro on the Feast of the Epiphany, Lima has historically been known as the "City of Kings."

11. Raúl Porras Barrenechea, "Palma Romántico," in *Ricardo Palma, 1833–1933*: 93. For traditions in which Pancho Sales appears see Ricardo Palma's *Tradiciones Peruanas completas* (Madrid: Aguilar, 1953); "Pancho Sales, el verdugo," 747–52; "Asunto concluido," 891–92; "El rey del monte," 903–7; "La venganza de un cura," 1103–6. María Abascal appears in "María Abascal," 954–58; and Juanita Breña in "Tauromaquía," 46–53; "¡¡Buena laya de fraile!!," 915–22; "Juana la Marimacho," 922–23. Palma also met notable characters from the era of independence, such as Rosa Campuzano and Manuela Sáenz; see "The Protectress and the Liberatrix."

12. Oviedo, 37. The traditions in which Aunt Catita or Granny are separately mentioned are: "¡Ahí viene el cuco!"; "Traslado a Judás (cuento disparatado de la tía Catita)"; "Croniquillas de mi abuela"; "La misa negra" (in this collection, "The Black Mass") in Ricardo Palma's *Tradiciones peruanas completas,* 667; 856–58; 1194–95; 833–35.

13. *La bohemia de mi tiempo, Tradiciones peruanas completas,* 1301.

14. Miró, 33.

15. *La bohemia . . . ,* 1307. The humorous poet and playwright Manuel Ascensio Segura (1805–1871) was a popular member of the romantic circle, and Palma collaborated with him on the comedy *El santo de Panchita,* published in 1886 but composed some time in the 1840s.

16. *Epistolario,* 140. One of the recurring themes in Palma's voluminous correspondence is his rejection of politics; see 134–39; 311–12.

17. Hector Bonilla, "Peru and Bolivia from Independence to the War of the Pacific," *The Cambridge History of Latin America, vol. III,* ed. Leslie Bethell (Cambridge: New York: Cambridge University Press, 1984), 547–48.

18. David P. Werlich, *Peru: A Short History* (Carbondale: Southern Illinois University Press, 1978), 87.

19. Werlich, 82.

20. Bonilla, 552.

21. Earlier, Palma had supported another alumnus of San Carlos, General Manuel Vivanco, who led an unsuccessful campaign against Castilla in 1856.

22. Oviedo, 64–65.

23. For Palma's account of his participation in the coup against Castilla, see Guillermo Feliu-Cruz's *En torno de Ricardo Palma* (Santiago: Prensas de la Universidad de Chile, 1933), 99–108.

24. Consider, for example, Palma's view of Gálvez as a monumental hero, an "immaculate man" whose "austere virtue" makes him morally invincible to calumny, Feliu-Cruz, 108.

25. Bonilla, 560–61.

26. Miró, 93–94.

27. Miró, 97.

28. The commemoration of the veterans of Callao was a result of Palma's participation in the siege, his loyalty to Gálvez, and also his own romanticism. As early as 1851, for example, when Palma was 18, he had been attracted to heroic martial themes; his third and final play, *Rodil,* celebrated the defense of Callao by the Spanish hero Rodil.

29. In a confidential letter to his friend Benjamin Vicuña Mackenna, Palma defended Balta and politely expressed his rejection of Manuel Pardo's presidency: "Without being a political friend of Mr. [don] Manuel Pardo, I always admired his talent, his activity, and his energy," *Epistolario,* 47.

30. He had six children, including Clemente, the author of *Cuentos malévolos* (1904) and *Historietas malignas* (1925) and his favorite, Angelica, author of nostalgic novels such as *Vencida* (1918) and *Coloniaje romántico* (1923).

31. *Epistolario*, 48. Palma wrote two substantive letters to Vicuña Mackenna defending his historical research on Bolívar, 43–52.

32. Palma felt that his problems with the Cáceres administration were a result of his friendship with President Miguel Iglesias. See his *Epistolario*, 124, 137–39, 156–57. Also, Angelica Palma's *Ricardo Palma* (Buenos Aires: Editorial Tor, 1933), 101–2.

33. *Epistolario*, 134–37. In the elections of 1889, Palma at first rejected all candidates, but he came to believe that the election of President Morales Bermúdez was probably best, simply because he thought it would avert violence: 228, 231.

34. As far back as 1878, Palma had written for Piérola's newspaper, "La Patria," Angelica Palma, 80.

35. Peter Flindell Klarén, *Peru: Society and Nationhood in the Andes* (New York: Oxford University Press, 2000), 201.

36. Flindell Klaren, 198. Also, see *Epistolario*, 158.

37. José Carlos Mariátegui, *Seven Interpretive Essays on Peruvian Reality*, trans. Marjory Urquidi (Austin: University of Texas Press, 1971), 199.

38. Palma's letters contain a wealth of commentary on his debates with the Royal Academy. In 1877 Palma wrote that he did not want to fracture Spanish with Latin American dialects, but rather to "enrich" the mother tongue with "general" Latin Americanisms, *Epistolario*, 29. A year later, when he was named the founding member of the Peruvian branch of the Spanish Royal Academy, Palma wrote that he hoped to serve the organization through the "preservation of the purity of the language" and the promotion of Spanish glory, 65. He also believed that the organization should only admit writers whose work was in Castilian, not "galli-speak," 66. For more on strengthening the ties between Peru and Spain, see 71; 149–50; 359–60; 464.

39. *Epistolario*, 392.

40. *Epistolario*, 395. For a detailed account of Palma's views on the dictionary, see his "Neologismos y americanismos" (1895), a linguistic inquiry included in his *Tradiciones peruanas completas*, 1377–83. Around the turn of the century, and until his death, he continued to complain bitterly about Spanish intransigence toward Latin America. In 1897, he declared himself in open rebellion against the academy and its dictionary: "When I need to . . . create a verb, I create it without the slightest scruple," *Epistolario*, 370. For his harshest critique of Spain over these linguistic issues, also see 449–50.

41. In his letter to Marcelino Menéndez y Pelayo dated March 17, 1912, Palma details how he came to resign from the library, *Epistolario*, 100–101.

42. Manuel González Prada, *Free Pages and Other Essays* (New York: Oxford University Press, 2003), 50

43. González Prada, 32. Palma, always protective of his reputation, was deeply hurt by these veiled attacks and authored an anonymous self-defense by suggesting that Ricardo Rosell, one of his disciples in the genre of the tradition, had been the target of González Prada's attack. For more on González Prada, see David Sobrevilla's "Introduction" to González Prada's *Free Pages and Other Essays*, xxiii–lvii.

44. In the years that followed, González Prada was fired and rehired, and Palma accepted a honorary directorship and resigned in protest over González Prada's second tenure.

45. Oviedo, 146.

46. Oviedo, 170.

47. Compton, 26.

48. The *costumbrista* sketch is a romantic genre of prose in which national types, landscapes, and settings are evoked.

49. Oviedo, 147.

50. Aníbal González, "Las tradiciones entre la historia y el periodismo," in Julio Ortega's anthology of Palma, *Tradiciones peruanas* (Madrid: Colección Archivos, 1993), 460–61.

51. For a full discussion of "The Magistrate's Ears" and its original documentary source, see Noel Salomon's "Comentario" to this tradition in *Orígenes del cuento hispanoamericano (Ricardo Palma y sus tradiciones)*, edited by Angel Flores (Mexico: Premia Editoria, 1982), 107–19.

52. Julio Ortega, "Las *Tradiciones peruanas* y el proceso cultural del siglo XIX hispanoamericano," *Tradiciones peruanas*, 429.

53. For a foundational discussion of how Palma's writing distances itself from "writerly" techniques and constructs his traditions through an adoption of the trappings of orality, see "Tensión, lenguaje y estructura: las *Tradiciones peruanas*" by Alberto Escobar, *Tradiciones peruanas*, 550–51. In the same volume, also see "Las Tradiciones y el proceso de su recepción" by Flor María Rodríguez-Arenas, 490–502.

54. González, 467.

55. For a discussion of Palma's use of humor, see Roy Tanner's *The Humor of Irony and Satire in the Tradiciones peruanas* (Columbia: University of Missouri Press, 1986).

56. González, 464.

57. In "Cháchara," Palma writes that his traditions are "little stones" that he offers to the nation, *Tradiciones peruanas completas*, 3; in "Preludio obligado," he writes: "I gather stones so that another may raise a triumphant arch . . . will national history disdain my stones?", 1457.

58. González Prada, 32.

59. Manuel Gonzalez Prada, *Pájinas Libres* (Lima: Ediciones PEISIA), 23.

60. Salazar Bondy, 13–14.

61. Jean Descola, *Daily Life in Colonial Peru, 1710–1820*, trans. Michael Heron (New York: Macmillan, 1968), 254. Also see Palma's own account of La Perricholi, "Genialidades de la 'Perricholi,' " *Tradiciones peruanas completas*, 616–21.

62. Mariátegui, 34.

63. Mariátegui, 198.

64. A facsimile of Palma's letter to Gálvez appears in José Gálvez's *Una Lima que se va* (Lima: PTCM, 1947), ix.

65. Gálvez, 133–34; 164.

66. Gálvez, 22.

67. Palma, "Cháchara," *Tradiciones peruanas completas*, 3. For other examples of Palma's critique of romanticism, also see "Carta tónico-biliosa a una amiga" (1874), 1453.

68. For a discussion of the division of nineteenth-century Latin American discourse into separate domains (literature, science, law, etc.) at the end of the century, see Julio Ramos's *Divergent Modernities. Culture and Politics in Nineteenth-Century Latin America* (Durham: Duke University Press, 2001), 41–78.

69. *Tradiciones peruanas completas*, 3.

70. *Epistolario*, 55.

71. *Epistolario*, 55.

72. "Carta tónico-biliosa a una amiga," *Tradiciones peruanas completas*, 1453.

73. *Epistolario*, 55. For similar allusions to the dead and their revival in his traditions, see Palma's *Tradiciones peruanas completas*, specifically "Cháchara," 3; "Carta tónico-biliosa a una amiga," 1453; "Preludio obligado," 1457. Moreover, Palma underlines the idea of the tradition as a transaction with the absent dead when he published some of his final traditions under the titles of *Ropa vieja* (old clothes) and *Ropa apolillada* (moth-eaten clothes).

74. "Preludio obligado," 1457.

75. See Palma's "Cháchara" and "Preludio obligado," 3, 1457.

76. Ortega, "Las Tradiciones peruanas y el proceso . . . ," 430.

77. *Epistolario*, 334.

78. Ricardo Palma, *Tradiciones peruanas* (Madrid: Calpe, 1923).

PERUVIAN TRADITIONS

First Series

Palla-Huarcuna

Whither marches the son of the Sun with so great a cortege?

Tupac-Yupanqui,[1] he who is rich in all the virtues, as the *haravicus*[2] of Cuzco call him, is proceeding in triumph through his vast empire, and wherever he passes unanimous cries of benediction are raised. The people are applauding their sovereign, because he brings them prosperity and good fortune.

Victory has accompanied his valiant army, and the unruly tribe of the Pachis has fallen before him.

Warrior of the red *llautu!*[3] Your body has been bathed in the blood of the enemy, and the people come forth to admire your courage as you pass.

Woman! Abandon your spinning wheel and lead your little ones by the hand so that they may learn from the soldiers of the Inca how to fight for the homeland.

The condor with giant wings, treacherously wounded and no longer possessed of the strength to cross the blue of the sky, has fallen on the highest peak of the Andes, tingeing the snow with its blood. The grand priest, seeing it dying, has said that the ruin of the empire of

---

[1] Tupac-Yupanqui, the eleventh Inca ruler, whose ambitious and successful military campaigns helped consolidate the empire in the fifteenth century.—Ed.

[2] Bards.

[3] Headband worn by Incas.

Manco[4] is approaching, and that others will come in pirogues with high sides to impose their religion and their laws upon it.

In vain do you raise your voice in prayer and offer sacrifices, O daughters of the Sun, for the omen will be fulfilled.

You are fortunate, old man, for only the dust of your bones will be trodden underfoot by the stranger, and your eyes will not see the day of humiliation for your kin! Until then, O daughter of Mama-Ocllo,[5] bring your sons, that they not forget the bravery of their fathers when the hour of conquest sounds in the life of the homeland.

Beautiful are your hymns, girl of the rosy lips; but in your accent there is the bitterness of the captive.

Perhaps you have left the idol of your heart behind in your native valleys; and today, as you march with your sisters in procession before the golden litter that the *curacas*[6] bear on their shoulders; you must hold back your tears and sing the praises of the conqueror. No, little wood-dove! . . . Your beloved is near you; for he too is one of the prisoners of the Inca.

Night is beginning to fall upon the mountains, and the royal cortege is stopping in Izcuchaca. Suddenly the alarm is sounded in the camp.

The beautiful captive, the young girl with the necklace of *guairuros*,[7] chosen for the monarch's seraglio, has been surprised as she fled with her lover, who has died defending her.

Tupac-Yupanqui orders the unfaithful slave girl put to death.

And she listens to the sentence joyfully, because she longs to be reunited with the master of her heart, and because she knows that the earth is not the abode of eternal love.

And therefore, O traveler! If you wish to know the place where the captive was sacrificed, the place that the inhabitants of Huancayo call Palla-Huarcuna, focus your eyes on the chain of hills, and between Izcuchaca and Huaynanpuquio you will see a rock in the form of an Indian maiden with a necklace at her throat and a turban of feathers

---

[4] Manco-Capac founded the Inca dynasty in the twelfth century. According to popular tradition, Manco-Capac was a divine entity that emerged from a sacred cave to disseminate the cult of the sun.—Ed.

[5] Mama-Ocllo Huaco was the sister of Manco-Capac and the mother of his son, Sinchi Roca, who succeeded him as Inca.—Ed.

[6] Great nobles.

[7] Indian currants.

on her head. The rock seems to have been sculpted by an artist, and the natives of the region, in their naive superstition, take it to be the evil spirit of their district, and believe that no one who dares pass by Palla-Huarcuna at night will escape being devoured by the phantom of the rock.

The Christ in Agony

(To Dr. Alcides Destruge)

I

San Francisco de Quito, founded in August, 1534, on the ruins of the ancient capital of the Scyris, is located on the western slope of Mount Pichincha or "mountain that boils," and today has a population of 70,000.

Mount Pichincha reveals to the curious gaze of the traveler two large craters, which are doubtless the result of its many eruptions. Three notable cones or vents can be seen, known as Rucu-Pichincha or Old Pichincha, Guagua-Pichincha or Young Pichincha, and Cundor-Guachana or Condors' Nest. After Sangay, the most active active volcano in the world, which is also in what was once the land of the Scyris, near Riobamba, Rucu-Pichincha is undoubtedly the most terrible volcano in South America. History has passed on to us only the record of its eruptions in 1534, 1539, 1577, 1588, 1660, and 1662. Almost two centuries had gone by without its torrents of lava and violent tremors giving rise to mourning and desolation, and there were many geologists who believed that it was an extinct volcano. But then March 22, 1859, came to give the lie to the high priests of science, for the picturesque city of Quito was very nearly destroyed at that time. Nonetheless, since the principal crater lies to the east, its lava pours forth in the direction of the Emerald deserts, a circumstance that saved the city that was the victim only of the tremors of the giant that serves it as a watch tower. It would be desirable, however, for the greater peace of mind of its habitants, to determine what basis there is in fact for Baron Humboldt's[1] opinion that an area of 6,300 square miles around Quito provides enough inflammable material for a single volcano.

For the sons of the America of new republics, Pichincha stands as a symbol of one of the most heroic pages of the great epic of the revolution. On the slopes of the volcano there took place, on May 24, 1822, the bloody battle that forever assured the independence of Colombia.

May you be blessed, land of the brave, and may the tutelary spirit of the future have in store for you happier hours than those of your present! You offered me hospitable refuge on the shores of the picturesque Guayas in days of exile and misfortune.[2] A grateful pilgrim ought never to forget the spring that quenched his thirst, the palm tree that afforded him cool shelter and shade, and the welcome oasis where he saw a horizon for his hope open before him.

For that reason I once again take up my pen of a chronicler to save from the dust of oblivion one of your most beautiful traditions, the memory of one of your most illustrious sons, who with the inspired revelations of his paintbrush won the laurels of genius, as Olmedo, another of your sons, won the immortal crown of the poet with his Homeric verses.[3]

II

I have already said as much: I am about to tell you of a painter, Miguel de Santiago.

The art of painting, which in colonial days was made illustrious by Antonio Salas, Gorívar, Morales, and Rodríguez, is embodied in the

---

[1] Alexander von Humboldt (1769–1859), German naturalist and author of the *Voyage de Humboldt et Bonpland aux régions équinoxiales de nouveau continent, fait en 1799* (1805–1834).—Ed.

[2] Palma visited Guayaquil twice: once in 1859, during a short war between Peru and Ecuador, and in 1865, when he sailed home from Europe because of increasing tensions between Spain and Peru over the Chincha islands, which ultimately resulted in war between the two countries.—Ed.

[3] José Joaquín Olmedo (1780–1847), author of "Victoria de Junín," a neoclassical epic in celebration of Bolívar's triumph at the Battle of Junín (1824).—Ed.

magnificent works of our protagonist, who must be considered to be
the true master of the Quito school. Like the creations of Rembrandt
and the Flemish school, they are distinguished by their attention to
light and shadow, by a certain mysterious chiaroscuro, and by the fe-
licitous disposition of groups of figures, just as the Quito school is noted
for its vivid color and its naturalness. Do not look to it for artistic
refinement, or expect to find accurate draftsmanship in the lines of its
Madonnas, but if you are fond of the poetic quality of the blue sky of
our valleys, the gentle melancholy of the *yaraví*[4] that our Indians sing,
accompanied by the sentimental harmonies of the *quena*,[5] then look to
the works of Rafael Sanas, Cadenas, or Carrillo in our day.

The church of La Merced, in Lima, today displays with pride a
painting by Anselmo Yáñez. The Quito style is not seen in all its details, but from the whole it is evident that the artist was strongly motivated by national sentiment.

The people of Quito have a feeling for art. One fact will suffice to
prove this. The cloisters of the convent of San Agustín are hung with
14 paintings by Miguel de Santiago, outstanding among which is one
of large dimensions entitled *La genealogía del santo Obispo de Hipona*.[6]
One morning in 1857, a portion of the painting showing a beautiful
grouping of figures was stolen. The city was alerted and the entire
populace turned out to search. The painting was found and restored to
its place. The thief was a foreign art dealer.

But now that we have spoken in passing of the 14 paintings by Santiago preserved in the convent of San Agustín, which are notable for
their use of lifelike color and their majestic composition, in particular
the one entitled *Bautismo*,[7] we shall acquaint the reader with the cause
that motivated them. Like most of the biographical information that
we are setting down about this great artist, we have taken this episode
in his life from a notable article written by the Ecuadorian poet don
Juan León Mera.[8]

[4] Yaraví is a song that fuses elements of Hispanic and native Andean culture and that
is commonly accompanied by guitar and flute.—Ed.

[5] A rustic flute.

[6] *The Genealogy of the Saint and Bishop of Hippo.*

[7] Baptism.

[8] Juan León Mera (1832–1894), author of the novel *Cumandá* (1879). Here Palma references *La vírgen del sol: leyenda; Melodías indígenas* (1887).—Ed.

A Spanish magistrate commissioned Santiago to paint his portrait. When it was finished, the artist left for a village called Guápulo, setting the painting in the sun to dry and leaving his wife to look after it. The hapless woman could not keep from letting the portrait get dirty, and called on the famous painter Gorívar, a disciple and nephew of Miguel, to repair the damage. On his return Santiago discovered from the joint of one finger that another brush had painted it over. The two culprits confessed.

Our artist was of a temperament more easily roiled than the sea when it is suffering from a stomach ache and cramps. He was enraged at what he believed to be a profanation, set upon Gorívar with the blade of his sword, and sliced off one of his poor wife's ears. The magistrate appeared and upbraided him for his violent behavior. Without respect for the magistrate's eminence, Santiago beat him too. He fled and brought charges against the enraged painter, who took refuge in the cell of a friar, and in the 14 months he was in hiding painted the 14 pictures that adorn the cloisters of San Agustín. One of these, the one entitled *Milagro del peso de las ceras,*[9] deserves special mention. It is said that one of the figures in it is a self-portrait of Miguel de Santiago.

III

By the time that Miguel de Santiago could freely breathe once again the air of his native city, the asceticism of his century had taken hold of him. One idea obsessed him: to translate to canvas Christ's supreme agony.

He set about to do this many times, but dissatisfied with his work, he would throw his palate down and destroy the canvas. But not for all this did he lose sight of his idea.

The fever of his inspiration consumed him, and yet his brush refused to obey his powerful intelligence and his stubborn will. But genius finds a way to emerge victorious.

Among the disciples who frequented his study was a young man of striking beauty. Miguel thought he saw in him the model he needed to fully carry out his idea.

He had him undress and placed him on a wooden cross. The position

[9] *The Miracle of the Weighing of the Candles.*

was not at all pleasant or comfortable. Nonetheless, a faint smile appeared on the young man's face.

But the artist was not seeking an expression of satisfaction or indifference, but one of pain and anguish.

"Are you suffering?" he kept asking his disciple.

"No, master," the young man answered, smiling calmly.

Suddenly Miguel de Santiago, his eyes out of their sockets, his hair standing on end, let out a horrible oath and pierced the young man's side with a lance.

The youth groaned, and the convulsions of the death agony began to be reflected in his face.

And Miguel de Santiago, in a state of inspired madness and in the delirium of his art, set about copying the mortal anguish and his brush, as swift as thought itself, flew over the smooth canvas.

The dying man strained, cried out, and writhed on the cross, and as the painter copied each one of his convulsions, he exclaimed with mounting enthusiasm:

"Good! Good, master Miguel! Good, very good, master Miguel!"

Finally the great artist untied his victim, saw him lying bloody and lifeless, passed his hand over his forehead as if trying to remember what had happened, and like someone waking from an exhausting nightmare, realized the enormity of his crime, threw down his palette and brushes, and ran out of the studio.

Art had caused him to commit murder!

But his *Cristo de la Agonía* was finished.

IV

This was Miguel de Santiago's last painting. His extraordinary merit served as his defense, and after a long trial he was absolved.

The painting was taken to Spain. Does it still exist, or can it have been lost because of the well-known carelessness of that country? We do not know.

Miguel de Santiago, who from the day of his crime for the sake of art suffered from frequent hallucinations, died in November of 1673. His last resting place is at the foot of the altar of San Miguel in the chapel of El Sagrario.

Second Series

The Knights of the Cape

A Chronicle of a Civil War

(To don Juan de la Pezuela, count of Cheste)

I

Who the Knights of the Cape Were and the Oath They Swore

On the afternoon of June 5, 1541, 12 Spaniards, all of whom had been rewarded by the king for their exploits during the conquest of Peru, were gathered together at the home of Pedro de San Millán.

The house that sheltered them consisted of a parlor and five other rooms, leaving a large plot of ground on which to build. Six leather armchairs, an oak bench, and a grimy table flush against the wall were the only furniture in the parlor. Hence the house, like the attire of those who lived there, revealed from a mile away one of those sorts of poverty that rubs elbows with beggary. And this was in fact the case.

The 12 hidalgos belonged to the number of those vanquished in the battle of Salinas on April 6, 1538.[1] The victor had confiscated their properties, but thankfully, he had allowed them to breathe the air of

---

[1] One of the many battles between Spanish factions in sixteenth century Peru. On April 26, 1538, at Salinas, Hernando Pizarro defeated Diego de Almagro, who had rebelled against Francisco Pizarro's authority in Peru.—Ed.

Lima, where they lived on the charity of friends. The victor could have hanged them without much ado, as was the custom of that era, but don Francisco Pizarro was ahead of his time and seemed to be a man of our day, when one's enemies are not always killed or imprisoned, but are deprived, in whole or in part, of their ration of bread. The fallen and the upright, the satiated and the starved: that was the colony, and that has been and is the republic. The law of the hammer and the anvil ruling every time the tables turned, or as the song has it:

> We got out of Guate-mala
> And entered Guate-peor:[2]
> the tambourine changes hands,
> but it sounds the same as before.

or as they say in Italy: being free of the barbarians only to end up with the Barberini.

The 12 cavaliers were named Pedro de San Millán, Cristóbal de Sotelo, García de Alvarado, Francisco de Chaves, Martín de Bilbao, Diego Méndez, Juan Rodríguez Barragán, Gómez Pérez, Diego de Hoces, Martín Carrillo, Jerónimo de Almagro, and Juan Tello.

Because of the importance of the role they play in this chronicle, we shall sketch a brief likeness of each one of the noblemen, beginning with the owner of the house. *A tout seigneur tout honneur.*[3]

Pedro de San Millán, Knight of the Order of Santiago, was 38 years old and was among the number of the 170 conquistadors who had captured Atahualpa. When the Inca's ransom was divided up, he received 135 silver marks and 3,330 doubloons. A loyal friend of Marshal don Diego de Almagro, he followed the latter's ill-fated colors, thereby falling into disgrace with the Pizarro brothers, who confiscated his fortune, leaving him as alms the dismantled property on the calle de Judíos, or as the saying goes: A small cage is quite big enough for a sparrow. In his earlier days when fortune smiled upon him, San Millán

---

[2] A play on words: "Guate-peor" is a punning comparative of "Guatemala." The proverb usually runs: "salir de Guatemala para ir a Guatepeor," to fall from the frying pan into the fire, see George W. Umphrey's *Tradiciones peruanas* (Chicago: B. H. Sanborn & Co., 1936), 19.

[3] Honor to whom honor is due [French].

had been an extravagant spendthrift; he was valiant, of graceful bearing, and his men were generally devoted to him.

Cristóbal de Sotelo was going on 55, and as a soldier who had fought in Europe his advice was held in great esteem. He was captain of infantry in the battle of Salinas.

García de Alvarado was a most arrogant young man of 28, with a martial air about him, instinctively overbearing, very ambitious, and paid what he deemed himself worth. There was something of the rogue and the rascal about him.

Diego Méndez, of the Order of Santiago, was the brother of the famous general Rodrigo Ordóñez who died in the battle of Salinas, in which he was leader of the losing army. Méndez was 43, and had a reputation not so much as a soldier as a Don Juan and a courtier.

As for Francisco de Chaves, Martín de Bilbao, Diego de Hoces, Gómez Pérez, and Martín Carrillo, the chroniclers tell us only that they were intrepid soldiers and beloved by their men. None of them lived to be 35. Juan Tello, the Sevillian, was one of the 12 founders of Lima, the others being Marquis Pizarro, the treasurer Alonso Riquelme, the Comptroller García de Salcedo, the Sevillian Nicolás de Ribera the elder, Ruiz Díaz, Rodrigo Mazuelas, Cristóbal de Peralta, Alonso Martín de Don Benito, Cristóbal Palomino, the Salamancan Nicolás de Ribera the younger, and Antonio Picado, the secretary. The first mayors of the town council of Lima were Ribera the Elder and Juan Tello. As is evident, the latter had been an important personage and at the time that we are portraying him he was 46 years old.

Jerónimo de Almagro had been born in the same city as Marshal Almagro and because of this circumstance and that of their common surname, they called each other cousin. In truth they were not related, for don Diego was a poor foundling. Jerónimo was approaching 40.

Juan Rodríguez Barragán was the same age, held to be a man of great daring as well as great experience.

It is common knowledge that, just as in our day no man who respects himself would go out on the street in his shirt sleeves, so in bygone days no man who aspired to be considered decent dared appear in public without his cape. Be it cold weather or hot, the Spaniard of old and the cape went together, whether it was out walking, banqueting, or on feast days of the Church. For this reason I suspect that the decree issued by the minister Monteagudo in 1822 forbidding Spaniards to wear the cape had for the independence of Peru the same importance as a battle won by the insurgents. Once the cape was abolished, Spain disappeared.

To make matters even worse for our 12 hidalgos, they had only one cape between them, and when one of them was obliged to go out, the rest of them were kept inside for lack of the indispensable garment.

Antonio Picado, Marquis don Francisco Pizarro's secretary, or better put, the demon who was dooming Pizarro to perdition, when speaking one day of the hidalgos called them the "Knights of the Cape." The nickname caught on and soon was on everyone's lips.

A brief biographical note on Picado is to the point here.

Picado came to Peru in 1534 as secretary to the Marshal don Pedro de Alvarado, he of the famous leap in Mexico.[4] When Alvarado, maintaining that certain territories in the North were not included within the boundaries of Pizarro's conquest as fixed by the emperor, was about to do battle with the forces of don Diego de Almagro, Picado sold the latter the secrets of his chief, and one night, fearing that his treachery would be discovered, he fled to the enemy camp. The marshal sent troops in pursuit of him, and when they were unsuccessful wrote to don Diego that he would not enter into any agreement whatsoever with him unless he handed over the person of his disloyal secretary. The chivalrous Almagro refused to accede to Pizarro's demand, thus saving the life of a man who later was to bring such disaster to him and his men.

Don Francisco Pizarro took Picado on as his secretary, and the latter exerted a fateful and decisive influence over the marquis, for it was Picado who, by getting the better of the governor's generous impulses, made him cling to a policy of hostility toward those whose only crime was having lost the battle of Salinas.

By the year 1541 it was known for a fact that the monarch, on being informed on what was happening in this realm, was sending out the bachelor-at-law don Cristóbal Vaca de Castro to impeach the governor, and the partisans of Almagro, readying themselves to ask for justice for the murder of don Diego, sent captains Alonso Portocarrero and Juan Balsa to report to this envoy of the crown so as to forewarn him. But

---

[4]Before arriving in Peru, Pedro de Alvarado (1485–1541) had participated with Hernán Cortés in the Conquest of Mexico. When the Spanish were forced from Tenochtitlan on July 1, 1519, by Aztec resistance (recorded in history as the "Noche Triste," or "Sad Night"), Alvarado used his lance to vault away from his pursuers.—Ed.

the investigating magistrate had not arrived as yet in the City of Kings; illness and bad weather at sea were delaying him.

Meanwhile Pizarro tried to win friends even among the Knights of the Cape and sent messages to Sotelo, Chaves, and others, offering to extricate them from the sorry state of paupers in which they were living. But to the honor of the Almagrists, it is only fitting to record that they did not humble themselves to accept this crust of bread thrown their way.

With matters having reached such a pass, Picado's insolence grew by the day, and there was no excuse for his way of insulting the "men from Chile," as Almagro's supporters were called. Incensed, the men from Chile hung three lengths of rope from the scaffold one night, with placards that read: "For Pizarro"—"For Picado"—"For Velázquez."

On learning of this affront, the marquis, far from being discountenanced, said with a smile:

"Poor wretches! We must give them some breathing room. They have had enough misfortune without our troubling them further. They are gamblers who have lost and as such they are going to extremes."

But Picado felt, as his name suggests, piqued, and that afternoon, the fifth of June, attired in a doublet and a short French cape with repoussé silver embroidery, and mounted on a spirited steed, paraded back and forth, making the horse caracole, in front of the gates of Juan de Rada, young Almagro's guardian, and those of San Millán's home, the residence of the 12 hidalgos, carrying his provocation to the point that, when a number of them showed themselves, he made a rude gesture, shouting: "For the men from Chile" and put his spurs to his mount.

The Knights of the Cape immediately summoned Juan de Rada.

Pizarro had offered Almagro the Younger, who was left an orphan at the age of 19, to be a second father to him, and to that end had taken him to live at his palace; but when the youth, tired of hearing words demeaning the memory of the marshal and his friends, he broke off with the marquis and became the ward of Juan de Rada. The latter, a lively and respected elderly man who belonged to a noble family of Castile, was held to be a man of great prudence and experience. He lived in rooms in the arcade of the Botoneros—the name passementerie workers who are known elsewhere as *pasamaneros* go by to this day— a few blocks of which is known to this day as the callejón de los Clérigos. Rada saw in the person of Almagro the Younger a son and a flag around which to rally to avenge the death of the marshal, and all the men from Chile, who numbered over 200, while recognizing the young don Diego as their leader, looked to Rada to give the revolutionary troops impetus and direction.

Rada swiftly answered the call of the Knights of the Cape. The elderly man presented himself, seething with indignation at Picado's most recent affront, and the group resolved not to await justice at the hands of the envoy that the crown was sending, but to proceed to punish the marquis and his insolent secretary themselves.

García de Alvarado, who was wearing the cape of the company of knights, threw it onto the ground, and stepping upon it, said:

"Let us swear, for the salvation of our souls, to die safeguarding the rights of young Almagro, and to cut from this cape the shroud of Antonio Picado."

II

Concerning the Daring Undertaking
Carried Out by the Knights of the Cape

Things could not be planned in secret to the point that the marquis would not notice that the men from Chile were frequently gathering together, that there reigned among them a pent-up excitement, that they were buying arms, and that, when Rada and Almagro the Younger went out on the street, they were followed, at a distance and under the guise of an escort, by a group of their supporters. Nonetheless, the marquis ordered no special measures.

In the midst of this lack of action on the part of the governor, the latter received letters from the authorities of different cities informing him that the men from Chile were openly paving the way for an uprising throughout the country. These accusations and others obliged him to send for Juan de Rada one morning.

The latter found the governor in the garden of the palace, at the foot of a fig tree that is still there today, and according to Herrera in his *Décadas*,[5] the following conversation took place between the two of them:

[5] Antonio de Herrera y Tordesillas (d. 1625), author of *Historia de los hechos de los Cas-*

"What is this, Juan de Rada? I am told that you've been buying arms to kill me."

"In all truth, sir, I have bought two cuirasses and a coat of mail to defend myself."

"But what moves you today, more than at some other time, to procure arms for yourself?"

"Because we are told, sir, and it is common knowledge that Your Lordship is collecting lances to kill all of us. Let Your Lordship finish us off and do with us as you please, for since you have lopped off our head, I've no idea why you should respect our feet. People are also saying that Your Lordship is thinking of killing the magistrate who is being sent by the king. If such is your intention and you decide to kill the men from Chile, do not kill all of them. Let Your Lordship send don Diego into exile on a ship, for he is innocent, and I shall go with him wherever fortune may take us."

"Who has made you suspect such great treachery and evil intent as that? Such a thought never entered my mind, and I am more anxious than you to see the magistrate arrive, as he already would have had he agreed to board the galleon that I sent to Panama to bring him here. As for the arms, I will have you know that I went out hunting the other day, and among all of those in our party none of us was carrying a lance, so I sent my servants to buy one, and they bought four. May it please God, Juan de Rada, that the royal envoy should arrive and these matters have an end, and may He uphold the truth!"

Not for nothing has it been said that good counsel comes from one's enemy. Perhaps Pizarro would not have come to his unhappy end if, as the keen-witted Rada advised him, he had exiled Almagro on the spot.

The conversation continued on a friendly note, and when Rada took his leave, Pizarro gave him six figs that he cut from the tree with his own hand; they were among the first to have been grown in Lima.

With this interview don Francisco thought that he had averted all danger, and he continued to disregard the warnings that he continually received.

---

tellanos en las Islas y Tierra Firme del Mar Océano en VIII décadas, desde 1492–1515 (1726–1730).—Ed.

On the afternoon of June 25, a priest sent word to the marquis that under the secrecy of the confessional he had learned that the Almagrists were plannning an attempt on his life in the near future.

"That priest is after a bishopric," the marquis replied, and with his usual disregard for danger went without an escort to take a stroll and play bowls, accompanied by Nicolás de Ribera the Elder.

As he was going to bed, the little page who was helping him undress said to him:

"Milord, there is nothing to be heard on the streets save that the men from Chile want to kill Your Lordship."

"Bah! Leave off listening to such prattle, my boy, for such matters aren't for your ears," Pizarro interrupted him.

Sunday June 26 dawned, and the marquis arose somewhat concerned.

At nine o'clock he summoned the mayor, Juan de Velázquez, and advised him to try to keep himself informed of the plans of the men from Chile, and if he suspected any serious attempt on his life, to proceed forthwith to arrest their leader and his principal friends. Velázquez gave him this answer, which in the light of what happened has a certain humor:

"Your Lordship need not worry, for as long as I have this ceremonial staff of office in my hand, I swear before God that no harm will be done you!"

Contrary to his habit, Pizarro did not attend Mass at a church, but ordered that one be said in the palace chapel.

It appears that Velázquez did not keep the marquis's order a secret as he should have, and spoke of it with the treasurer Alonso Riquelme and several others. It thus came to the attention of Pedro de San Millán, who went to Rada's residence, where many of the conspirators were forgathered. He shared what he knew with them and added: "It is time to act, for if we set aside our plan till tomorrow, we will be quartered today."

As the others scattered throughout the city to carry out various tasks, Juan de Rada, Martín de Bilbao, Diego Méndez, Cristóbal de Sosa, Martín Carrillo, Pedro de San Millán, Juan de Porras, Gómez Pérez, Arbolancha, Narváez and others, until they numbered 19 conspirators, set out in a hurry from the calle de los Clérigos (and not that of the mat makers, as is commonly believed), heading for the governor's palace. Gómez Pérez skirted a puddle so as not to step into it, and Juan de Rada upbraided him: "We're about to bathe ourselves in human blood, and milord is being careful not to get his feet wet? Turn around and go back; you're of no use to us."

More than 500 persons, passersby or people going to twelve o'clock Mass, were in the Plaza de Armas at the time and indifferently watched the group go by. Certain suspicious individuals confined themselves to saying: "Those men are going to kill the marquis or Picado."

The marquis, governor, and captain general of Peru, don Francisco Pizarro was chatting in one of the drawing rooms of the palace with the bishop-elect of Quito, Mayor Velázquez, and some 15 friends more, when a page rushed in shouting: "The men from Chile are coming to kill milord the marquis."

The confusion was frightful. Some of them rushed down the halls to the garden, and others climbed out the windows to the street, among the latter Mayor Velázquez, who, in order to get a better hold on a balustrade, placed his ceremonial staff between his teeth. He thereby kept the oath he had sworn to three hours before, for if the marquis found himself in danger, it was because Velázquez did not have his staff in his hand but in his mouth.

Pizarro, whose cuirass was not tightly fastened because he did not have enough space to finish girding himself for battle, with his cape across his chest as a shield and sword in hand, came out to fight the conspirators, who had already killed a captain and wounded three or four servants. The marquis was accompanied by his half brother Martín de Alcántara, Juan Ortiz de Zárate, and two pages.

Despite his 64 years, Pizarro fought with the verve of youth, and the conspirators were unable to get past a door defended by the marquis and his four companions, who emulated his brio and his bravery.

"Traitors! Why do you want to kill me? How shameful! Attacking my house like brigands!" Pizarro shouted in a fury, brandishing his sword. As he wounded one of the conspirators whom Rada had pushed toward him, Martín de Bilbao ran his sword through his neck.

The conqueror of Peru uttered only one word: "Jesus!" and fell, tracing a cross of blood on the ground with his finger and kissing it.

Then Juan Rodríguez Barragán broke a jug of Guadalajara earthenware over his head, and don Francisco Pizarro breathed his last.

Martín de Alcántara and the two pages died with him, and Ortiz de Zárate was left badly wounded.

The conspirators later tried to take Pizarro's body away and drag it through the plaza, but the pleas of the bishop of Quito and the influence of Juan de Rada prevented this barbarous act. During the night two humble servants of the marquis washed the body; dressed it in the habit of the Order of Santiago but did not put the marquis's gold spurs on for they had disappeared; dug a grave on the site of what today is the cathedral, in the courtyard that is still called the Patio de los Naranjos,[6] and buried the corpse. Pizarro's bones today lie beneath the main altar of the cathedral in a velvet-lined chest with gold clasps. At least that is the general belief.

Once the murder had been committed, those responsible for it proceeded to the Plaza de Armas, shouting: "Long live the king! The tyrant is dead! Long live Almagro! May justice be done on earth!" And Juan de Rada rubbed his hands together in satisfaction, saying: "O happy day when it was seen that Marshal Almagro had loyal friends to take their vengeance on his murderer!"

Jerónimo de Aliaga, the factor Illán Suárez de Carbajal, the municipal magistrate Nicolás de Ribera the Elder, and many of the eminent citizens of Lima were immediately imprisoned. The residences of the marquis, his brother Alcántara, and Picado were sacked. The booty from the first of these was estimated to be 100,000 pesos, that of the second 15,000 pesos, and that of the third 40,000.

By three in the afternoon, more than 200 of Almagro's supporters had set up a new municipal government, installed Almagro the Younger in the palace with the title of governor until the king ordered otherwise, recognized Cristóbal de Sotela as lieutenant governor, and given command of the army to Juan de Rada.

The Mercedarian friars, who in Lima as in Cuzco were supporters of Almagro, carried their monstrance in procession and hastened to recognize the new government. The friars always played a large role in the quarrels of the conquistadors. It was they who turned the pulpit of the church of Santo Espíritu into a platform for slandering the side that did not share their sympathies. And as proof of the influence that the sermons had on the soldiery, we shall copy a letter that Francisco Girón[7] sent to Father Baltasar Melgarejo. The letter reads: "Most Mag-

---

[6] Patio of the Orange Trees.

[7] After the events described in this tradition, Francisco Hernández de Girón (d.1554)

nificent and Reverend Sir: I have learned that Your Paternity does me more battle with his tongue than do soldiers with their arms. I beg you to be so kind as to remedy this, for otherwise, God granting me victory, Your Paternity will oblige me to turn a blind eye to our friendship and to the position that Your Paternity holds, the most magnificent and reverend person of whom may He keep. From this my camp at Pachamac. Your servant kisses the hand of Your Paternity. Francisco Hernández Girón."

A historical observation. Rada was always the soul of the conspiracy, and Almagro the Younger was ignorant of all the plans of his supporters. He was not consulted regarding the murder of Pizarro, and the young leader played no role in it save to accept it as an accomplished fact.

Once Mayor Velázquez found himself in prison, he was helped to escape by his brother the bishop of Cuzco, Fray Vicente Valverde, that fanatic of the Dominican order who exerted such influence with regard to the capture and torture of Atahualpa.[8] The two brothers then boarded ship to go join Vaca de Castro, but on the island of La Puná the Indians shot them to death with their arrows, together with 17 Spaniards. We do not know for certain whether the Church venerates Father Valverde among its martyrs.

Velázquez went from the frying pan into the fire. The Knights of the Cape would not have forgiven him either.

At the first signs of revolt, Antonio Picado hid in the house of the treasurer Riquelme. His place of refuge having been discovered the following day, Almagro's supporters came to seize him. Riquelme said to them: "I do not know where señor Picado is," even as with his eyes he made signs for them to look for him under the bed. My pen declines to comment on such a base act.

---

became a military ally of the first Viceroy of Peru, Blanco Núñez de Vela, who was defeated by Gonzalo Pizarro in the Battle of Iñaquito in 1546. After Gonzalo Pizarro's execution in 1548, Girón associated himself La Gasca, a representative of the Spanish king who executed him for leading a bloody revolt against his authority. For more on these events, see "The Magistrate's Ears" and "The Demon of the Andes."—Ed.

[8] Vicente de Valverde (d.1542) was the Dominican friar who gave the signal to capture Atahualpa when the Inca ruler threw down a bible that Valverde had offered him.

The Knights of the Cape, headed by Juan de Rada and with the consent of don Diego, set themselves up as a tribunal. Each of them threw up to Picado the insults to which he had been subjected when as Pizarro's secretary Picardo was all-powerful; he was then tortured to make him reveal where the marquis had hidden treasure; and finally, on September 29, he was beheaded in the Plaza de Armas with the following proclamation, read aloud by Cosme Ledesma, a Spanish-speaking black, to the roll of drums and accompanied by four soldiers with pikes and two others with matchlock harquebuses: "His Majesty has ordered the death of this man because he has been a troublemaker in this realm; and because he burned or seized many royal decrees, concealing them since they would bring harm to the marquis; and because he was extorting and had extorted as bribes from the country a large sum of gold pesos."

The oath of the Knights of the Cape had been kept to the letter. And the famous cape served as Antonio Picado's shroud.

III

The End of the Twelve Knights of the Cape and Their Leader

It is not our intention to go into details concerning the 14 months and a half that Almagro the Younger acted as caudillo, or to write a history of the campaign that Vaca de Castro was obliged to undertake to vanquish him. Hence we shall speak only briefly of the principal events.

With few sympathies among the residents of Lima, don Diego found himself forced to abandon the city in order to reinforce his troops in Guamanga and Cuzco, where he had many supporters. Days before beginning his retreat, Francisco de Chaves came to him with a complaint, and seeing that no remedy for it was forthcoming, he said to him: "I do not wish to be your friend any longer, and I return to you my sword and my horse." Juan de Rada arrested him for insubordination, and had him beheaded immediately. Thus ended the life of one of the Knights of the Cape.

Juan de Rada, worn out by his years and his tribulations, died in Jauja as the campaign began. This was a fatal blow to the rebel cause.

García de Alvarado replaced him as general, and Cristóbal de Sotelo was named field marshal.

Discord soon broke out between the two heads of the army, and as Sotelo lay ill, García de Alvarado went to demand satisfaction for certain bits of gossip that had come his way. "I do not recall having said anything about you or about the Alvarados," the marshal answered. "But if I have said something, I shall say it again, because, being who I am, I couldn't care less about the Alvarados. And wait until I have recovered from the fever that has laid me low before you ask me for further explanations at sword's point." Thereupon the impetuous García de Alvarado committed the villainy of wounding Sotelo, and one of García's partisans finished him off. Such was the death of the second Knight of the Cape.

Almagro the Younger would have liked to punish the treacherous murderer immediately, but it was not an easy undertaking. García de Alvarado, proud of his prestige among the troops, was plotting to rid himself of don Diego, and then, depending on what best suited him, either fight Vaca de Castro or come to an agreement with him. Almagro craftily dissembled, won Alvarado's trust, and succeeded in luring him to a banquet that Pedro de San Millán was giving in Cuzco. There, in the middle of the feast, a confidant of don Diego's threw himself upon don García, saying to him:

"You're a prisoner!"

"Not a prisoner, dead," Almagro added and stabbed him, with the other guests finishing him off.

Thus three of the Knights of the Cape left this world before doing battle with the enemy. It was written in the stars that all of them would die a violent death, bathed in their own blood.

Meanwhile, the decisive moment was approaching, and Vaca de Castro made peace overtures to Almagro and declared an amnesty, from which only the nine Knights of the Cape who were still alive, and two or three Spaniards besides, were excepted.

On Sunday, September 16, 1542, the civil war ended with the bloody battle of Chupas. Almagro, at the head of 500 men, was almost the victor over the 800 who were following the colors of Vaca de Castro. During the first hour victory seemed to favor the side of the young leader, for Diego de Hoces, who was in command of one wing of his army, totally routed a division on the other side. Without the daring of Francisco de Carbajal, who restored order in the ranks of Vaca de Castro and in addition to that, had it not been for the lack of experience or the treason of Pedro de Candia, who was in command of Almagro's artillery, the victory of the men from Chile would have been assured.

The number of dead on both sides was over 240, and the number of wounded was also considerable. In view of such a small a number of combatants, carnage such as that can be explained only by keeping in mind that the supporters of young Almagro had for their leader the same fanatical devotion that they had professed for his father the marshal, and it is a well-known fact that fanaticism for a cause has always made for heroes and martyrs.

Those were indeed the days when great valor was needed to enter the fray. Battles ended in hand-to-hand combat, and strength, skill, and high morale determined the outcome.

Firearms were three centuries away from rifles with a firing pin and were, rather, a bother for the soldier, who could not use his musket or harquebus unless he was equipped with a steel, a flint, and tinder for lighting the fuse. Artillery was in its infancy; if stone-throwing mortars or falconets were of any use, it was to make noise as did petards. In a word, gunpowder was wasted by firing in salvos, and since calibrated range finding was as yet unknown, cannon balls landed wherever the devil guided them. Today it is a joy to fall on the battlefield, for the cowardly as for the brave, with the same exactitude with which an equation in the third degree is solved. One's fellow dies mathematically, according to the book, clean as a whistle, and in short it must be a consolation that the soul is being taken to another neighborhood. No question about it, a cannon ball today is a scientific one, born educated and knowing precisely where it is going to land. This is progress, and the all rest is sparks and fizzles.[9]

With all hope of victory gone, Martín de Bilbao and Jerónimo de Almagro refused to leave the battlefield and flung themselves on the enemy's ranks shouting: "Kill me; I killed the marquis!" They soon lay lifeless. Their dead bodies were quartered the following day.

---

[9] This passage is a fine example of how Palma ironically interjects the republican present into his evocation of the colonial era.—Ed.

Pedro de San Millán, Martín Carrillo, and Juan Tello were taken prisoner, and Vaca de Castro immediately ordered them beheaded.

Diego de Hoces, the brave captain who caused such havoc among the royalist troops, managed to escape from the battlefield, only to be beheaded in Guamanga a few days later.

Juan Rodríguez Barragán, who had remained behind as lieutenant governor in Cuzco, was taken prisoner in the city and put to death. On learning of his defeat, the same authorities who had appointed don Diego went over to the victor's side in the hope of obtaining amnesties and rewards.

Diego Méndez and Gómez Pérez managed to find asylum with the Inca Manco, who had refused to capitulate to the conquest and was maintaining a large army of Indians on the peaks of the Andes. They lived there until the end of 1544. In the middle of a quarrel with the Inca Manco one day, Gómez Pérez stabbed him to death, whereupon the Indians murdered the two Knights of the Cape and four other Spaniards who had sought refuge with them.

Almagro the Younger fought desperately until the last moment, when, the battle now lost, he spurred his horse on, galloped toward Pedro de Candia, and crying out "Traitor!" ran him through with his lance. Thereupon Diego Méndez made him take flight with him to go join the Inca, and the two of them would have succeeded in doing so had not Méndez taken it into his head to enter Cuzco to bid his mistress farewell. Because of this imprudence the valiant youth was taken prisoner, while Méndez managed to escape, only to die later at the hands of the Indians, as we have already recounted.

Almagro was brought to trial and emerged a condemned man. He appealed the verdict to the Royal Tribunal of Panama and to the king, and the appeal was denied. Then he said forthrightly: "I place Vaca de Castro before God's tribunal, where we will be judged without passion, and then I shall go to my death in the same place where my father was beheaded. I ask only that I be buried in the same grave, beneath his remains."

"He met death courageously," we are told by a chronicler who witnessed his execution. "He refused to have his eyes blindfolded so that he might fix them on the image of Christ Crucified until his last moment; and as he had asked, he was buried in the same grave as his father the marshal."

He was a young man 24 years old, born of a noble Indian mother from Panama, of medium height, fair of face, a fine horseman, very courageous, and skilled in the use of arms; he shared the cleverness of his progenitor, exceeded his father in liberality, for he was most generous, and like him, knew how to win the devotion of his followers.

Thus, with the sad end of their leader and of the Knights of the Cape, the band of men from Chile was annihilated.

The Magistrate's Ears

I

A Chronicle of the Era of the Second Viceroy of Peru

The imperial town of Potosí was, in the middle of the sixteenth century, the place to which fortune hunters chose to flock. This explains why, five years after the discovery of its rich mines, the town's population numbered over 25,000 souls.

"A mining town," the proverb goes, "is a lustful, lawless town." And never was a proverb more apt than in the case of Potosí during the first two centuries of the conquest.

The year of grace 1550 was drawing to a close, and the municipal magistrate of the town was the bachelor-of-laws don Diego de Esquivel, an irascible and covetous man, who was reputed to be capable of auctioning off justice in exchange for bars of silver.

His Honor was also fond of the fruit of paradise, and in the imperial town there was much gossip about his exploits as a philanderer. Don Diego had not gotten himself into the fix of having the parish priest read him the famous epistle of Saint Paul and prided himself on belonging to the brotherhood of bachelors, who in my opinion constitute, if not a social plague, a threat to other people's property. There are those who affirm that communists and bachelors are bipeds closely resembling each other.

In those days His Honor was infatuated with a girl from the town; but she, wanting no more to do with the magistrate, had very politely sent him packing, placing herself in the safeguard of a soldier of the Tucumán infantry regiment, a lad who had fallen madly in love with the damsel's charms. Hence the magistrate was eager for the chance to take his vengeance on the ungrateful girl who had snubbed him, as well as on the lad who had won her favor.

Since the devil never sleeps,[1] it happened that one night a great commotion broke out in one of Potosí's many gambling houses, swarms of which, contrary to the ordinances and decrees of the viceroy, were to be found in the calle de Quinto Mayu. A gambler, a novice when it came to prestidigitation and lacking the skill to make the little cubes behave, had allowed three dice to roll out of his hand when the stakes were high, whereupon another of the gamblers, possessed of a short temper, had brought out his dagger and pinned the neophyte's hand to the gaming table. The shouts and the fracas that ensued brought the night watch, and with it the magistrate, armed with his ceremonial sword and staff.

"Shut your traps and to jail with all of you!" he ordered.

And the constables, siding with the gamblers as is usual in such rows, allowed them to escape through the lofts overhead, confining themselves, for the record, to nabbing two of the least quick witted.

Don Diego was overjoyed when, on visiting the jail the next day, he immediately caught on to the fact that one of the prisoners was his rival, the soldier from the Tucumán regiment.

"Hello there, my good man! So you're something of a gambler as well?"

"What does Your Honor mean? A devil of a toothache was keeping me awake last night, so to see if I could relieve it I went to that gambling house looking for a countryman of mine who always carries with him in his purse a couple of Saint Apollonia's molars, which are said to cure the toothache as if by magic."

"I'll cast a magic spell over you, you rogue," the judge muttered, and

---

[1] The devil frequently appears in the *Peruvian Traditions* (see for example, "The Countess Who Was Summoned," "A Mother's Love," and "The Black Mass"). In another tradition, "El Alcalde de Paucarcolla," Palma writes: "We need the Devil; they must return him to us. . . . In the name of a pyrotechnic history and a phosphorescent literature I protest against the supression of the bad enemy. To eliminate the devil is to kill the tradition" (my translation) in *Tradiciones peruanas completas* (Madrid: Aguilar, 1953), 270–71.—Ed.

turning to the other prisoner, he added: "The two of you know what the law is: 100 duros' fine or a dozen lashes. I'll be back at noon and . . . be careful what you decide!"

Our soldier's fellow prisoner sent a message home and managed to get himself the money for the fine, and when the magistrate returned he found that the prisoner had rounded up the entire sum.

"And what about you, you scoundrel, are you paying or aren't you?" he asked the other prisoner.

"I haven't a peso to my name, sir; and Your Honor can decide as he will, but even though they quarter me, they won't get a quarter of a peso out of me. I beg your pardon, brother, but I've no money to give you."

"Well, running the gauntlet will make good on what you owe."

"That's not possible either, Your Honor, for even though I'm a soldier, I come from a well-known lineage and my father is a full 24th part Sevillian. Ask my captain, don Alvaro Castrillón, and Your Lordship will learn that I have a don before my name, as does the king himself, may God keep him."

"You a hidalgo, don Slyboots? Master Antúnez, give him 12 lashes at once."

"Be careful what you order, Your Honor, for, by Christ, a Spanish hidalgo is not treated so basely."

"A hidalgo! A hidalgo! Tell that to me in my other ear."

"Well then, don Diego," the soldier replied in a fury, "if that dastardly and cowardly act is carried out, I swear by God and the Virgin that I shall take my vengeance on Your Honor's ears."

The magistrate gave him a contemptuous look and left to take a turn about the courtyard of the jail.

Shortly thereafter, Antúnez the jailer, accompanied by four of his familiars or satellites, brought the hidalgo out in shackles and dealt him 12 resounding lashes in the presence of the magistrate. The victim bore the pain without the slightest murmur, and once the flogging was over Antúnez set him free.

"I don't hold this against you, Antúnez," the victim of the punishment told him, "but let the magistrate know that from today on his ears belong to me, and tell him that he should take as good care of them for me as if they were my most precious possession."

The jailer let out a stupid guffaw and muttered to himself:

"This fellow's brain is addled. If he's a raving madman the magistrate has only to turn him over to me, and we'll see if there's any truth to that proverb that says that punishment makes the madman sane."

II

Let us pause, friend reader, and make our way into the labyrinth of history, inasmuch as in this series of Traditions we have obliged ourselves to devote a few lines to the viceroy under whose rule our story takes place.

After the tragic fate that befell the first viceroy, don Blasco Núñez de Vela, the court of Spain deemed it best not to send another such high-ranking official to Peru immediately.[2] For the moment, invested with broad powers and signed blank orders from Charles V, the Licenciate La Gasca arrived in these parts with the title of governor, and history tells us that rather than to arms, he owed his victory over Gonzalo Pizarro to his astuteness and intelligence.

The country once pacified, La Gasca pointed out to the emperor the necessity of naming a viceroy for Peru, and suggested for this office don Antonio de Mendoza, marquis of Mondéjar and count of Tendilla, as a man already experienced in matters of government since he had ruled as viceroy of Mexico.

The marquis of Mondéjar, second viceroy of Peru, made his entry into Lima with modest pomp on September 23, 1551. The viceroyalty had just gone through a long and disastrous war, party passions were rampant, immorality was widespread, and Francisco Girón was preparing to lead the bloody uprising of 1553.[3]

The omens on the occasion of the viceroy's taking command were not, certainly, auspicious. His first step was to adopt a conciliatory policy, rejecting—so a historian affirms—the denunciations on which hostility feeds. "The story is told of him," Lorente[4] adds, "that when a captain once came to him to denounce two soldiers for having gone

---

[2] Reference to the defeat and execution of Viceroy Blasco Núñez de Vela at the hands of Gonzalo Pizarro, Francisco Pizarro's brother.—Ed.

[3] See "The Knights of the Cape," note 7.—Ed.

[4] Sebastián de Lorente (1813–1884), author of *Historia del Perú bajo la dinastía Austriaca, 1542–1598* (1863). "The Magistrate's Ears" is loosely based on a brief anecdote in Lorente's text.—Ed.

over to the Indians, living on what they could hunt and making gunpowder for their own exclusive use, the viceroy said to the captain in a stern voice: "Such deeds deserve to be rewarded rather than punished, because I fail to see what crime has been committed if two Spaniards are found living among Indians, eating what they kill with their harquebuses, and making gunpowder for themselves instead of to sell; there is, rather, much virtue in that and an example worthy of being imitated. Go with God, and let no one come to me another day with a tale like that, for it displeases me to hear such stories."

Would that those who govern always give such a splendid answer to troublemaking courtiers, professional accusers, and plotters of revolts and infernal machinations! The world would be the better for it.

Though he had the very best of intentions, the marquis of Mondéjar managed to carry out very few of them. He sent his son don Francisco to visit Cuzco, Chucuito, Potosí, and Arequipa and draw up a report on the needs of the natives; he appointed Juan Betanzos to write a history of the Incas; he created the guard of halberdiers; he handed down a number of sensible decrees concerning the municipal police of Lima; and he severely punished duelists and their seconds. Duels, even for ridiculous reasons, were the vogue of the period, and many of them took place with the duelists wearing blood-red tunics.

Good don Antonio de Mendoza planned to institute beneficial reforms. Unfortunately ill health dulled his energetic spirit, and death carried him off in July of 1552, after he had served as viceroy for only ten months. A week before his death on July 21, a clap of thunder was heard, accompanied by lightning flashes, a phenomenon seen and heard in Lima for the first time since the foundation of the city.

III

On the following day don Cristóbal de Agüero, for such was the name of the soldier, presented himself before the captain of the Tucumán regiment, don Alvaro Castrillón, and said to him:

"I beg you, sir, to grant me permission to leave the service. His Majesty wants soldiers with honor, and I have lost mine."

Don Alvaro, who held Agüero in great esteem, brought up several arguments to dissuade him, but all of them were dashed to pieces against the soldier's unbending resolve. The captain finally granted his request.

The humiliation suffered by don Cristóbal had remained a secret, for the magistrate forbade the jailers to speak of the incident. Perhaps don Diego's conscience cried out to him that his ceremonial staff as magistrate had served him to take his vengeance on the gambler for having had his amorous overtures rebuffed.

And three months had thus gone by when don Diego received letters summoning him to Lima to take possession of an inheritance, and having obtained permission from the chief magistrate to leave town, he began to make preparations for the trip.

He was taking a stroll through Cantumarca on the eve of his departure when a man with his face muffled in a cape approached him, asking him:

"Is your trip to begin tomorrow, Your Honor?"

"Is that any concern of yours, you most impertinent fellow?"

"Any concern of mine? I should say so! Seeing as how I must take care of those ears of yours."

And the man in the cape disappeared down a back street, leaving Esquivel amid a sea of puzzling thoughts.

Early the next morning don Diego began his trip to Cuzco. Once he had reached the city of the Incas, he was on his way to visit a friend that same day, when on turning a corner he felt a hand on his shoulder. He turned around in surprise and came face to face with the man he had ordered lashed in Potosí.

"Fear not, Your Honor. I see that those ears of yours are still in their rightful place, and that pleases me."

Don Diego was petrified.

Three weeks later, after our traveler had arrived in Guamanga and gone to his room at the inn, there was a knock on the door as darkness fell.

"Who is it?" the magistrate asked.

"Praised be The Most Holy!" the person outside answered.

"May He ever be praised, amen." And don Diego went to the door.

Neither the ghost of Banquo at Macbeth's feast, nor the appearance of the statue of the Knight Commander in don Juan's room caused more astonishment than that experienced by the magistrate on suddenly finding himself confronted by the man flogged in Potosí.

"Calm yourself, Your Lordship. Have those ears of yours suffered no deterioration? Well then, till we meet again."

Fear and remorse left don Diego speechless.

He reached Lima at last, and while on his first stroll met our ghost of a man, who this time did not say a word to him, but cast a telling glance at his ears. There was no avoiding him. In church and on his strolls the man dogged him like his shadow, his eternal nightmare.

Esquivel was in a state of constant anxiety, and the slightest noise made him give a start. Neither wealth, nor the esteem in which, beginning with the viceroy, the society of Lima held him, nor the city's banquets, nothing, in short, could calm his fears. The image of his relentless pursuer was forever etched on the pupils of his eyes.

And thus there arrived the anniversary of the scene in jail.

It was ten o'clock at night, and don Diego, having made certain that the doors of his town house were securely locked, was sitting comfortably in a leather armchair, engaged in writing letters by the light of a dim lamp. Suddenly a man stole in through a window in the next room, two sinewy arms held Esquivel fast, a gag smothered his cries, and in a moment strong ropes bound his body to the armchair.

The hidalgo of Potosí was before him, and a sharp dagger gleamed in his hands.

"Your Honor," he said to him, "the year is up today and I have come in the name of my honor."

And with diabolical serenity he sliced off the ears of the hapless magistrate.

IV

Don Cristóbal de Agüero managed to get himself transferred to Spain, making a mockery of the pursuit of him ordered by the viceroy, the marquis of Mondéjar. He asked for an audience with Charles V, made him judge of his cause, and was granted not only the sovereign's pardon, but promotion to captain of a regiment that was being organized to serve in Mexico.

The magistrate died a month later, not so much as a consequence of his wounds as on account of his humiliation at hearing himself called The Man with No Ears.

A Heretical Viceroy and a
Rascally Bell Ringer

A Chronicle of the Era of the
Seventeenth Viceroy of Peru

I

A Thrashing for Ringing a Bell

The church and the convent of the Augustinian Fathers were at first (1551) located at the site where the parish church of San Marcelo stands today, until in 1573 they were moved to the vast area they now occupy, not without a great legal battle and much controversy with Dominicans and Mercedarians who were opposed to the establishment of other monastic orders.

In a short time the Augustinians, because of their ascetic customs and their learning and science, gained a sort of supremacy over the other orders. They acquired very valuable properties, both rural and urban, and their income was so well managed and increased so greatly that for more than a century they were able to distribute 5,000 pesos in alms each year during Holy Week. The most eminent theologians and the most distinguished preachers belonged to this order, and the cloisters of San Ildefonso, a seminary that the Fathers founded in 1606 for the education of their novices, turned out truly illustrious men.

Around the year 1656, a Limeñan named Jorge Escoiquiz, a young man 20 Aprils old, succeeded in persuading the Fathers to allow him to take the habit, but since he showed more inclination toward knavery than toward study, the Fathers, who did not like to have scamps and idlers as novices, tried to expel him. But the scalawag found a patron in one of the outstanding Fathers of the order, and the monks charitably agreed to let him stay and gave him the important post of bell ringer.

The bell ringers of rich convents had as subordinates two slave boys, who wore the habit of lay brothers. So the post was not one to be scorned when the one who held it had, in addition to six pesos' salary, boarding, lodging, and money earned on the side, assistants under him to give orders to.

In the time of the viceroy and count of Chinchón the town council of Lima created the post of curfew ringer, a position that was done away with a half century later. The curfew ringer had the best job in the guild of bell ringers, for his only duty was to ring the bell in the tower of the cathedral at nine o'clock each night. It was a prestigious post much sought after and earned a salary of a peso a day.

Nor was it an office that allowed sleeping on the job, for if there was and is a demanding post in Lima that requires alertness, it is that of bell ringer, and even more so in colonial days, in which there were any number of religious feasts and the bells were rung for at least three days whenever the mail packet arrived form Spain with the earthshaking news that the royal infante had cut his last tooth or recovered from measles or chicken pox.

The office of bell ringer was not free of risk, as witness the little wooden cross that even now can be seen by the Lima reader, set in the wall of the little square of San Agustín. It so happened that, at the end of the last century, a bell ringer got caught in the framework of the Mónica,[1] a revolving bell, flew through space with no need for wings, and did not stop until he was dashed against the wall facing the tower.

Until the middle of the seventeenth century the only carriages in Lima were those of the viceroy and the bishop, and four or so calashes

---

[1] The great bell of the convent of San Agustín in Lima.

belonging to magistrates or nobles of Castile. Philip II, in a royal decree of November 24, 1577, had forbidden the manufacture of carriages or their importation from Spain, giving as his reason for prohibiting the use of such vehicles the fact that, in view of the scarcity of horses, they should be reserved for military purposes. The penalties laid down for offenders was severe. This royal decree, which was not rescinded by Philip III, began to be disobeyed in 1610. Little by little the luxury of having oneself horse-drawn in a carriage began to spread, and it is a well-known fact that by the time of Amat[2] more than a thousand such vehicles were to be seen on the Alameda de los Descalzos on the day of Our Lady of Porciúncula.[3]

The bell ringers and their assistants, who lived on permanent watch in the towers, had orders to ring the bells whenever the viceroy or the archbishop passed through the little square of the convent, a practice that was continued until the time of the marquis of Castell-dos-Rius.[4]

It seems that the viceroy and count of Alba de Liste, who, as the reader will see farther on, had his reasons for being wary of the clergy, went out one Sunday in his carriage with an escort to pay visits. The sound of a carriage was in those days such an event that families, taking it to be the one that precedes earthquakes, rushed helter-skelter to the doors of their houses.

The carriage had to pass though the little square of San Agustín, but the bell ringer and his helpers were probably out merrymaking and far from the nest, for not a bell clapper in the tower moved. This discourtesy shocked His Excellency, and on speaking of it at his nightly gathering of friends he was indiscreet enough to blame the prior of the Augustinians, who was a personal friend of his, and when the matter had been investigated the bell ringer, rather than confessing that he had not been at his post, said that although he saw the carriage pass by, he did not believe it necessary to ring the bells, for there was no

[2] Manuel de Amat y Junient (1704–1782) was Peru's 31st viceroy, 1761–1776.—Ed.

[3] August 2, the day of Our Lady of Porciúncula, commemorates the founding of the Franciscan Order in 1208.—Ed.

[4] Manuel de Oms y Santa Pau, Marquis of Castell-dos-Rius (d. 1710), was the 24th viceroy of Peru, 1707–1710.—Ed.

need for the blessed bronzes to rejoice at the passage of a heretical viceroy.

Jorge's reply was different from that of the bishop don Carlos Marcelo, when in 1621, after being consecrated in Lima, he arrived in Trujillo, his birthplace and his future diocese, and exclaimed: "The bells that are ringing most joyously are doing so because they are members of my family, since they were cast by none other than my father." And this was the truth.

Jorge's offense, which might have caused serious discord between the representative of the crown and the Augustinian community, was deemed by the governing body of the Augustinians to merit severe punishment, and the bell ringer's excuse to be of no avail, for no impertinent bird roosting in a bell tower was called upon to pass judgment on the viceroy's conduct in his quarrels with the Inquisition.

And each Father, armed with his scourge, unleashed a penitential lash on the bare back of Jorge Escoiquiz.

II

The Heretical Viceroy

His Excellency don Luis Henríquez de Guzmán, count of Alba de Liste and Villaflor and a descendant of the royal house of Aragon, was the first grandee of Spain to come to Peru with the title of viceroy, in February of 1655, after having held the same office in Mexico. He was the uncle of the count of Salvatierra, whom he relieved as ruler of Peru. As a Guzmán, his arms were: flanched shield, chief and base of azure, and a basin of gold, checked in gules, with seven serpents' heads, flanches of silver, and five sable ermines saltierwise.

A magistrate of fine administrative abilities and a man with rather advanced ideas for his time, his rule has gone down in history only because of the large number of misfortunes that took place during it. His six years as viceroy were six years of tears, mourning, and public unrest.

The galleon commanded by the marquis of Villarrubia that was carrying almost six million in gold and silver and 600 passengers, was shipwrecked off the cliffs of Chanduy, and only 45 persons were saved.

There was scarcely a family in Lima that did not lose a relative in the disaster. A private company managed to bring up from the sea bottom nearly 300,000 pesos, a third of which was handed over to the crown.

A year later, in 1656, the marquis of Baides, who had just served as governor of Chile, was returning to Europe with three ships loaded with treasure; having been vanquished in a naval battle near Cádiz by English pirates, he chose to set fire to the magazine of the ship rather than surrender.

And finally, the squadron of don Pablo Contreras, which in 1652 set sail for Peru with a cargo of merchandise, was caught in a storm and seven ships were lost.

But for Lima, the worst of the disasters was the earthquake of November 13, 1655. Publications of the time describe in great detail its damages, the penitential processions, and the repentance of great sinners, and it struck such terror in people's consciences that by a miracle many scoundrels gave fortunes that had been stolen back to their legitimate owners.

On March 15, 1657, another earthquake, which lasted for more than a quarter of an hour, caused great grief in Chile, and finally, the tremendous eruption of Pichincha,[5] in October 1660, were events that sufficed to prove that this viceroy had come under an unlucky star.

To further strike terror in people's spirits, in 1660 there appeared the famous comet observed by the learned Limeñan don Francisco Luis Lozano, who was Peru's first great cosmographer.

And for nothing to be lacking in this gloomy picture, civil war overtook part of the territory. The Indian Pedro Bohorques, on escaping from prison in Valdivia, raised his standard after proclaiming himself the descendant of the Incas, and after having himself crowned placed himself at the head of an army. Defeated and taken prisoner, he was taken to Lima, where the gallows awaited him.

Jamaica, which until that time had been a Spanish colony, was captured by the English and turned into a center of pirate activity, which for a century and a half kept this territory in a state of continual alarm.

The viceroy and count of Alba de Liste was not well liked in Lima because of his indifferent religious beliefs, and the people, in their naive fanaticism, thought that he was the one drawing the wrath of heaven

---

[5] Pichincha is a volcano in Ecuador, see "The Christ in Agony."—Ed.

down upon Peru. And although he played an important role in having the University of Peru, under the rectorate of the illustrious Ramón Pinelo, celebrate with great pomp Pope Alexander VII's brief on the Immaculate Conception of Mary, this did not suffice to rid him of the nickname of the "heretical viceroy" that an eminent Jesuit, Father Alloza, had helped to make popular; for once, when His Excellency attended a ceremony in the church of San Pedro, that preacher had severely upbraided him for not listening to the Divine Word and conversing instead with one of the magistrates.

Archbishop Villagómez appeared in the procession of Corpus Christi one year with a sunshade, and when the viceroy reprimanded him, he withdrew from the procession. The king put the two of them on a equal footing by ruling that neither the viceroy nor the archbishop should use a sunshade.

The count of Alba de Liste was opposed to the consecration of Friar Cipriano Medina as bishop of Guamanga, maintaining that the bulls appointing him were not in order. But the archbishop went at midnight to the seminary of San Francisco for novices and there consecrated Medina.

When the royal magistrates arrested the scribes of the ecclesiastical tribunal for contempt of court, the archbishop excommunicated the magistrates. The viceroy, backed by the Royal Tribunal, obliged His Reverence to rescind the excommunication.

The count of Alba de Liste had countless conflicts with the archbishop over the question of ecclesiastical benefices, conflicts that contributed to causing the fanatical people to regard him as an unbeliever and a bad Christian, when in reality he was simply a zealous defender of royal patronage.

The viceroy also had the misfortune of living in open war with the Inquisition, which was then at the height of its power and prestige. Among other prohibited books, he had brought from Mexico a pamphlet written by the Dutchman Guillermo Lombardo, which he showed in confidence to an inquisitor or familiar of the Holy Office. But the latter denounced him, and on the first day of the feast of the Holy Spirit, when His Excellency was in the cathedral with all the municipal corporations, a member of the Holy Office mounted to the pulpit and read an edict compelling the viceroy to hand over the pamphlet and place his doctor, César Nicolás Wandier, who was suspected of being

a Lutheran, at the disposal of the Office. The viceroy left the church in
great indignation, and sent Philip IV a well-founded complaint. Serious
conflicts arose from this, to which the monarch put an end by reproving
the overbearing conduct of the Inquisition, and by advising Alba de
Liste as a friend to hand over the pamphlet that had caused the quarrel.

As for the French doctor, the noble count did everything possible to
free him from the clutches of the fierce inquisitors, but it was no easy
matter to snatch a victim away from the Holy Office. On October 8,
1667, after more than eight years' imprisonment in the dungeons of the
Holy Office, Wandier was tried and condemned. He was accused,
among other trumped-up charges, of having in his cell a crucifix and
an image of the Virgin in order to pass for a devout man, and of
addressing them in blasphemous words. After the auto-da-fé, in which
the accused was fortunately not condemned to the stake, there were
held in Lima three days of rogations, a procession of atonement, and
other religious ceremonies, which ended with the transfer of the images
of the cathedral to the church of El Prado, where we presume they still
exist today.

In August of 1661, after handing over the government to the count
of Santisteban, the viceroy returned to Spain, more than happy to leave
a land where he risked being turned into a crackling by being burned
to death as a heretic.

III

A Bell Ringer's Vengeance

It is likely that Escoiquiz did not get over the sting of the lash all that
quickly, for he vowed to himself to take his vengeance on the over-
demanding viceroy who attached such importance to one bell more or
less ringing. A week had not yet gone by since the day of his flogging,
when one night, between twelve and one, the bells of the tower of San
Agustín gave a long and joyous peal. All the inhabitants of Lima were
in their beds and sleeping like logs at that hour, and they immediately
rushed into streets asking one another what the good news was that
the bells were celebrating with their tongues of bronze.

His Excellency the viceroy, without being thereby a libertine, was
having an affair with an aristocratic lady; and when, after ten, there

was no longer anyone who would venture out on the streets of Lima, the viceroy slipped out of a hidden door leading to the calle de los Desamparados, well muffled in his cape and accompanied by his steward, headed off to visit the beauty who had enslaved his heart. He spent a couple of hours in delightful intimacy, and was returning to the palace after midnight with the same caution and secrecy.

On the following day the news spread all over the city that a nocturnal stroll of the viceroy had occasioned the untimely pealing of the bells. And there was whispering and much gossip on the steps of the cathedral, and the rumors and conjectures that had grown and spread most widely were that the count had taken such precautions in order to attend a mysterious secret meeting of heretics, for no one could believe that such a serious-minded gentleman would muffle up like a smuggler to indulge in an escapade worthy of some love-smitten youth.

But His Excellency had his misgivings, and fearing an indiscretion by the bell ringer, summoned him secretly to the palace, and when he was alone with him in his private office, said to him:

"You wretch! Who told you that I was passing by last night?"

"Your Excellency," Escoiquiz answered without turning a hair, "there are owls in my tower."

"And what the devil does that have to do with me?"

"Your Excellency, who has had many a run-in with the Inquisition and is continually at odds with it, must know that witches take the form of owls."

"And to scare them off you disturbed the whole city with your bells? You're a first-rate rascal, and I'm tempted to send you off to jail."

"It would not be worthy of Your Excellency to punish someone as discreet as I am so severely, someone who hasn't even told his shirt collar what takes the viceroy of all Peru up and down the street of San Sebastián at night."

The chivalrous count needed no more more prompting to realize that his secret, and with it the reputation of a lady, lay in the hands of the bell ringer.

"Very well, very well!" he interrupted him. "Keep your tongue tied short and see to it that the clappers of your bells are silent too."

"I for my part will be as silent as the dead, for I don't like to talk about other people's affairs. But as for what has to do with the dignity of Mónica and my other bells, I won't yield as much as the end of a fingernail, for they were not cast by their maker for accomplices and intermediaries of sinful strollers. If Your Excellency doesn't want them to ring out, the remedy is easy. If you don't walk through the little square the problem is solved."

"Agreed. And now tell me: What can I do for you?"

Jorge Escoiquiz, who, as is evident, had his wits about him, asked the viceroy to intercede with the prior to have himself readmitted as a novice. His Excellency promised to do so, and three or four months later the superior of the Augustinians allowed the bell ringer to return. And his eminent protector was of such service to him that in 1660 Friar Jorge Escoiquiz celebrated his first Mass, with his sponsor being none other that the heretical viceroy.

According to some, Escoiquiz never got beyond being an ordinary friar; according to others, he became a dignitary of his convent. I cannot say which version is true.

What for me is certain fact is that the viceroy, being afraid of the pealing of the bells, never again passed through the little square of San Agustín when he took a notion to go acourting in the calle de San Sebastián.

> Y aquí hago punto y fin,
> sacando de esta conseja
> la siguiente moraleja:
> que no hay enemigo chico.[6]

---

[6] And here I write finis and end, / drawing from this tale / the following moral: / no enemy is ever small.

Drink, Father, It Will Keep You Alive!

A Chronicle of the Era When
the Wife of a Viceroy Ruled

Doña Ana de Borja, countess of Lemos and wife of the viceroy of Peru, was a great lady, more tempered than Toledo steel. She was found to be such by Her Majesty doña María of Austria, who govered the Spanish monarchy during the minority of Charles II, for on naming her husband viceroy of Peru, doña María provided him with a royal warrant that stipulated that in case the better service of the kingdom obliged him to leave Lima, he should place the reins of government in the hands of his consort.

Accordingly, when His Excellency deemed it indispensable to go in person to put down the disturbances in Laycacota by hanging the rich miner Salcedo, doña Ana remained in this city presiding over the Tribunal, and her rule lasted from June of 1668 to April of the following year.

The count of Bornos said that the most learned woman is capable of governing only twelve hens and one rooster. Nonsense! Surely this statement did not apply to doña Ana de Borja y Aragón, who, as you readers will see, was one of the countless exceptions to the rule. I know women capable of governing twenty-four hens . . . and up to two roosters.

Just as I am telling you, like it or not we Peruvians were governed by a woman for ten months . . . and frankly it did not go all that badly for us, for the tambourine was in hands that knew how to play it.

And so that you won't say that we chroniclers pay no tax on lies, and that I force you to take what I say on faith, I shall copy what the erudite gentleman señor Mendiburu writes on this subject in his *Diccionario Histórico*[1]: "On undertaking his journey to Puno, the Count of Lemos entrusted the government of the kingdom to doña Ana, his wife, who exercised this power during his absence, resolving all matters without anyone making the slightest objection, beginning with the Tribunal, which recognized her authority. We have in our hands a dispatch of the vicereine, appointing a member of the accounting tribunal, which is headed as follows: "don Pedro Fernández de Castro y Andrade, count of Lemos, and doña Ana de Borja, his wife, countess of Lemos, by virtue of the power she has been granted for the government of these realms, attentive to the opinion of the tribunal, has been pleased to appoint and most willingly appoint, etc., etc."

Another proof. In Odriozola's *Documentos históricos*[2] collection there can be found a decree of the vicereine ordering that military preparations against pirates be made.

Doña Ana, in her period in command, was a lady 29 years old, with an elegant figure albeit a plain face. She dressed in splendor and was never seen in public when she was not decked with diamonds. Of her disposition it is said that she was extremely haughty and dominating, and that she was inordinately proud of her lineage and titles of nobility.

And the pride of someone like her, when she counted among the saints of the celestial court none other than her grandfather Francisco de Borja, must have been a mere nothing![3]

The mischievous ladies of Lima, who were so fond of doña Teresa de Castro, the wife of the viceroy don García, never looked favorably on the countess of Lemos, and baptized her with the nickname of Bigfoot. I presume that the vicereine was a woman with a firm foundation.

---

[1] Manuel de Mendiburu (1805–1888) was a Peruvian soldier and political figure who authored the *Diccionario histórico-biográfico del Perú* (8 vols., 1874–1890).—Ed.

[2] Manuel de Odriozola (1804–1889) was director of the *Biblioteca Nacional* during the War of the Pacific and the compiler of the *Colección de Documentos históricos del Perú en las épocas del Coloniaje después de la Conquista y de la Independencia hasta la presente* (10 vols., 1863–1877).—Ed.

[3] Umphrey's translation, 113.

But to go on with our story, doña Ana was said to have had an idea that would not have occurred to the most resolute governor, and that proves, in essence, how great feminine cleverness is, and likewise proves that when a woman becomes involved in politics or in what is a man's business, she knows how to leave a well-planted banner.

Among the passengers whom the galleon from Cádiz brought to Callao was a Portuguese friar of the order of Saint Jerome. His name was Father Núñez. His Paternity was a chubby little man with wide shoulders, a pot belly, a short neck, bulging eyes, and a reddish Roman nose. Imagine, reader, a candidate for a sudden attack of apoplexy, and you will have a perfect portrait of the Hieronymite friar.

Father Núñez had only just arrived in Lima when the vicereine received an anonymous letter in which the aforementioned friar was said to be not a friar at all, but a spy or secret agent for Portugal who, for the greater success of some political machination, appeared wearing the holy habit as a disguise.

The vicereine summoned the judges and submitted the accusation to them. Their lordships decided that, there and then and without further ado, Father Núñez should be arrested and hanged, *coram populo*.[4] Of course! In those days there was no such thing as guarantees of the individual or other such foolishness of the sort that today are customary and give the individual as much protection as does a silken doublet from a clubbing from the back.

The sage vicereine was reluctant to take matters hither and yon, and when something that Garcilaso said of Francisco de Carbajal occurred to her, she remarked to her fellow members of the Tribunal: "Leave things to me, and with no need to make a great to-do or offend him, I can discover if he is a friar or a monk, for the habit does not make the monk but the monk the habit. And if he turns out to be a priest tonsured by a barber and not by an archbishop, then without more kyries or litanies we can call Gonzalvillo to hang him by the neck on the gallows in the main square."

This Gonzalvillo, a double-dyed black and ugly as the devil, was the official hangman of Lima.

That very same day the vicereine had her steward invite Father Núñez to the palace "to share a modest meal."

[4] Before the populace [Latin].

The three judges accompanied the noble lady at table, and Gonzalvillo the Terrible waited in the garden.

The guests were splendidly served, not those delicacies that today are common and are like nun's food, a mere puff of air, but, rather, dishes that were succulent and solid and stick to the ribs. The best birds in the poultry yard, turkey, chicken, and even pig in a blanket were served in profusion.

Father Núñez did not eat; he devoured. He did full honor to all the dishes.

The vicereine winked at the judges as though to say to them:

"He gobbles down his food. He's a friar."

Father Núñez had unwittingly passed the test. There was yet another.

Spanish cuisine is loaded with spices, and this naturally makes one thirsty. It was fashionable to place on the table large Guadalajara earthenware vessels that have the property of keeping water cool and give it a most agreeeable taste.

After consuming as dessert a big helping of macaroons, pastries, and sweets made by nuns, the guest couldn't help but feel an imperious thirst; he who has a dry gullet neither growls nor sings.

"Show us how you go about this!" the countess murmured.

This was the decisive proof she was waiting for. If her guest was not what he revealed himself to be by his habit, he would drink the water down sparingly, with a neatness not customary in the refectory.

The friar took the heavy Guadalajara pitcher, raised it almost as high as his head, which he leaned on the back of his chair, tipped the pitcher, and began to drink his fill.

The vicereine, seeing that his thirst was like that of a sand dune and his way of satisfying it typical of a friar, said to him with a smile:

"Drink, father, drink, it will keep you alive!"

And the friar, taking the advice to be a friendly interest in his health, did not take his mouth from the pitcher until there wasn't a drop left. His Paternity immediately passed his hand across his forehead to wipe away the sweat that was pouring out of him, and gave a belch like the snort of a harpooned whale.

Doña Ana got up from the table and went out on the balcony, followed by the judges.

"What do Your Lordships think?"

"That he's undeniably a friar, Your Ladyship" the judges answered as one.

"So I believe, in the name of God and my soul. Let the good priest go in peace."

Now, then, it's up to you to say whether or not the woman who governed Peru was very much a man!

The Countess Who Was Summoned

A Chronicle of the Era of the
Archbishop Who Was the Viceroy

I confess that among the many traditions that I have brought to light, none has caused me more trouble than the one that I am consigning to paper today. The plot of it is so thorny and delicate that the ink turns to sediment on the tip of my pen. But to Rome for everything, and may a good numen permit me to come through with flying colors and cover with a veil of decorum, although not a very thick one, this, my faithful account of an event that echoed all over Lima more resoundingly than the loudest nose blowing.

I

Doña Verónica Aristizábal, despite her 40 flowering Easters, was, around the year 1688, what in every land, of heretics and Christians alike, is called a good-looking woman. Never was ham better preserved, not even in Westphalia.

The widow of the count of Ellipsis Dots—a title like any other, for I don't care to set the real one down in print—had been named on the death of her husband the tutor of their two sons, of whom the elder was five years old at the time. The count's fortune was what is called a sizeable one, and consisted, in addition to a town house and valuable city properties, of two magnificent haciendas situated in one of the most fertile valleys near this City of Kings. And kindly forgive me, reader, if I change the names and do not specify where the action took place, for if I did so I would be dotting my i's and perhaps mischievously cause you to point out, quite accurately, the descendants of the countess of Ellipsis Dots, as we have agreed to call this interesting widow. As for discretion, I am the keeper of the seal of secrecy.

Once the first months of mourning had passed and all the polite formulas of social etiquette had been observed, Verónica abandoned the house in Lima and went off with trunks and valises to live on one of the haciendas. In order that the reader may have some idea of the importance of this country fiefdom, it will suffice us to note that the number of slaves came to 1,200.

Among them was a robust and attractive mulatto 24 years old, for whom the deceased count had stood as godfather at his baptism, and as his godson he had always been treated with special affection and favor. At the age of 13, Pantaleón, for this was his name, was brought to Lima by his godfather, who set him to learning the everyday empiricism that in those days was called medical science, a very clear idea of which has been bequeathed to us by Juan de Caviedes, the Quevedo[1] of Lima, in his most amusing *Diente del Parnaso*.[2] Perhaps Pantaleón, who was the contemporary of Caviedes, belonged to one of the types that stand out in this book of our original, caustic poet.

When the count decided that his godson now knew enough to correct a prescription of Hippocrates himself, he sent him back to the hacienda as doctor and apothecary, assigning him a room outside the quarters occupied by the other slaves, permitting him to dress decently and fashionably, and allowing him to occupy a seat at the table where the steward or administrator, a dimwitted Galician; the head overseer, who was cast in the same mold as the latter; and the chaplain, a chubby Mercedarian friar with a fatter neck than a Bujama deer, took their meals. Though not without muttering under their breath, the three of them were obliged to accept the doctor with the brand-new medical degree; and to make a long story short, either because of the useful

[1] Francisco de Quevedo, a Spanish Golden Age satirist (1580–1645).—Ed.
[2] Juan del Valle Caviedes (1652–1694) was a notable satirist whose most famous work is *El diente del parnaso* (Tooth of Parnassus).—Ed.

services that the latter offered them, rescuing them from more than one brawl, or because they found him likable on account of his sharp wit and the distinction of his manners, the fact is that chaplain, steward, and overseer could not do without the company of the slave, whom they treated as a close friend and equal.

Around that time milady the countess arrived at the hacienda to live, and along with the chaplain and the two Galicians, who were the most notable employees on the estate, she admitted the slave to her nightly social gathering, for to her, apart from his being the godson and protégé of her late husband, he had the reputation of being don Exactly the Right Man to administer a sedative against a headache or a potion for any one of the complaints to which our frail nature is so prone.

Pantaleón not only enjoyed the prestige accorded him by science, but in addition his politeness, his youth, and his vigor and handsomeness were a contrast to the coarseness and the physical appearance of the Mercedarian friar and the two Galicians. Verónica was a woman, and this said, I have said that her imagination must have made the contrast seem still greater. The idleness and isolation of life on a hacienda, the ever impressionable nerves of the daughters of Eve, the trust that lemon balm water will calm them, especially if the doctor who administers it is young, good looking, and intelligent, the frequency and degree of intimacy of their relations, and—all the rest: what do I know?—caused Cupid to plant a well-aimed dart in the very center of the countess's heart. And just as when the devil has no need to make a fly swatter of his tail, and loves tricks know no measure, there happened . . . what you readers, without being soothsayers, will already have guessed. As the song rightly has it:

> The sun suffers few eclipses
> and the moon a thousand;
> for women are apt to go wrong
> more often than men.[3]

---

[3] Pocos eclipses el sol / y mil la luna padece; / que son al desliz más prontas / que los hombres las mujeres.

II

Reader, a cigar or a toothpick, and let us speak of colonial history.

Don Melchor de Liñán y Cisneros entered Lima as archbishop in February, 1678, but with the groundwork so well laid in the court of Madrid that five months later Charles II, removing the count of Castellar from his post, named His Reverence viceroy of Peru as well; and among other rewards, he later gave him the title of count of Puebla de los Valles, a title that the archbishop later transferred to one of his brothers.

His arms were those of the Liñán family: a shield, banded gules, and gold.

The viceroy and count of Castellar handed over the royal treasury with well-filled chests, and the archbishop and viceroy took care not to fall into the category of spendthrift. While the country was not rich, its state under the rule of Liñán y Cisneros was not one of penury; as he very wittily put it, speaking of the Treasury, it was necessary to guard it against the many who guarded it, and defend it against the many who defended it.

Unfortunately, his hauteur and the spirit of petty rivalry that he harbored against his predecessor, harassing him despicably in the trial over residence, detract from the name of the archbishop and viceroy in the eyes of history.

It was under his administration that the residents of Lima sent casks of gold for the "queen's necklace," the name given to the gift that the various peoples gave the monarch when he married: It was, let us say, the wedding present offered by his vassals.

The Brazilians took possession of a part of the terrritory bordering on Buenos Aires, and His Reverence promptly sent troops that, under the command of Field Marshal don José de Garro, the governor of Río de la Plata, dislodged them after a hard-fought battle. The Peace of Utrecht put an end to the war, with Portugal obtaining advantageous concessions from Spain.

The freebooters Juan Guarín (Warlen) and Bartolomé Chearps, abetted by the Indians of Darién, made incursions into the Southern Sea, took a number of important prizes in Panama, such as the vessel *Trinidad,* sacked the ports of Barbacoas, Ilo, and Coquimbo, razed Serena, and on February 9, 1681, disembarked in Arica. Gaspar de Oviedo, a royal lieutenant and supreme magistrate of the province, placed himself at the head of the people, and after eight hours of bloody combat, the pirates were forced to take refuge on their ships, leaving Captain Guarín behind among the dead and 11 men taken prisoner. Liñán y Cisneros hurriedly had two ships fitted out in Callao, armed them with 30 pieces of artillery, and gave command of them to General Pantoja; and although it is true that our squadron did not give chase to the pirates, its maneuvers played an important role in causing the latter, already demoralized by the disaster of Arica, to abandon our waters. As for the 11 prisoners, they were executed in the main square of Lima.

This era was one of great religious controversies. The rivalry between friars and Jesuit fathers in the missions of Mojos, Carabaya, and Amazonas; a stormy chapter in the history of the nuns of Saint Catherine in Quito, many of whom abandoned the cloister; and the dispute between Bishop Mollinedo and the canons of Cuzco over details of discipline, could be written about at length. But the most serious upheaval was that of the Franciscans of Lima who, on December 23, 1680, at 11 at night, set fire to the cell of the general commissar of the order, Friar Marcos Terán.

During the rule of Liñán y Cisneros, the 21st viceroy of Peru, the first copies of the *Recopilación de leyes de Indias,*[4] printed in Madrid in 1680, was received in Lima; the distilling of brandy not made from the pure dregs of wine was forbidden; and the little convent of Saint Rose of Viterbo for Franciscan lay sisters was founded.

III

Jealousy, The Greatest Monster is the title of a famous comedy of the Spanish Golden Age, and the poet certainly hit the nail on the head.

A year after the countess had established herself on the hacienda, she brought to it from a convent of nuns in Lima a little slave girl, 15 or 16 Aprils old, as fresh as a sherbet, as mischievous as an elf, as joyful as a Christmas Mass, and with a pair of black eyes so black that they seemed made of the darkness of night. She was Verónica's pampered favorite. Before sending her to the convent to complete her education

---

[4] The official law code for the Indies.

by learning needlework and other arts in which the good nuns are so skillful, her mistress had paid for her music and dance teachers, and the girl took such good advantage of the lessons that in Lima there was no harpist more expert, no timbre of voice purer and more pliant for singing the arias *Bella Aminta* and *Pastor Feliz,* no feet more nimble for tripping a *sajuriana,*[5] no waist more slender and patriotic for dancing a little dance of this homeland of ours.

It would be a Herculean task for me to describe Gertrudis's beauty. Any portrait of this girl of color that I were to draw would be a pale one beside the original, and it suffices for the reader to imagine a mixture of one of those sorts of refined sugar and Ceylon cinnamon that caused the licentious blind friar of the Order of Our Lady Of Mercy to sing, in a ballad that I shall take care to reproduce exactly:

> canela y azúcar fué
> la bendita Magdalena . . .
> quién no ha querido a una *china,*[6]
> no ha querido cosa buena.[7]

The arrival of Gertrudis on the hacienda awakened in the chaplain and the doctor all the appetite that a tasty morsel awakens. His friarly Reverence began to be distracted when he opened his breviary; and the doctor-apothecary's mind was so preoccupied with the girl that, on one occasion, he administered jalap to one of his patients instead of gum arabic and thereby came within an inch of dispatching him to the land of skulls without a postillion.

Someone has said (and in case no one has thought of saying something so nonsensical I shall do so) that a rival has eyes like a telescope to discover, not a comet with a tail, but a flea in the heaven of his affair of the heart. This explains why the chaplain soon tumbled to the truth and acquired proof that between Pantaleón and Gertrudis there existed what, in politics, one of our eminent leaders called criminal complicity. The resentful rival then decided to take his vengeance, and went to the

---

[5] A traditional Peruvian dance.
[6] A girl of color.
[7] the blessed Magdalena / was sugar and cinnamon . . . / he who has not loved a *china* / hasn't loved a good thing.

countess with the piece of gossip, hypocritically maintaining that it was a scandal and a disgrace for such an honorable house that two slaves should be involved in knavery that morality and religion condemn. Nonsense! Bells are not cast to make people frightened when they ring.

It is probable that if the Mercedarian had suspected that Verónica had made of her slave something more than a doctor, he would have refrained from accusing him. The countess had enough strength of will to control herself, thanked the chaplain for his piece of Christian information, and simply said that she would be able to put her house in order.

Once the friar had left, Verónica shut herself up in her bedroom to allow the storm that was roiling in her soul to do its worst. She, who had deigned to descend from the pedestal of her pride and preoccupations to raise a miserable slave to her own height, could not forgive him for treacherously deceiving her.

An hour later Verónica, affecting a serenity of spirit, went to the sugar mill and summoned the doctor. Pantaleón, thinking that the summons had to do with coming to the aid of someone who was ill, appeared at once. The countess, in the stern tone of voice of an examining magistrate, questioned him about his relations with Gertrudis, and exasperated by the lover's stubborn answers in the negative, ordered the blacks to tie him to an iron ring and whip him mercilessly. After half-an-hour's torture, Pantaleón was almost lifeless. The countess put a stop to the punishment and questioned him once more. The victim did not back down from his denials, and more exasperated than before, the countess threatened to have him thrown into a cauldron of boiling honey.

Even in the face of this cruel threat the unfortunate Pantaleón persisted in answering in the negative, and abandoning the respectful air with which up to that moment he had answered his mistress's questions, he said:

"Do that, Verónica, and within a year, on the same day as today, at five in the afternoon, I shall summon you before God's tribunal."

"Insolent wretch!" the countess shouted in a fury, lashing the hapless Pantaleón across the face with her riding crop. "To the cauldron! To the cauldron with him!"

Horrors!

And the terrible command was immediately obeyed.

IV

The countess was taken to her apartments in a state of total delirium. The months went by, her illness grew worse, and science declared defeat. In her frightful attacks the furious madwoman kept shouting:

"I am summoned!"

And there thus arrived the morning of the day when the fateful appointed date came round, and wonder of wonders, the countess's delirium was gone when she awakened. The new chaplain, who had replaced the Mercedarian friar, was summoned and heard her confession, pardoning her in the name of Him Who is ever merciful.

The priest gave Gertrudis her letter of emancipation and a sum of money from her mistress. The unfortunate girl of color, whose fatal beauty was the cause of the tragedy, left an hour later for Lima, and took the habit of a lay sister in the convent of the Poor Clares.

Verónica spent the rest of the day in peace.

The bell of the hacienda sounded the first stroke of five. On hearing it the madwoman leapt from her bed shouting:

"It's five o'clock! Pantaleón! Pantaleón!"

And fell dead in the middle of her bedroom.

A Mother's Love

A Chronicle of the Era of the Viceroy "Silver-Arm"

(To Juana Manuela Gorriti)[1]

We have considered it advisable to alter the names of the principal characters in this Tradition, a venal sin that we have committed in "The Countess Who Was Summoned" and several others. Names matter little if one takes care not to falsify historical truth, and the reader will readily guess the very powerful reason we had for rebaptizing our fellows.

I

In August of 1690 His Excellency don Melchor Portocarrero Lazo de la Vega, count of La Monclova, knight commander of Zarza of the Order of Alcántara, and 23rd viceroy of Peru by the Grace of His

---

[1] Juana Manuela Gorriti (1819–1892) an Argentinian novelist and cultural critic whose Lima literary salon Palma attended in his adolescence. Gorriti authored *Panoramas de la vida* (1876) fiction and prose, and a memoir of her Lima salón, *Veladas literarias de Lima (1876–1877)* (1892). See *Dreams and Realities: Selected Fiction of Juana Manuela Gorriti,* trans. Sergio Waisman, ed. Francine Massiello (2003)—Ed.

Majesty Charles II, entered Lima. In addition to his daughter, doña Josefa, and his family and servants, several soldiers accompanied him on the journey from Mexico. Don Fernando de Vergara, a nobleman from Extremadura and captain of gentleman lancers, stood out from the others thanks to his dashing and martial air, and it is said of him that even in the company of Mexican beauties he had not lost his reputation as an austere Benedictine monk. A swashbuckler, a gambler, and a lover who besieged the ladies, it was more than difficult to make him settle down, and the viceroy, who professed a paternal affection for him, proposed to find him a bride himself, so as to see if the proverbial saying that has it that "a change of condition is a change of habit" is true.

Evangelina Zamora had, along with her youth and beauty, other qualities that made her the most enviable match of the City of Kings. Her great-grandfather had been, after Jerónimo de Aliaga, the municipal magistrate Ribera, Martín de Alcántara, and Diego Maldonado the Rich, one of the conquistadors most favored by Pizarro, who rewarded them with shares of land in the Rimac Valley. The emperor gave him permission to use a *don* before his name, and a few years later the valuable gifts that he sent the crown secured for him the honor of a habit of the Order of Santiago. With a hundred years behind him, rich, and a nobleman, our conquistador concluded that he no longer had a mission to rule over this vale of tears, and in 1604 he departed it, bequeathing to his eldest son a country estate and urban properties worth a fortune that was estimated at the time to be a fifth of a million pesos.

Evangelina's grandfather and father added to the inheritance, and the young lady found herself orphaned at the age of 20, under the protection of a guardian and envied for her fortune.

The daughter of the count of La Monclova, who was in modest circumstances, and the wealthy young Evangelina soon cemented the most cordial friendship. The latter thus had a reason to visit the viceroy's palace, and while there frequently found herself in the company of the captain of lancers, who, as a young man attentive to women, wasted no opportunity to pay court to the young lady who finally, without confessing to the amorous inclination that the nobleman from Extremadura had succeeded in awakening in her breast, listened with secret pleasure to the proposal of marriage to don Fernando. The intermediary was the viceroy himself, and a well-bred young lady would never think of saying no to so distinguished a sponsor.

During the first five years of their marriage, Captain Vergara forgot his former life of dissipation. His wife and children were his one source of happiness; he was, let us put it thus, an exemplary husband.

But one fateful day the devil caused don Fernando to accompany his spouse to a festive family gathering, and caused there to be a gaming room where not only was the classic card game *malilla abarrotada* played, but many devotees of the little cubes of the dice box were also gathered round a table covered in green baize. The passion for gambling was merely slumbering in the captain's soul, and it is no cause for surprise that at the sight of the dice it awakened stronger than ever. He gambled, with such bad luck that he lost 20,000 pesos that night.

From that time on, the model husband changed his habits completely, and returned to his feverish existence as a gambler. Because luck turned against him more and more frequently, he was obliged to squander the fortune of his wife and children in order to pay his gambling debts and plunge into that bottomless abyss that goes by the name of making good one's losses.

Among his companions in vice was a young marquis whom the dice persistently favored, and don Fernando took it into his head to fight against such mad luck. On many nights he took the marquis to dine at the home of Evangelina, and once dinner was over, the two friends shut themselves up in another room to wager the "shirt off their backs," an expression that, in the language of gamblers, has a literal meaning.

The gambler and the madman are decidedly one and the same. In my opinion, if any shortcoming diminishes the historical figure of Emperor Augustus, it is the fact that, according to Suetonius, he gambled at odds and evens after dinner.

In vain did Evangelina make every effort to lead the unrestrained gambler away from the precipice. Tears and tenderness, quarrels and reconciliations were useless. The good lady had no more weapons to bring to bear on the heart of the man she loved.

One night the unhappy wife had already retired to her bed when don Fernando awakened her to ask her for her engagement ring, a diamond solitaire of very great value. Evangelina gave a start in surprise, but her husband calmed her fears, telling her that it was simply a matter of curiosity of some friends who doubted the worth of the precious jewel.

What had happened in the room where the rival gamblers had been? Don Fernando had lost a large sum, and not having anything of his own left to gamble, had agreed that he would bet his wife's splendid ring.

Bad luck is inexorable. The precious jewel gleamed on the ring finger of the marquis who had won.

Don Fernando shook with shame and remorse. The marquis took his leave, and Vergara accompanied him to the drawing room, but on reaching it he turned his head toward a glass screen adjacent to Evangelina's bedroom, and through the panes he saw her sobbing as she knelt before an image of Mary.

A horrible vertigo overcame don Fernando, and swift as a tiger he threw himself on the marquis and thrust his dagger in his back three times.

The ill-fated marquis fled to the bedroom and fell lifeless at the foot of Evangelina's bed.

II

At a very early age the count of La Monclova sent a company he commanded into the fray at Arras in 1654. His courage took him into the thick of the battle, and he was carried from the field in a state near death. He eventually recovered, though with the loss of his right arm, which it was found necessary to amputate. It was replaced by a silver one, and this was the source of the nickname he was known by in Mexico and in Lima.

The viceroy "Silver Arm," on whose coat of arms there appeared this motto: "*Ave Maria gratia plena*," succeeded the illustrious don Melchor de Navarra y Rocafull as viceroy of Peru. "With prestige equal to that of his predecessor, albeit with fewer gifts for governing," Lorente says, "of pure habits, devout, conciliatory, and moderate, the count of La Monclova edified the people through his example, and the needy found him ever ready to give his emoluments and the rents from his house as alms."

In the fifteen years and four months that the rule of "Silver Arm" lasted, a rule whose duration no viceroy attained either up until then or afterward, the country enjoyed total peace, governance was orderly, and magnificent residences were built in Lima. It is true that the public treasury did not particularly flourish, but this was for causes unrelated to politics. The magnificence and luxury of the processions and religious feast days of the time were reminiscent of the days of the count of Lemos. The arcades with their 85 arches, which cost 25,000 pesos to build, the city hall, and the gallery of the palace were constructed in this era.

In 1694 a freak was born in Lima with two heads and two pretty faces, two hearts, four arms, and two chests joined by cartilege. From its waist to its feet there was little about it that was out of the ordinary, and the erudite scholar and encyclopedist don Pedro de Peralta of Lima wrote a curious book, with the title of *Desvios de la naturaleza,*[2] in which, as well as offering a minute anatomical description of the freak, he endeavors to prove that it was endowed with two souls.

Following the death of Charles the Bewitched in 1700, Philip V, who succeeded him, rewarded the count of La Monclova by making him a grandee of Spain.

Ill, an octogenarian, and weary of ruling, the viceroy "Silver Arm" urged the court to replace him. The count of La Monclova died on September 22, 1702, without seeing this desire realized, and was buried in the cathedral; his successor, the marquis of Castell-dos-Ríus, did not arrive in Lima until July of 1707.

Doña Josefa, the daughter of the count of La Monclova, continued to live in the palace after the death of the viceroy; but one night, with the connivance of her confessor, Father Alonso Mesía, she climbed out a window and sought asylum with the nuns of Saint Catherine, taking her vows in the habit of Saint Rose, whose cloister was under construction. In May of 1710 doña Josefa Portocarrero Lazo de la Vega entered the new convent, of which she was the first abbess.

III

Four months after his imprisonment, the Royal Audience sentenced don Fernando de Vergara to death. From the first, the latter declared that the killing of the marquis was a premeditated act committed in

---

[2] Freaks of nature.

a fit of desperation at being a ruined gambler. Confronted with such a frank confession, the tribunal was forced to apply the death penalty.

Evangelina used every possible resource to free her husband from a shameful death, to no avail, and in the midst of her grief, the day set for the criminal's execution arrived. The unselfish and courageous Evangelina then resolved to make, for the love of her children, an unprecedented sacrifice.

Dressed in mourning she presented herself in the drawing room of the palace, as the viceroy, the count of La Monclova, was conferring with the magistrates. She stated that don Fernando had murdered the marquis, his right to do so being protected by law; that she was an adulteress; and that, having been surprised by her husband, she had fled from his wrath, and her partner in crime had received his just due at the hands of the offended husband.

The frequency of the visits by the marquis to Evangelina's residence, her ring on the dead man's hand that was taken to be a love token, the stab wounds in his back, the fact that the body had been found at the foot of the lady's bed, and other small details were reason enough for the viceroy, giving credence to the revelation, to order a stay of the sentence.

The magistrate who had heard the case made his appearance in the prison in order to have don Fernando attest to the truth of his wife's declaration. But the clerk had only just finished reading it when Vergara, in prey to a thousand contrary sentiments, let out a frightful peal of laughter.

The wretch had gone mad!

A few years later, death folded its wings about the chaste bed of the noble spouse, and an austere priest offered the dying lady the consolations of religion.

Evangelina's four children knelt at their mother's bedside to await her final blessing. The unselfish victim, obliged by her confessor, thereupon revealed to them the tremendous secret: "The world will forget," she said to them, "the name of the woman who gave birth to you, but it would have been relentless with you had your father mounted the steps of the scaffold. God, who reads into the crystal of my conscience, knows that I have lost my honor in the eyes of society so that you would not be one day called the children of a father hanged to death."

A Viceroy and an Archbishop

A Chronicle of the Era of
the Twentieth Viceroy of Peru

The colonial era, rich in events that were providentially paving the way for the day of Independence in the New World, is a source barely tapped as yet by American intelligences.

Therefore, and pardon our bold presumption, each time that the feverish desire to write takes possession of us, a demon of temptation that youth can scarcely resist, we evoke in our nocturnal solitude the mysterious genius that watches over the history of the bygone days of a people that lives on, nourished not by memories or hopes but by realities.

We repeat: In America tradition is barely alive. America still enjoys the novelty of a discovery and values a fabulous treasure that has barely begun to be exploited.

Either because of the indolence of governments with respect to the conservation of their archives, or because of the negligence of our forefathers as regards the recording of the facts, it is undeniable that it would be very difficult today to write a complete history of the era of the viceroys. The early days of the empire of the Incas, after which there follows the bloody trail of the conquest, have come down to us depicted in fabulous and implausible colors. It appears that a similar fate awaits the three centuries of Spanish domination.

Meanwhile, it is up to our young people to do something to keep tradition from being completely lost. That is therefore the purpose on which our attention is focused by choice, and in order to attract that of the people we believe it useful to adorn every historical narrative with the trappings of romance. If in writing down these notes on the founder of Talca and Los Angeles we have not achieved our objective, forgive us in the name of the good intention that guided us and the immense quantity of dust that we have breathed in on leafing through chronicles and reading manuscripts letter by letter in countries where, in addition to the scarcity of documents, the archives are not easily available to the person who wishes to consult them.

I

The Number Thirteen

His Excellency don José Manso de Velazco, who earned the title of count of Superunda for having rebuilt Callao (destroyed by the famous earthquake of 1746), took command of the viceroyalty of Peru on July 13, 1745, replacing the marquis of Villagarcia. The importance that a chronicler might assign to this date would be beneath our notice had it not had, as old documents recount, a noticeable influence on the viceroy's spirits and future; and here, with your permission, dear reader, my pen is going to allow itself a few moments' idle talk and moralizing.

The more intelligent or bold a man, the more his spirit appears to be susceptible of welcoming a superstition. The flight or the song of a bird is for many a grim omen, whose influence is not powerful enough to overcome the force of reason. Only the fool is not superstitious. Caesar placed his trust in luck during a storm. Napoleon, who distributed thrones as the booty of war, remembered, on giving battle, the brightness of the sun at Austerlitz, and is even said to have had his future read in the cards by a fortune teller (Mademoiselle Lenormand).

But this preoccupation is never so obvious as when it is a question of the number 13. It so happened that a number of times when there were 13 guests at a banquet, one of them would die within the year; it is certain that this is the source of the exhaustive care with which Cabalists count how many persons are seated at table. The devout explain that the bad luck of the number 13 stems from the fact that at the divine Last Supper Judas was the 13th at table.

Another of the peculiarities of the number 13, also known as "the friar's dozen," is that it designates the number of coins given as an earnest when a close friend or relative decides to have himself one last spree before marrying. This is the origin of the instinctive horror of marriage that bachelors profess, a horror that we will not deign to say whether or not it is well founded, just as we would not dare to declare ourselves either advocates or enemies of the sacred bonds of matrimony.

A close friend complained of having attended a banquet at which the guests at table numbered 13. "And did anyone die? Did anything unfortunate occur?" "Certainly!" (the friend being interrogated replied). "I got married during that year."

The truth is that once the viceroy was alone in the palace with his secretary Pedro Bravo de Ribera, he could not keep himself from saying to him:

"I think, Pedro, that my government will bring me great misfortune. My reason tells me that the next 13 years do not bode well."

The secretary smiled derisively at the superstition of his lord and master, in whose life, with which he was intimately acquainted, there would no doubt be a turn of events in which the fateful number to which he had just alluded would play an important role.

And the fact that his heart was a faithful prophet for the viceroy (since during his 15 years as viceroy catastrophes abounded) is substantiated by a rapid review of the history of those years.

Don José Velazco had been viceroy for a little over a year when the destruction of Callao took place, followed by a devastating epidemic in the highlands, and the fire in the government archives housed in the residence of the marquis of Salinas, a fire that was held to be arson. Tremendous earthquakes in Quito, Latacunga, Trujillo, and Concepción de Chile, the Santa flood, a fire that destroyed Panama, and the rebellion of the Indians of Huarochiri, which was put down by hanging the principal ringleaders, figure among the dire calamities of that era.

In August of 1747, immediately following the destruction of Callao, the town of Bellavista was founded; the convent of Ocopa, dedicated to the propagation of the faith, was erected; the church of the Discalced Fathers was consecrated; the nun and woman of letters Sor María Juana, along with four other Capuchin sisters, founded a convent in Cajamarca; the so-called Newton's comet was seen; the state tobacco monopoly was established; the Royal Tribunal of Panama was done away with; and in 1755 a census was taken in Lima, resulting in the registration of 54,000 inhabitants.

II

*Regarding an Excommunication, and How because of
It the Viceroy and the Archbishop Became Enemies*

The obligation to motivate the following chapter would doubtless make us run the risk of mentioning facts that might wound touchy sensibilities were we not to adopt the tactic of changing names and telling of the event at a gallop. On a country estate in the Ate valley, near Lima, there lived a poor priest who was acting as chaplain of the estate. The owner, who was no less than a grandee of Castile, owing to matters of little importance that, moreover, are irrelevant here, caused the good chaplain to be paraded through the patio one morning, riding on a donkey and being given a good taste of the lash; he is said to have died shortly thereafter of pain and shame.

This horrifying punishment, suffered by one anointed of the Lord, caused a great commotion among the peaceloving people. The crime was unheard of. The Church issued a decree of total excommunication of the owner of the estate, in which it was ordered that the walls of the patio where the chaplain had been put to shame be torn down and that the land of the estate be sown with salt, not to mention many other rituals concerning which we shall spare the reader.

Our estate owner, who enjoyed great prestige in the mind of the viceroy and who, moreover, was a relative by marriage of his secretary Pedro Bravo, found himself protected by the two aforementioned, who had recourse to every means at their disposal to diminish to some degree the severity of the excommunication. The viceroy went several times to visit the archbishop to that end, but the latter stood firm.

Meanwhile a sort of alarm spread in the town and fears of a serious conflict for the government grew. The people, more and more incensed, were demanding the prompt punishment of the author of the sacrilegious act, and the viceroy, convinced that the archbishop was not a man who could be used for his purposes, found himself obliged to give in despite himself.

Praised be the Lord, those were good days for the Church! The people, as yet not contaminated by impiety, which according to many, is today taking giant steps forward, believed at the time with simple faith. Wicked society that has succumbed to the accursed fever of combating the concerns and errors of the past! Perverse human race that tends toward freedom and progress, and bears imprinted on its banner the imperative of civilization: *Forward! Forward!*

We repeat that we have recorded this curious fact only in embryonic form and with great caution, wanting nothing to do with adorning it with myriad glosses and incidental details concerning it. Old women recount that when the owner of the estate died, his corpse disappeared, for of a certainty it did not receive a Church burial, having been carried off by the one who appears in paintings at the foot of Saint Michael, and who in the wee hours traveled through the streets of Lima in a coach afire with infernal flames and drawn by a team of four diabolical horses abreast. Today there are still individuals who firmly believe in such nonsense. Let us leave such people to their mad beliefs and write: period, and *da capo.*

III

How the Archbishop of Lima Celebrated Mass after Having Had Lunch

It is a well-known fact that for the good inhabitants of the republic of Lima quarrels over privileges and prerogatives between the civil and ecclesiastic powers have always been a source of scandal. Even those of us who were born in these trying times remember many disputes between our presidents and the archbishop or the bishops. But in the era in which, by order of His Majesty Ferdinand VI, His Excellency the count of Superunda governed this viceroyalty of Peru, the two powers nearly counterbalanced each other, and His Excellency was far too timid to have recourse to his authority. Trifling questions, perhaps futile from the start, such as the one that we have consigned to another chapter, embittered the spirits of both the viceroy and of Archbishop Barroeta to the point that they gave rise to a bitter hatred between the two.

"Great was the rivalry," Córdova Urrutia says, "between the archbishop and the viceroy, because the former had ordered the organ to be played for him as he entered the cathedral and not to be played for the king's representative, and that a sunshade be raised for him, as for the latter, in processions. The complaints ended up in the court, which decided against the archbishop.

The count of Superunda, in his account of his rule, says, speaking of the archbishop: "He had the misfortune of excommunicating fiery geniuses known to be unruly and capable of changing the best ordered republics. These latter induced him to govern without reflection by persuading him that he ought to govern his jurisdiction with vigor, and that it was without limits. And inasmuch as he acted without experience, he fell out in short order with his council and various tribunals. The paths that many times I induced the archbishop to follow, with an eye to his decorum and the tranquillity of the city, were maxims quite the opposite of those of his advisors, who lost no time in persuading him that his subordination was a snub to his dignity and that he should make it known that he was the archbishop, clearly differentiating his authority from that of the viceroy who so badly humiliated him. The idea that those who thus counseled him deserved him, and the archbishop's inclination to rule despotically made them hasten to write me a confidential note having to do with a certain personal question, telling me to give him a free hand, but he endeavored to distance himself as much as possible from my message. In a short time rivalries with almost all the tribunals increased and the city was filled with edicts and orders, its inhabitants falling into vast confusion. If all of the incidents and obstacles that were later met with by the government in its dealings with the archbishop were recorded, they would constitute a bulky volume or history."

And the count of Superunda goes on to tell of the famous quarrel of the sunshade or canopy in the procession of the novena of the Conception, an incident that took place around the year 1752. Since it does not serve our purpose, we prefer to leave it in the inkwell and confine ourselves to the final quarrel between the representative of the crown and the archbishop of Lima

It was the practice that only when the archbishop officiated did he seat himself directly beneath a canopy directly adjacent to the viceroy's, and in order to keep the archbishop from suffering what vanity would describe as a snub, a servant of his always went to the palace on the eve of the feast day, with instructions to ask whether or not His Excellency would be present.

On the feast day of Saint Clare, also the name of a convent founded by Saint Toribio of Mongrovejo to which he bequeathed his heart, Manso found the means, in his opinion infallible, to humiliate his adversary, answering the messenger that he felt ill and that he therefore would not attend the ceremony. Chairs were set out for the Royal Tribunal, and at twelve noon Barroeta headed for the church and made himself comfortable beneath the canopy; but to his great surprise he saw the viceroy enter shortly thereafter, preceded by the various municipal corporations.

What had made His Excellency decide to change the ceremony in this way? Something of little moment. The certainty that His Reverence had just had for his lunch, eaten in the presence of laymen and clerics, either a consumptive or a robust stewed pullet, which of the two the chronicler took no pains to ascertain.

Let us agree that the archbishop's position was rather difficult, that without being subject to what he believed to be immense ridicule, he could not have his canopy lowered. His Reverence felt all the more confused the more the smiles and glances of the courtiers were haughty and mocking. Five minutes thus went by and still the ceremony did not begin. The viceroy was enjoying Barroeta's confusion and all those present were assured of His Excellency's triumph. The sword was humiliating the soutane.

But the good viceroy had not reckoned with this guest, or what amounts to the same thing, he was forgetting that he who lays down the law lays a trap for himself. Manso whispered in the ear of one of his officials, who approached the archbishop, pointing out to him in the name of His Excellency how odd it was for the viceroy to remain beneath a canopy and on an equal footing with someone who could not celebrate Mass because of the aforementioned pullet that he had eaten for lunch. The archbishop stood up, cast a sidelong glance at the ruffs of the Tribunal present, and said with remarkable self-possession:

"Officer! Announce to His Excellency that I am officiating."

And he headed with resolute step to the sacristy, from which he emerged dressed in liturgical vestments.

And what is notable about this account is that he did just as he said he would.

IV

In which the Pullet Begins to Cause Indigestion

We leave it to the imagination of our readers to calculate the scandal that the appeararance of the archbishop doubtless caused, a scandal that reached a climax when he was seen to consume the Divine Form. The viceroy did not miss the opportunity to sow discord among the people, so that the flock would declare that its pastor had been caught in the act of *flagrante sacrilegio.* The suspicion that His Excellency didn't know that long-suffering lamb called the people is well founded. The Creoles, after commenting on the event at length, broke up after making the following declaration, typical of the fanaticism of that era:

"In view of the fact that His Reverence took communion after having eaten lunch, he no doubt had God's permission to officiate."

Perhaps because of such trifles, the ill will of the cloistered religious toward Viceroy Manso was aroused, for a friar, on preaching the sermon on Palm Sunday, had the insolence to say that Christ had entered Jerusalem mounted on a gentle[1] donkey, a bit of buffoonery by means of which he believed that he had held His Excellency up to ridicule.

Meanwhile, the archbishop was not asleep, and even as the viceroy and the Royal Tribunal sent off to the king and his Council of the Indies a well-founded accusation of Barroeta, the latter called the ecclesiastic council together in his palace. In point of fact, minutes of the proceedings were drawn up in which, after citing the holy fathers, turning to the secret papal bulls of Paul II and other pontiffs, and undermining canon law, the conduct of the dignitary, which did not stop at eating pullets or buns, was approved, with the aim of furthering what goes by the name of the code of prerogatives and privileges of the Church of Christ. The archbishop thereupon appealed to His Holiness, who gave his approval of the step taken.

The Council of the Indies was not altogether satisfied, and although it did not openly rebuke Barroeta, it called him inconsiderate to have turned to Rome without first taking the matter to the crown. And to prevent the bickering between the political and religious authorities

---

[1] A play on Viceroy Manso's name. Gentle is *manso* in Spanish.

from happening again, His Holy Royal Majesty saw fit to transfer Barroeta to the archiepiscopal seat of Granada, and to appoint to that of Lima His Lordship don Diego del Corro, who entered the capital on November 26, 1785, and died in Jauja after two years as archbishop.

Among the archbishops that Lima has had, one of the most notable for the morality of his life and for his education and talent was don Pedro Antonio de Barroeta y Angel, born in Rioja in Castilla la Vieja. He had the synodal record of Lobo Guerrero reprinted,[2] and during the seven years that, according to Unanue,[3] his authority as archbishop lasted, he issued a number of edicts and regulations to reform the manners and morals of the clergy that, according to one writer of the time, were not very evangelical. Judging from the portrait of him in the sacristy of the cathedral, his eyes reveal his energetic nature and his broad forehead shows clear signs of intelligence. He succeeded in making himself loved by the people, but not by the canons, whom he frequently had cause to bring into line, and he vigorously supported those whose awareness of their century and their education he regarded as privileges of the Church.

As for ourselves, if we were to be frank, we declare that we can scarcely imagine excusing the conduct of the archbishop during the feast of Saint Clare, for we believe—a belief from which all the theologians of Christendom will not dissuade us—that the religion of the Crucified, truly a demanding religion, can permit neither deceitful practices nor melodramatic liturgical incidents. Before allowing pride to triumph, before stretching sacred laws, before abusing the faith of a people and sowing within it alarm and doubt, the minister of the Lord on High should have remembered the words of the immortal book: "Woe to him whence scandal cometh." "Let the house burn down without smoke pouring out" was the proverb wherewith our grandfathers condemned scandal.

---

[2] Lobo Guerrero (1546–1622) was Archbishop when he organized a synod that resulted in new regulations for the Archdiocesis of Lima.—Ed.

[3] *Guía política, eclesiástica y militar del virreynato del Perú para 1793 y 1794* (2 vols., 1793–1797) by Hipólito Unanue (1755–1833).—Ed.

V

Episcopal Witticisms

And in case the opportunity to speak of Archbishop Barroeta does not present itself again, I shall take advantage of this one and bring up a few witticisms of his. When radishes come your way, buy them.

As His Reverence was visiting the cloisters of Lima, he arrived at one in which he found the friars in a turmoil directed at their provincial or superior. The community complained that the latter was tyrannizing his inferiors to the point of forbidding anyone to cross the threshold and go outside without permission. The provincial began to defend his conduct, but Barroeta interrupted him, saying to him:

"Shut up, father, shut up, shut up, shut up."

The provincial shut his mouth, the archbishop said a blessing and headed for the door, and the friars were altogether delighted to see their keeper humiliated.

When the provincial recovered from his stupefaction, he went to the palace of the archbishop and respectfully complained to him that in the presence of the community His Reverence had forced him to hold his tongue.

"I am far, very far, from being rude to anyone, much less to Your Reverence, whom I esteem. What were my words?"

"Your Paternity interrupted me as I was unburdening myself by saying: 'Shut, up, shut up, shut up!' "

"Blessed be God! What were the friars asking for? Complaining about being shut up? Well then, let Your Reverence allow them out for a stroll along the street and they will leave you in peace. It is no fault of mine that Your Paternity didn't understand me and took hold of the live coal where it is red hot."

And the provincial took his leave, satisfied that señor Barroeta had not intended to offend him.

This archbishop was the one who, the story goes, on leaving the town of Mala, a miserable hole in which His Grace and his retinue were obliged to put up with a bad supper and a worse bed, exclaimed:

> Entre médanos de arena
> para quién bien se regala
> no tiene otra cosa Mala[4]
> que tener el agua buena.[5]

And in conclusion, here is another of His Reverence's witticisms.

The marquise of X was a relative of his and a person whose every desire was always satisfied by the archbishop. Her Ladyship took great interest in his appointing a certain cleric, her protégé, to a curateship. Barroeta, who had little idea of the purity and morality of the candidate, turned the marquise down. She took it into her head to go to Spain, spent money lavishly, and instead of a curateship obtained a bishopric for her protégé. With the royal decree in hand, the marquise went to visit the archbishop and told him:

"Señor don Pedro, the king is making a canon of the person whom you refused to make a parish priest."

"And a good deal of money it has cost you to obtain it, Your Ladyship."

"Naturally," the marquise answered. "But I would willingly have spent my entire fortune so as to keep your snub from lingering in my bones."

"Well, milady, if your purpose had been to secure a curateship, I would have granted one for nothing, but to give the care of souls to a good-for-nothing . . . *nequaquam*.[6] A good parish requires a head; to be a good canon requires but one good thing."

"What is that?" the marquise asked.

"A good backside so as to sit comfortably in a choir seat."

VI

In Which His Excellency's Star Grows Dim

After 17 years' rule, not counting those that he had spent as president of Chile, the count of Superunda, who had asked the court to be re-

---

[4] The archbishop is punning on the name of the town, since Mala suggests bad, *malo*.
[5] Amid sand dunes / for one to indulge himself / Mala has nothing to offer / save its good water.
[6] By no means [Latin].

lieved, handed command of it over to His Most Excellent Lordship don Manuel de Amat y Juniet on October 12, 1761.

The count of Superunda is, without dispute, one of the most notable figures of the colonial era. Chile owes to him the founding of its most important cities, and history, ever just, devotes honorable pages to him. The people are never ungrateful toward those who dedicate themselves to its good, a pleasing truth that, unfortunately, frequently causes public men in South America to be forgotten. While he exercised the presidency of Chile, he governed uprightly, was conciliatory toward the conquered and conquering races, tireless in promoting material improvements, tenacious in awakening in the common people the habit of work. With such worthy antecedents he went on to the viceroyalty, where he did battle with base, creeping intrigues that hindered the advance of his rule and made his disposition of his troops useless. His predecessor, moreover, had handed the country over to him in a state of violent upheaval. Apu Inca, at the head of a number of rebel tribes proud of the petty triumphs they had won over the Spanish forces, was threatening to make a sudden attack on the capital from Huarochirí. Manso marshaled all his vigor and energy and within a short time managed to imprison and kill the caudillo, whose head was placed on the arch of the Lima bridge. Do not tax us with lacking in love for the American cause because we call Apu Inca a rebel. Nations always find themselves disposed to receive the beneficent dew of freedom, and to our mind, trusting in the documents that we have been able to consult, Apu Inca was neither the apostle of the idea of redemption or the descendant of Manco Capac. His pretensions were those of the ambitious man without talent, who, by usurping a name, becomes the leader of a horde. He proclaimed the extermination of the white race without offering the native his political rehabilitation. His cause was that of barbarism against civilization.

Growing weary of the hazards that surrounded him in Peru, Manso was returning to Europe via Costa Firme when, to his misfortune, the boat that was transporting him put in at the island of Cuba, under siege at the time by the English.

Don Modesto de la Fuente, in his *Historia de España*, recounts curious details regarding the famous siege of Havana, during which the reader will see what a sad role it fell to Superunda to play. As lieutenant general, he presided over the military tribunal assembled to decide on either the surrender or the resistance of the threatened fortresses, but "whether because Manso had become short of breath over the years," as the Marquis of Obando supposes, or because he truly believed it to be impossible to resist, he led the tribunal to decide to surrender, thereby allowing an English ship to take Manso and his companions to the port of Cádiz.

From the trial to which they immediately became subject it turned out that the surrender was cowardly and the articles set down with regard to it ignominious, and that the count of Superunda, the principal cause of the disaster, deserved to be condemned to the loss of honors and offices, with the added sentence, in no way satisfactory, of two years' imprisonment in the fortress of Montjuich.

Don José Manso, a man of exemplary charity, did not, certainly, make a fortune from his prolonged rule in Peru. It is said that having been asked one day for alms by a beggar, he answered by giving him the hilt of his sword, of solid silver, and he is famous for the benefits he showered on the multitude of families that suffered the consequences of the horrible earthquake that ruined Lima in 1746.

VII

In Which His Reverence's Star Grows Brighter

Spring of the year 1770 was beginning when, strolling one afternoon in La Vega, the archbishop encountered an army of youngsters who, with childish larkishness, were frolicking about in the alleys of trees. We can explain the fondness for children that old people feel if we recall that old age and childhood, "the coffin and the cradle," are both very close to God.

His Reverence halted and looked with a fatherly smile at that happy crowd of young scholars enjoying the day off from school that the preceptors of those days gave their pupils. The dominy was seated on a bench on the lawn, absorbed in reading a book, until a servant of the archbishop's came to rouse him from his reading, summoning him in the name of His Reverence.

The dominy was a venerable old man with bold and noble features who, despite his poverty, wore his threadbare gown with a certain air of distinction. Having settled in Granada a short time before, he was head of a school, going under the name of Master Velazco, with nothing of his life story being known.

The Archbishop had scarcely set eyes on him when he recognized him to be the count of Superunda and embraced him. Once his initial transport was over, it was followed by confidences shared, and finally Barroeta made him promise to live at his side and accept his favors and protection. Manso obstinately refused, until His Reverence said to him:

"It seems to me, señor count, that Your Excellency still holds a grudge against me, leading me to believe that he is refusing my support, or that he is offending me by presuming that I am endeavoring to humiliate him in his adversity."

"Power, glory, wealth are no more than vanity of vanities! And if you imagine, señor archbishop, that I do not accept your protection out of hauteur, I shall abandon the school and come live with you this very day."

The archbishop embraced him once again and invited him to climb into his carriage.

"Fair enough," the count added. "Your ministry obliged you to cure me of my mad hauteur. Down with the proud!"

VIII

From that day on, though he had been embittered by the memory of his misfortunes and the ingratitude of the king, who in the end gave him back his status and honors, the days of the unfortunate Superunda were more bearable and peaceful.

The Corregidor[1] of Tinta

A Chronicle of the Era of the
Thirty-third Viceroy

Ahorcaban a un delincuente
Y decía su mujer:
No tengas pena, pariente
todavía puede ser
que la soga se reviente.[2]

ANONYMOUS

I

It was November 4, 1780, and the parish priest of Tungasuca, in order to celebrate his saint's day, which was also that of His Majesty Charles III, had gathered together for a splendid lunch the most important members of the parish as well as friends from nearby towns, who had been arriving since daybreak to congratulate him.

The priest, don Carlos Rodríguez, was a good-natured cleric, char-

---

[1] A *corregidor* is a chief administrative officer or mayor whose jurisdiction is called a *corregimiento*. The *corregidor's* responsibilities included the collection of tribute, the maintenance of roads, and the administration of justice.—Ed.

[2] A felon was about to be hanged / and his spouse said: / don't worry, good husband, / there's always a chance / that the rope will break.

itable, and not very demanding when it came to collecting taxes and other parish benefit due him as a parish priest, qualities worthy of an apostle that made him the idol of his parishioners. He was seated at the head of the table that morning, with a descendant of the Incas, don José Gabriel Tupac-Amaru, on his left, and on his right doña Micaela Bastidas, the wife of the cacique.[3] The wine flowed freely and as a result the most exuberant good cheer reigned. Suddenly the sound of a horse galloping up to the door was heard, and the horseman, without removing his spurs, strode into the dining room.

The new arrival was don Antonio de Arriaga, the corregidor of the province of Tinta, a Spanish hidalgo who was inordinately proud of his lineage going back generations, and who lorded it over Europeans and Creoles as befitted, as he saw it, those of less noble birth. Coarse of speech, overbearing in manner, cruel to Indians conscripted for forced labor, and so miserly that had he been born a clock, he wouldn't have told anyone what time it was: such was His Lordship. And as a crowning touch to his disrepute, the vicar general and the canons of Cuzco had solemnly excommunicated him for certain infringements upon the authority of the Church.

All the guests stood up as the corregidor came in. Paying no attention to the cacique, the corregidor thereupon sat himself down in the seat that the latter had been occupying, and the noble Indian went to sit down at the other end of the table, disregarding the lack of courtesy on the part of the vainglorious Spaniard. After a few trite phrases, and once he had filled his stomach and wet his whistle, His Lordship said to the priest:

"Don't get the idea, Your Reverence, that I've ridden at a gallop all the way from Yanaoca simply to congratulate you on your saint's day."

"Your Lordship knows that whatever it is that brings you here you are always welcome in this, my humble dwelling," the good curate replied.

"I am pleased that Your Reverence personally convinced me that a message I received yesterday was false, for had I found it to be true I give you my word that I would have taken no notice of your cassock or your tonsure and would have seized Your Reverence so as to give you a thrashing you would have remembered for all your days. So long

[3] An Indian leader.—Ed.

as I hold the staff of authority, no cassock-wearing Sunday sermonizer is going to threaten me."

"As God is my witness I don't know the reason for Your Lordship's wrathful words," the priest murmured, overawed by Arriaga's insolent remarks.

"I know my reasons better than anyone else, don Carlos. A fine impression I'd make if I were to tolerate in my district the public reading of those reprimands or those confounded notices of my excommunication that that old crackpot of a vicar general in Cuzco is sending around under my very nose, so to speak. And I swear by the soul of my father, may he rest in peace, that I will deal harshly with the first priest that gets out of line in my district! And be forewarned that if I get hot under the collar, I'll plant my feet in Cuzco, to put it baldly, and turn those pot-bellied, womanizing sots of canons into liver and lung stew!"

And absorbed as he was in his rude boasting, which he interrupted only to gulp down big swallows of wine, the corregidor did not notice that don Gabriel and other of the guests were stealing out of the dining room.

II

At six that afternoon the insolent hidalgo was galloping toward the town where he lived when his horse was lassoed, and don Antonio found himself in the midst of five armed men, whom he recognized as guests of the priest. "Give yourself up, Your Grace," said Tupac-Amaru, who was leading the men.

And without giving the wretched corregidor time to put up the slightest resistance, they clapped a pair of irons on him and took him to Tungasuca. Indian couriers left immediately with messages for Upper Peru and other locations, and Tupac raised his colors in rebellion against Spain.

A few days later, on November 10, a gallows could be seen in front of the chapel of Tungasuca, and the haughty Spaniard, in his uniform and accompanied by a priest who was exhorting him to die a Christian death, heard the town crier proclaim:

"This is the justice that don José Gabriel I, by the grace of God Inca, king of Peru, Santa Fe, Chile, Buenos Aires, and the continent of the Southern Seas, duke and lord of the Amazons and of the great Paititi, has ordered carried out against the person of Antonio de Arriaga as a tyrant, a traitor, an enemy of God and His ministers, and a corrupter and liar."

The executioner, a black slave of the hapless corregidor, stripped him of his uniform as a sign of his disgrace, dressed him in a shroud, and put a rope around his neck. But as the corregidor's body hung suspended a few inches from the ground, the rope broke. Taking advantage of the natural surprise that this incident caused the Indian onlookers, Arriaga began to run toward the chapel, shouting: "I am saved! Give me sanctuary!"

The hidalgo was about to enter the church when the Inca Tupac-Amaru blocked his path, and grabbing him by the neck, said to him:

"The Church is of no use to a blackguard like you! The Church will not give sanctuary to a scoundrel who has been excommunicated!"

And the executioner again laid hands on the condemned man and soon his gruesome mission was accomplished.

III

Our Tradition should end here, but the plan for our work requires that we devote a few lines by way of an epilogue to the viceroy under whose rule this incident took place.

His Excellency don Agustín de Jáuregui, a native of Navarre and of the family of the counts of Miranda and of Teba, knight commander of the order to Santiago and lieutenant general of the royal armies, was acting as governor of Chile when Charles appointed him to replace the viceroy of Peru, don Manuel Guirior, whom he had unjustly and summarily removed from his post. The knight commander arrived in Lima on June 21, 1780, and to be frank, none of his predecessors took command under less favorable omens than he.

On the one hand, the savages of Chanchamayo had just razed and sacked a number of civilized settlements, and on the other, the increased taxes and the steps taken by the tyrannical royal inspector Areche had given rise to serious disturbances, in which many corregidors and tax collectors fell victim to the wrath of the people. It may be said the entire country had been set afire, despite the fact that Guirior had suspended the levying of the hateful and exorbitant taxes until such time as the monarch reflected on the matter.

Moreover, war between Spain and England had been declared, and repeated dispatches from Europe informed the new viceroy that the queen of the seas was readying a fleet that was to be sent to the Pacific.

Jáuregui (a name that means "too gentlemanly" in Basque), in preparation for pirate attacks, was to fortify the coast and arm it with artillery, organize militias, and enlarge the battle fleet, all of these measures that required great expenditures, thereby further increasing the public debt.

Don Agustín de Jáuregui had occupied the viceroy's palace for barely four months when news came of the execution of the corregidor Arriaga, and along with it the news that the cacique Tupac-Amaru had been proclaimed Inca and sovereign of Peru, ruling over an area of more than 300 square leagues.

This is not the place to give an account of this tremendous revolution that, as is well known, put the colonial government in grave danger. Independence came close to being achieved at that point.

On April 6, Good Friday of the year 1781, the Inca and his principal vassals were taken prisoner and the most barbarous atrocities practiced on them. There were tongues cut off and hands severed, bodies quartered, the gallows, and the garrote, for Areche permitted every sort of savagery imaginable.

With the execution of the Inca, of his wife doña Micaela, of his children and his brothers, the revolutionaries were left without a rallying point. Nonetheless the spark of revolt was not put out until July of 1783, when there took place in Lima the execution of don Felipe Tupac, the brother of the unfortunate Inca and chieftain of the Indians of Huarochiri. "Thus there ended this revolution, and history would find it difficult to find another more justified or less favored by fortune," Dean Funes writes.[4]

The arms of the house of Jáuregui were: a shield mantled, the first quarter in gold with a crested oak and a boar passant, the second in

---

[4] Gregorio Funes (1540–1830), an Argentinian cleric and orator who authored the *Ensayo de la historia civil del Paraguay, Buenos Aires y Tucumán* (1816).—Ed.

gules and a castle with a pennon, the third in azure with three fleurs-de-lis.

It is said that on April 26, 1748, the viceroy don Agustín de Jáuregui received as a gift a little basket of cherries, a fruit that His Excellency was very fond of. He had barely eaten two or three of the cherries when he fell senseless to the floor. Thirty hours later the great door of the reception hall swung open, and there in an armchair, under a canopy, was Jáuregui, in his dress uniform. In keeping with the ceremony for such an occasion, the palace notary, followed by the judges of the Royal Tribunal, advanced to within a few steps of the canopy, and said three times in a loud voice:

"Most Excellent señor don Agustín de Jáuregui!"

And then, turning to address those present, he uttered this ritual phrase: "Sires, he does not answer. He has died! He has died! He has died!"

He immediately produced a document testifying to this fact, and the members of the tribunal signed it.

Thus did the Indians avenge the death of Tupac-Amaru.

Third Series

The Inca's Achirana

(To Teodorico Olachea)

In 1412 the Inca Pachacutec, accompanied by his son the imperial prince Yupanqui and his brother Capac-Yupanqui, undertook the Conquest of the Valley of Ica, whose inhabitants, though peace loving by nature, lacked neither the resources nor the army to wage war. That was the wise monarch's understanding, and before resorting to arms he proposed to the Iqueños that they submit to his paternal government. The latter willingly agreed, and the Inca and his 40,000 warriors were cordially and splendidly received by the Icans.

As Pachacutec was visiting the unruly territory that he had just subjected to his domination, he stopped for a week in the *pago*[1] called Tate. The owner of Tate was an elderly woman who lived with beautiful young girl, her daughter.

The conqueror of peoples believed that it was equally easy to win the damsel's heart. But she loved a handsome young man of the region and had the strength, which only true love inspires, to resist the love-smitten pleas of the prestigious and all-powerful sovereign.

Finally Pachacutec lost all hope of his love being returned, and taking the girl's hand in his, told her, not without first breathing a sigh:

"Set your mind at ease, dove of this valley, and may the mist of sorrow never spread its veil over the sky of your soul. Ask a favor of

[1] Country property or estate.

me that will make you and yours remember forever the love that you inspired in me."

"Your Lordship," the young girl answered him, kneeling and kissing the hem of the royal mantle, "you are great and nothing is impossible for you. Your nobility would have won my heart had my soul not already been the slave of another master. I shall ask you for nothing, since the one who receives gifts is placed under an obligation. But if the gratitude of my people satisfies you, I beg you to bring water to this region. Sow benefits and you will reap blessings. Reign, Your Lordship, over grateful hearts rather than over men who timidly bow before you, dazzled by your splendor."

"You are modest, damsel with the black hair, hence you captivate me with your words as with the fire of your gaze. Farewell, illusory dream of my life! Wait ten days, and you will see that what you seek has come about. Farewell, and do not forget your king!"

And the chivalrous monarch, climbing into the litter adorned with gold that the nobles of the kingdom carried on their shoulders, continued his triumphal progress.

For ten days the 40,000 men of the army were occupied in opening the bed of the river that takes its rise on the estates of El Molino and El Trapiche and ends at Tate, the country property on which there lived the beautiful young lady with whom Pachacutec had fallen passionately in love.

The Inca's irrigation system supplied abundant water to the haciendas that today are known by the names of Chabalina, Belén, San Jerónimo, Tacama, San Martín, Mercedes, Santa Bárbara, Chanchajaya, Santa Elena, Vista-Alegre, Sáenz, Parcona, Tayamana, Pongo, Pueblo Nuevo, Sonumpe, and, finally, Tate.

Such, according to tradition, is the origin of Achirana, a word that means "what flows purely toward what is beautiful."

A Letter Sings

Up to the middle of the sixteenth century we see the phrase "letters speak" used by the purest of Spanish prose writers, meaning that such and such a fact is referred to in letters. But all of a sudden letters weren't content to speak, but broke into song; and even today, in order to put an end to a dispute, we are in the habit of putting a hand in our pocket and taking out a missive as we say: "Well, sir, a letter sings." And we read in public the truths or lies that it contains, and the battleground is ours. Creoles don't refer to letters as either speaking or singing, and confine themselves to saying: "a bit of paper speaks."

Last night while reading the Jesuit Acosta, who, as you know, wrote about the events of the conquest at length and in detail,[1] I came upon a story and said to myself: "The phrase already appears here," or what amounts to the same thing, even though Father Acosta doesn't say so, he examines the origin of the little phrase in question, for which I am going to claim before the Royal Spanish Academy the honors of a Peruvianism.

And this said, enough of beating about the bush and on to the main concern.

I believe I have recounted before, and in case I left it in the inkwell

---

[1] José de Acosta (1540–1600) was a Spanish Jesuit who resided in Lima for 15 years and wrote *De procuranda indorum salute* (1588), which called for better treatment of the Indians, and the *Historia natural y moral de las Indias* (1590), which surveyed the natural history and geography of Mexico and Peru.—Ed.

I make it appear in print here, that when the conquistadors took possession of Peru wheat, rice, barley, sugar cane, lettuce, radishes, cabbage, asparagus, garlic, onions, eggplant, mint, chickpeas, lentils, broad beans, mustard, anise, lavender, cumin, oregano, sesame, and other products of the land that would be too long to enumerate, were unknown in this country. As for beans, we had them at home, along with various other produce and fruit that made the Spaniards lick their fingers with pleasure after tasting them.

Some of the new seeds grew more abundantly and bore more fruit in Peru than in Spain; and with great seriousness and self-assurance several respectable chroniclers and historians recount that in the valley of Azapa, in the jurisdiction of Arica, such a colossal radish was grown that a man could not get his arms around it, and that don García Hurtado de Mendoza, who at the time was not yet viceroy of Peru, but governor of Chile, was ecstatic and looked at such a wonder openmouthed. I say, that radish was no trifle!

Around the year 1558 don Antonio Solar was one of the richest inhabitants of the City of Kings. Although he was not among Pizarro's companions at Cajamarca, he arrived in time to get himself a good share of the division of land after the conquest, a share that consisted of a spacious parcel on which to build his house in Lima, 200 *fanegas*[2] of uncultivated land in the valleys of Supe and Barranca, and 50 *mitayos* or Indians to serve him.[3]

For our grandfathers the following catchy saying had the value of an aphorism or of an article of the Constitution: "The house in which you live, the wine you drink, and all the pieces of land you see and can seize."

Don Antonio put together a valuable hacienda in Barranca, and to further the work he brought from Spain two teams of oxen, an act that in those days gave agriculturalists the same importance as that given in our day to ships propelled by steam engines that transport people from London or New York. "The Indians came," says one chronicler, "to see them plow, amazed by something that to them was monstrous, and

[2] Here, a measure of land; about $1^{1}/_{2}$ acres.
[3] The *mita* was a system of enforced Indian labor; *mitayos* were the Indian laborers of the *mita*.—Ed.

they said that the Spaniards were idlers who used those huge animals so as not to have to work themselves."

Don Antonio Solar was the rich *encomendero* whom the viceroy Blasco Núñez de Vela wanted to hang, accusing him of being the author of a lampoon in which, alluding to the reforming mission given His Excellency, the following inscription was written on the wall of the inn at Barranca: "The one who throws me out of my house and land I will throw out of this world."

And since I have used the word *encomendero,* it will not be out of place for me to note the origin of it. In the title deeds or documents in which each conquistador was assigned parcels of land, the following clause was placed: "Likewise, you are entrusted with[4] *x* (here the number was inserted) Indians for you to indoctrinate in matters of our holy faith."

Along with the teams of oxen there arrived seeds or plants of melon, medlars, pomegranates, citrons, lemons, apples, apricots, quince, sour cherries, cherries, almonds, nuts, and other fruits of Castile unknown to the natives of the country, on which they gorged themselves to such a point that not a few of them died. More than a century later, under the rule of the viceroy and duke of La Palata, an edict was published that priests read to their parishioners after Sunday Mass, forbidding the Indians to eat cucumbers, a vegetable known as *mataserrano*[5] for its fatal effects.

The time came when Barranca's melon patch produced its first harvest, and here our story begins.

His steward chose ten of the best melons, carefully setting them in a couple of crates, and put them on the shoulders of two *mitayos,* giving them a letter for their master.

When the melon bearers had covered several leagues, they sat down to rest next to a wall. As was only natural, the perfume of the fruit awakened the curiosity of the *mitayos,* and there began within them a hard-fought battle between appetite and fear.

"Do you know, brother," one of them finally said in their native dialect, "that I have thought of the way we can eat a melon without its

[4] In Spanish, *se os encomiendan.*
[5] Indian killer.

being discovered? Let us hide the letter behind the wall, for if it doesn't see us eat it won't be able to accuse us."

The simple ignorance of the Indians attributed to writing a diabolical and marvelous power. They believed, not that the letters were conventional signs, but spirits, that not only functioned as messengers but also as lookouts or spies.

This must have seemed right to the other *mitayo,* for without a word he put the letter behind the wall, placing a stone on top of it, and this done, the two of them set themselves to devouring, not eating, the inviting and delectable fruit.

Once they were already near Lima, the second *mitayo* smote his forehead, saying:

"Brother, we're making a mistake. It would be best if we divide our loads equally, for if you are carrying four melons and I'm carrying five our master will be suspicious."

"Well spoken," said the other *mitayo.*

And once again they hid the letter behind another wall as they finished off a second melon, that delicious fruit that as the proverb says, when fasting it is gold, at midday silver, and at night it kills; for in all truth, there is no fruit more indigestible and liable to produce colic when one has a bellyful of it.

Arriving at don Antonio's house they placed in his hands the letter, in which the overseer announced to him that he was sending him ten melons.

Don Antonio, who had promised the bishop and other notables to present them with the first melons harvested, happily headed for the crates to inspect the load.

"What's this, you thieving rascals!" he exclaimed, snorting with rage. "The overseer is sending me ten melons, and two are missing," and don Antonio consulted the letter again.

"He's sending just eight, *taitai,*"[6] the *mitayos* answered, trembling.

"The letter says ten and you ate two of them on the way. Well then! Have a drubbing be given these rogues."

And the poor Indians, after getting a good thrashing, sat sulking in a corner of the patio, and one of them said:

"Do you see, brother, a letter sings!"

---

[6] A respectful form of address. Also *taitay.*

Don Antonio overheard him, and shouted to them:

"Yes, you rascals, and take care that I don't give you another thrashing. You know now that a letter sings."

Don Antonio told his social circle about it, and the phrase became widespread and traveled across the sea.

An Adventure of the Poet-Viceroy

I

The faction of the *vicuñas,* who were called that because its members wore vicuña hats, was getting the worst of it in the civil war that was raging in Potosí. For the moment, the Basques were winning because the corregidor[1] of the imperial town, don Rafael Ortiz de Sotomayor, was altogether on their side.

The Basques had taken over Potosí, for they held all the important public offices. Of the 24 town councilors, half were Basques, and even the two magistrates were of that nationality, despite the fact that this was expressly forbidden by royal decree. The Creoles, Castilians, and Andalusians formed an alliance to destroy or at least counterbalance this predominance of the Basques. Such was the origin of the open war that for many years made this region the stage of bloody slaughter, to which the ever-victorious general of the *vicuñas,* don Francisco Castillo, put an end in 1626, by marrying his daughter, doña Eugenia, to don Pedro de Oyanume, one of the most important Basques of the town.

In 1617 the viceroy and prince of Esquilache wrote a long letter to Ortiz de Sotomayor regarding several matters of government, which reads more or less as follows:

[1] See note 1, "The Corregidor of Tinta."—Ed.

And kindly note, my dear don Rafael, that there is a smell of rebellion about those factions in Potosí that is overwhelming. The hour has come for the harshest of measures to be taken to put an end to them, for mild measures would prove to be a disservice to His Majesty, an offense to Our Lord God, and a discredit to these realms. Hence I have nothing to recommend to the discretion of Your Excellency, who, as a valiant and astute soldier, will apply the cautery to the place where the wound appears, for the devil has a free hand in these matters concerning Potosí, and disorder may spread like oil on a cloth. I expect Your Excellency to answer that you have brought a satisfactory end to these disorders, and not otherwise, for it is high time to end them before those *vicuñas* catch their breath and come to be as much a problem as the *comuneros*[2] in Castile.

The *vicuñas* had sworn not to allow their daughters or sisters to marry Basques, and one of the latter, on learning of the solemn pledge of the enemy faction, proclaimed right in the middle of the main square: "If the *vicuñitas* are not willing to be our wives, we are men enough to take them at the tip of our swords." This boast further aroused the *vicuñas'* hatred, and there were daily skirmishes in the streets of Potosí.

Ortiz de Sotomayor was not one to embrace a conciliatory policy. A firm supporter of the Basques, he believed that the viceroy's letter authorized him to use treachery as a weapon against the *vicuñas*, and so one night he had don Alfonso Yáñez and eight or ten of the leading *vicuñas* secretly seized, decapitated, and their heads placed on the top of a post in the main square.

With the break of day the *vicuñas* came face to face with this terrible sight and immediately set upon the corregidor's men with daggers, and the latter were forced to take asylum in a church. But fearing, with good reason, the vengeance of his enemies, don Rafael mounted his horse and came to Lima, while letting it be known that he had done nothing save to follow the viceroy's instructions to the letter. As we have seen, this was not precisely true, for His Excellency had given no authorization to behead anyone who had not first been sentenced to death by a court.

---

[2] Supporters of the *Comunidades* in Spain who staged a bloody rebellion against Charles V.

II

Thursday of Holy Week in the year 1618 was celebrated with all the solemnity that characterized that century of strict observers. His Excellency don Francisco de Borja y Aragón, prince of Esquilache, left the viceroy's palace, with a splendid retinue, to go visit seven of the most important churches of the city.

As he was leaving the church of Santo Domingo, after having prayed at the first station of the cross with the devotion that befitted a kinsman of Saint Francis Borja, duke of Gandía, he found himself face to face with a supremely beautiful lady followed by a slave carrying the indispensable small rug for her mistress to kneel on. The lady's eyes fixed on the viceroy one of those glances that give off magnetic currents. Don Francisco returned her gaze with a barely visible smile, raising his hand to his heart as if to tell the young lady that Cupid's dart had found its mark.

> A la mar, por ser honda
> se van los ríos,
> y detrás de tus ojos
> se van los míos.[3]

His Excellency was a real don Juan, and there was much talk in Lima of his good fortune in love. Along with his dashing demeanor, his martial bearing, and his urbanity, he enjoyed the vigor of a man in the prime of life, for the prince of Esquilache was barely 35. Possessed of a fiery imagination, gracious of speech, brave to the point of recklessness, and generous to the point of extravagance, don Francisco de Borja y Aragón was the perfect examplar of those chivalrous hidalgos who laid down their life for their king and their lady.

There are historical figures whom we become fond of, and I for one am a devoted admirer of the poet-viceroy, doubly noble by reason of his titles of nobility and by the parchments that he filled with his elegant pen of a prose writer and the favorite of the muses. I concede that he allowed the Jesuits to have too free a hand during his rule, but it must be borne in mind that the descendant of a general of the Com-

---

[3] Into the deep blue sea / the rivers flow, / so into your eyes / do mine go.

pany of Jesus, canonized by Rome, would necessarily share the prejudices of his kind. If he sinned thereby, the blame lay with his era, and it is folly to demand that men be superior to the times in which they live.

In the other six churches he visited, the viceroy kept meeting the same lady, and the same exchange of smiles and glances ensued.

> If you don't love me
> don't trade glances with me;
> if you won't ransom me,
> don't make me your captive.[4]

At the last station of the cross, when a page was about to place a little cushion of crimson velvet with a gold fringe on his prie-dieu, the prince of Esquilache leaned over and quickly whispered:

"Jeromillo, there is big game behind that pillar. Follow the trail."

It would appear that Jeromillo was skilled at this sort of hunting and was endowed with both the sense of smell of a setter and the swiftness of a falcon, for by the time His Excellency returned to the palace and dismissed his retinue, the page was already awaiting him in his chamber.

"Well, Mercury, who is she?" the viceroy said to him. Like all the poets of his century, he was fond of references to mythology.

"This note, which smells of perfume, will tell Your Excellency," the page replied, taking it out of his pocket.

"By Santiago de Compostela! So we've received a note, have we? Ah, little page, you're worth twice your weight in gold, and I must immortalize you in verses that surpass my poem on Naples."

And drawing closer to a lamp, he read:

> Siendo el galán cortesano
> y de un santo descendiente,
> que haya ayunado es corriente
> como cumple a un buen cristiano.
> Pues besar quiere mi mano,

---

[4] Por dios, si no me quieres / que no me mires; / ya que no me rescates, / no me cautives.

según su fina expresión,
le acuerdo tal pretensión,
si es que a más no se propasa,
y honrada estará mi casa
  si viene a hacer colación.[5]

The mysterious lady knew very well that she was going to be dealing with a poet, and the better to impress him she had had recourse to the language of Apollo.

"I say!" don Francisco murmured. "So the lady is a bluestocking, or to put it differently, Minerva in the person of Venus. Jeromillo, we're off on a love-adventure. My cape, and give me the address on Olympus of this godess." Half an hour later the viceroy, muffled in his cape so that no one would recognize him, was on his way to the lady's house.

III

Doña Leonor de Vasconcelos was a striking Spanish beauty and the widow of Alonso Yáñez, the man beheaded by the corregidor of Potosí. She had come to Lima determined to avenge her husband, and she had cleverly put Cupid's artillery into play to attract the viceroy of Peru to her home. To her the prince of Esquilache was her husband's real murderer.

The widow of Alonso Yáñez lived in a house on the calle de Polvos Azules, with grounds in the rear that ran down to the river. This circumstance, together with the frequent sound of male footsteps in the courtyard and the interior of the house, was a cause for alarm in the mind of the adventurous gallant.

Don Francisco had been engaged for half an hour in ceremonious conversations with the lady when the latter revealed who she was, trying to bring the conversation round to an explanation of what had happened in Potosí. But the shrewd prince skirted the subject and chose to follow instead the winding path of amorous artfulness.

---

[5]The gallant being a courtly gentleman / And the descendant of a saint, / has today fasted / As befits a good Christian. / Since he would kiss my hand / as he politely puts it, / I grant him this desire / if he will propose nothing more, / and my house will be honored / should he come to take refreshment here.

A man as keen witted at the prince of Esquilache needed to be told no more to realize that he had fallen into an ambush, and that he was in a house that was probably the headquarters that night of the *vicuñas*, of whose animosity toward his person he had already had some indication.

The moment came to proceed to the dining room to partake of the promised refreshments. It consisted of that pleasing salad of mixed fruits we Limeños call *ante*, three or four different preserves made by the nuns, and the classic *pan de dulce*.[6] After sitting down at the table the viceroy picked up a Venetian glass decanter full of a delicious Malaga wine, and said:

"I regret, doña Leonor, not doing honor to so excellent a Malaga, but I've made a vow to drink only a superb sherry that comes from my own vineyards in Spain."

"Your Excellency need not deprive himself of the wine he likes best. I can easily send one of my servants to Your Excellency's steward."

"Your Ladyship has read my mind."

And turning to a servant he said to him:

"Look here, you rascal. Go to the palace, ask for my page Jeromillo, give him this little key, and tell him to bring me the two bottles of sherry that he'll find in the cupboard of my chamber. Don't forget this message, and here's a doubloon to buy yourself some *pan de dulce*."

The servant left and the prince of Esquilache went on in a jovial vein:

"My wine is so fine that I have to keep it locked up in my chamber, for that knave of a secretary of mine, Estúñiga, has the same predilection for wine as mosquitoes for blood, and a scribe's inclination to give every bottle of wine his personal seal of approval. I'm going to get cross with him one of these days and slice off his ears to set other topers an example."

The viceroy placed his hopes in Jeromillo's quick wits and kept up his gallant small talk. To get out of a snare, it's head first and then arms, as the proverb has it.

When Jeromillo, who was nobody's fool, received His Excellency's message, he realized without further prompting that his master was in grave danger. The only thing in the bedroom closet was a pair of pistols

[6] Sweet buns.

with gold inlays, a splendid royal gift that Philip III had given don Francisco on the day he took his leave of the monarch before sailing for America.

The page had doña Leonor's servant arrested, and from the few words that escaped the latter in his surprise, Jeromillo gathered that he must come to His Excellency's aid without a moment to lose.

Luckily the house that was the scene of the viceroy's love-adventure was only a block from the palace, and a few minutes later the captain of the guard, with a squad of halberdiers, surprised six of the *vicuñas* who had sworn to kill the viceroy or force him into making some sort of concession to the Basque faction.

Don Francisco said to the lady with a mocking smile:

"The meshes of your net were made of silk, milady, so you needn't be surprised that the lion has broken through them. It is indeed a pity that we weren't able to play out our roles to the end, you as Judith and I as Holofernes!"

And turning to the captain of the guard, he added:

"Don Jaime, let those men go free, and take care that this incident doesn't come to light and set people's tongues to wagging! And you, milady, don't take me for an accomplice to murder. Honor, rather, the prince of Esquilache, who swears to you by the quarters of his coat of arms that even if he ordered the disturbances in Potosí put down, he never authorized the beheading of anyone not sentenced to death according to the law.

IV

A month later doña Leonor and the *vicuñas* set out on the road back to Potosí. But on the same night that they left Lima, a patrol found the body of don Rafael Ortiz de Sotomayor in an alleyway with a dagger buried in his chest.

Everyone the Master in His Own House

I

I don't know in exactly what year of the last century a Mercedarian, a friar of great influence and importance with the title of Visitor General of the Order, came from Spain to this City of Kings. The date doesn't matter one iota, for even though I am of two minds as to when it took place, my story is nonetheless true.

The Visitor brought with him royal documents and pontifical decrees that accorded him any number of powers and privileges. The sons of Nolasco received him with great festivities, poems in his honor and banquets, giant figures in procession, and I don't know what other nonsense.

Not so much to warmly receive the guest as to figure out the extent of the Visitor's powers, the Very Reverend archbishop went with great ceremony to visit him and proposed that they have lunch together three times a week in the archbishop's palace.

To emphasize the importance of the friar, we need only point to the fact that he was addressed as Your Excellency, as paper and parchment documents testify.

I don't dare say for certain, but I have reason to suspect that His Excellency the Visitor was none other than Friar José González de Aguilar Flores de Navarra, the king's theologian, lord of the baronetcies of Algar and Escala in Valencia, and (to top it all off!) grandee first class of Spain.

The first morning that His Reverence and His Excellency were to lunch together in each other's cordial company, the former sent his coach round to the door of the convent of La Merced a little before eight, and the Visitor made himself comfortable on the soft cushions.

Once he had reached the drawing room of the bishop's palace and after exchanging greetings and other mumbo-jumbo as etiquette required, the Visitor said:

"In order not to keep Your Reverence waiting, I have come without saying the Divine Office."

"Well, there is time for Your Excellency to fulfill your duty in *my* cathedral."

And with a servant accompanying him, after walking through the Patio of the Orange Trees, the two of them entered the sacristy. The Visitor then dressed in vestments and, attended by an altar boy, said Mass at the high altar.

When the canons gathered at nine o'clock in the choir and found out what had just taken place, they were beside themselves.

"What!" they cried out in a fury. "How does a friar dare say Mass at *our* high altar!"

Given the canons' pride, the incident was something that cried out to high heaven and had to be remedied.

After a delicious lunch of cracklings, tamales, *sanguito de ñajú*,[1] little cakes made of almond paste and candied fruit, and other appetizing Creole dishes, the guest departed and the indignant canons entered with their complaint, and what with their melodramatic show of anger and their recriminations they made the good-natured archbishop's head spin.

He turned every shade of red, for to tell the whole truth the fault was largely his because it had not occurred to him to assign the celebrant a chapel of his own. In high dudgeon the canons brought up rules and briefs and other foolishness, and after a long controversy it was agreed that if the Visitor took it into his head to say Mass in the cathedral again, he would do so at a portable altar.

[1] Cornmeal pudding with okra.

II

And several weeks went by, and when there was no longer anyone who remembered what had happened, a Sunday morning came round, and the Visitor arose in a cheerful mood, saying that he had taken a notion to put a reform into effect in *his* church immediately.

And secretly summoning a dozen carpenters, he ordered that the altar of Our Lady of Antigua, located near the door, be partitioned off with planks from the central nave and the remainder of the church.

The Dominicans argue with the Mercedarians as to which order was first established in Lima, but it is historically proven that the first Mass in our capital was celebrated by a Mercedarian monk, Friar Antonio Bravo; that in 1535 Father Miguel Orenes was at the time provincial or commander of the Order; and that when the conquistador Pizarro was assassinated in 1541, the Mercedarians, who had been branded as supporters of Almagro, had already almost finished building their convent and church, investing in them the sum of 700,000 pesos.

Let us continue this Tradition.

The friars murmured, sotto voce, that His Excellency's brain had become addled, but respect kept them from making the slightest comment about their superior's order.

On the following day the enclosure of the altar was finished, with its own little door. The workers had labored all night.

This was the first of the three Rogation Days that precede the feast of the Ascension of Our Lord, and following the ritual, the archbishop and his choir visited each of the great churches in turn. That Monday it was the turn of the church of La Merced.

With all the friars of his convent, His Excellency went to the door of the church to solemnly receive the visit.

The group was about to enter the central nave leading to the high altar, when the Visitor headed them off, saying:

"Stop; this is not the right way."

And turning to the archbishop he added:

"Your Reverence: since the canons do not approve of a friar celebrating Mass at *your* high altar, I have decided that they can officiate only at the altar by the door of *my* church."

"But Your Excellency . . ." the archbishop stammered.

"There is nothing for it, Your Reverence. Everyone is master in his own house."

"And God in everyone's house, brother," a choirmaster murmured.

And that was that. The archbishop and his canons turned around and proceeded to celebrate Rogations in another church that, if we are not mistaken, was La Concepción.

It would appear that the canons still hold a grudge against the Mercedarians that has become traditional, and that they are unwilling to forgive them for the arrogance of the Visitor. A good proof is that they have never again come to celebrate Rogation Days in the church of La Merced.

The Latin of a Young Lady of Lima
(To José Rosendo Gutiérrez)

It is well known that in the system of education in the past, it was very important to make youngsters waste three or four years studying the language of Virgil and Cicero, and that in the end they were left not rightly knowing either Latin or Spanish.

A boy asked his father:

"Papa, what is Latin?"

"Something that takes three years to learn and three weeks to forget."

I am of the opinion that Heinecius with his *Metaphysics* in Latin, Justinian with his *Institutes* in Latin, and Hippocrates with his *Aphorisms* in Latin must have left little trace in the minds of young scholars. And I don't say that because I think—heaven free me from talking such nonsense!—that in the past there were not eminent men learned in letters and science among us, but because it worries me to imagine a university proceeding in which a doctoral thesis, always greeted with loud applause, was read for 60 minutes, when the gathering of ladies and prominent personages who did not know the slightest thing about Nebrija and the professors who taught Duns Scotus and Digestus the Elder were sometimes left as much in the dark as the last lay brother.

So it is not surprising that students left the classrooms with little of substance in their brains, while at the same time their heads were chock full of sophistries and their speech distressingly pedantic.

In medicine, the doctors, by dint of Latinisms more than by pre-scriptions, dispatched their fellows to rot in the ground.

The sick chose to die in Spanish and this preference in matters of taste was responsible for the great prestige of household remedies and of charlatans who gave them out. Among the medicines of that inno-cent age, none amuses me more, being both cheap and speedy, than the virtue attributed to prayers of Christian doctrine. Thus those suf-fering from typhoid fever were to take a *salve,* which in the naive opin-ion of our grandfathers was something cooler and less irritating than a cold drink made from melon seeds. The *credo,* on the other hand, was deemed to be a hot remedy, and was a better sudorific than borage water or punch laced with brandy. And I leave in the inkwell the opin-ion that the Gospels, when applied on the stomach, were an excellent poultice, not to mention the blessed buns of Saint Nicholas, or the ejaculatory prayers against the seven-day fever, or the little crystal balls sold by certain friars to keep children from becoming scrawny or from being sucked by witches.

On the platforms of tribunals, men who wore judge's togas and ac-ademic robes devised pleas that were half in Latin and half in Spanish, and besides the hodge-podge of tongues, justice, which by itself is blind, suffered as though its cataracts were being removed.

The language of Latium was so much the fashion that not only was there a Latin of the sacristy but also a Latin of the kitchen; a good proof of this is the story of a pope, who, tiring of polenta and macaroni, ventured one day to eat a certain dish from America, and His Holiness apparently found it so tasty that he must have gone round the bend, and forgetting Tuscan, exclaimed in Latin: *Beati indiani qui manducant pepiani.*[1]

When a certain bishop reprimanded a cleric who was going about armed with a sword, the latter excused himself by claiming that he used to it to defend himself against dogs.

"But you don't need a sword for that," His Reverence replied, "for if you recite the Gospel of Saint John you won't be bitten."

"Well and good, Your Reverence, but if the dogs don't understand Latin, how do I escape danger?"

In literature Gongorism was all the rage, and writers vied to see

---

[1] Blessed be the Indians who eat peppers [Latin].

which of them could outdo the other in extravagance. In order not to be accused of being a liar, I mention here the works of two distinguished Lima poets: the Jesuit Rodrigo Valdez[2] and the encyclopedic Peralta,[3] the two of them most estimable from another point of view. And I shall say nothing of Lunarejo, a wise Cuzcan who, among other books, published one with the title *Apologética de Góngora*.

In the days of the viceroy and count of Superunda we had a woman poet, the fruit of our Lima orchard, named doña María Manuela Carrillo de Andrade y Sotomayor, a lady of great importance, who martyrized not only the Spanish muses but Latin ones as well. And I say that she martyrized them and subjected them to public shame because (and forgive me the lack of gallantry) the verses by my fellow Limeñan that I have read are worse than bad. Doña María filled reams of Catalonian paper with her scribbles, and even wrote short plays and comedies that were performed in our coliseum.

And I leave in the inkwell any further mention, among other women poets from Lima who were intimately related to the mischievous nymphs who dwell on Parnassus, of doña Violante de Cisneros; doña Rosalía Astudillo y Herrera; sor Rosa Corbalán, a nun of the Order of The Conception; doña Josefa Bravo de Lagunas, abbess of Santa Clara; the Capuchin sor María Juana; sor Juana de Herrera y Mendoza, of the Order of Saint Catherine; doña Manuela Orrantía; and doña María Juana Calderón y Vadillo, daughter of the marquis of Casa Calderón and wife of don Gaspar Ceballos, a Knight of the Order of Santiago and also a devotee of letters. Doña María Juana, who died in 1809 at the age of 83, had the Cuzcan bishop Gorrochátegui as her teacher of literature, and was a very skillful translator of Latin, French, and Italian.

Many of these women knew not only Latin, but Greek as well; and there were some, such as doña Isabel de Orbea, who was denounced to the Inquisition as being a philosopher, and the Trinitarian nun doña Clara Fuentes, who could trump and win every trick from the theologians, jurists, and canon lawyers of Christendom.

I have recounted what I have of doña María Manuela Carrillo de

---

[2] Rodrigo de Valdez (1609–1682), author of *Poema heroyco hispano-latino pagegyrico de la fundacion, y grandezas de la muy noble, y leal ciudad de Lima* (1687).—Ed.

[3] Pedro de Peralta Barnuevo (1664–1743), author of the epic poem *Lima fundada* (2 vols., 1732).—Ed.

Andrade y Sotomayor and other of her martyred companions to show that even women acquired the knack of Latinizing, and that many had at their fingertips Ovid's *Metamorphoses* and his *Ars Amandi*[4] and translated them, meaning that there existed even a Latin of the bedroom.

Now, with your permission, I am going to bring to light a brief story that I heard many times when I was a boy . . . and it has rained more than than once from then till now!

Well then, in the days of Amat, there was a girl in Lima named Mariquita Castellanos, a young lady of many comings and goings, of whom I had occasion to speak at length in my first book of Traditions.[5] Such as the fact that she was the source of a saying that became proverbial: "I'm a pretty girl: la Castellanos!"

It appears that Mariquita spent her early years in the convent of Santa Clara, until she reached the age of *chivateo* (the name our forebears gave to puberty), whereupon she abandoned convent bars and began to gambol about in this City of Kings. The girl was as pretty as a nosegay of flowers, and what is more, sharp witted, as is proved by the reputation that her clever remarks had in Lima.

There existed at the time a poetaster, a great Latinist whose name is irrelevant, whom Mariquita kept on the string. The suitor had offered to bring her as a present a satin skirt worth three bull's eyes, the vulgar expression for doublons. But it is the fate of poets to have an abundance of consonants and not of money, and days and days went by while the promised garment remained where it was, running the danger of growing moldy, in the shopkeeper's display window.

Mariquita was piqued at being mocked and resolved to put an end to it by dismissing the informal courtship, as long in the promising as it was short in the fulfilling. The swain came to visit her, and since at the time nerves and spleen, two complaints very helpful as excuses for doing or saying a vulgar thing, had not yet been invented, the nymph received him with an air of displeasure, avoiding conversation and venturing only an occasional monosyllable. The poet lost his temper and his language became Latinized as he said to the girl:

[4] *The Art of Love* [Latin].
[5] A reference to "¡Pues bonita soy yo, la Castellanos!"—Ed.

Háblame, niña, con pausa.
Estás triste? *Quare causa?*[6]

And Mariquita, remembering the Latin that she had heard spoken
by the chaplain of the sisters of Saint Clare, shot back this rejoinder:

Tristis est anima mea,
hasta que la saya vea.[7]

The love-smitten poet, seeing that the girl had hit upon his sore
spot, had to come up with this excuse that, in situations such as this,
is enough to cut through the Gordian knot:

Et quare conturbas me
si sabes que no hay con qué?[8]

Whereupon the girl, showing him to the door, said to him:

Entonces, *fugite in allia,*
Que otro gato dará algalia.[9]

And raw rice for the devil with a tail, messhall rice for the bobtailed
devil, Calcutta rice for the devil who's a son of a . . . dog, and that's
the end of the story.

---

[6] Speak slowly to me, girl, / Are you sad? What is the cause?
[7] I'm in sad spirits / Until I see the skirt.
[8] And why do you upset me, / If you know I haven't the means?
[9] Then flee elsewhere, / for another cat will give me civet.

Santiago the Flier

It would be difficult to find anyone from Lima who, in his childhood at least, has not attended a puppet show. It was a Spanish woman, doña Leonor de Goromar, who in 1693 asked for and obtained the permission of the viceroy, the count of La Monclova, to put on a show that has been and will be the delight of children, and that has immortalized the names of ño[1] Pancho, ño Manuelito, and ño Valdivieso, the most famous puppeteer of our day.

Among the puppets, the ones that are most popular are ño Silverio, ña Gerundia González, Chocolatito, Mochuelo, Piticalzón, Perote, and Santiago the Flier. The first of these are fanciful characters, but the last was as much a man of flesh and blood as those of us who today eat bread. And he was not a nobody either, but a man of genius, and the proof lies in the fact that he wrote a very original book that is in the Biblioteca Nacional in manuscript, a copy of which I own.

This manuscript, with ink that with the years has taken on a color between white and red, must have passed through many a customs house and gone through severe storms before becoming part of the manuscript section of the library, for not only are its last pages missing, but, most regrettably, some mischief-maker has torn out a number of its pen-and-ink drawings, which, from what I gather from reading the text, must have numbered 15.

[1] A popular abbreviated form of *señor*.

The work is entitled *Nuevo Sistema de Navegación por los aires, por Santiago de Cárdenas, natural de Lima en el Peru.*[2]

It is evident that, when it came to written style, the author was very plainspoken, a circumstance to which he naively confesses. The son of an impoverished father and mother, he learned to read haltingly and to write signs like scrawled letters that would try the patience of a paleographer.

In 1736 Santiago de Cárdenas was ten years old, and went to sea as a cabin boy on a merchant ship that plied the route between Callao and Valparaíso.

The flight of a bird, which he calls a *tijereta*, awakened in Santiago the idea that a man could also master space, aided by an apparatus that fulfilled the conditions he lays down in his book.

Many of the most admirable human inventions and discoveries are in fact owed to trivial causes, if not to chance. The oscillation of a lamp gave Galileo the idea for a pendulum; the fall of an apple suggested to Newton his theory of attraction; the vibration of his voice at the bottom of a derby hat inspired Edison to conceive of the phonograph; without the shudders of a dying frog Galvani would not have appreciated the power of electricity and invented the telegraph; and finally, without having observed a sheet of paper thrown casually into a fireplace rising because of the smoke and heat, Montgolfier would not have invented the hot-air balloon in 1783. Why, then would Santiago not have found in the flight of a *tijereta* the primary cause of a marvel that would immortalize his name?

Santiago spent ten years at sea, and his constant preoccupation was to study the flight of birds. Finally, as a consequence of the disastrous earthquake of 1746 that caused the sinking of the ship on which he had hired on, he was obliged to settle in Lima, where he found employment in mechanical trades, at which, according to what he himself recounts, he was very proficient; later he made gloves, clerical caps, and pumps from one piece of *vicuña*, so that "the finest cloth does not match the delicacy of my work, for I enter and leave various trades with the same

---

[2] The text was published in Valparaíso by the publishing house Jover, in one volume of 230 pages in octavo, with four engravings, with this article serving as a prologue [Author's note].

dexterity as though I had learned them by the rules; but unfortunately, I wasted the improvements I made without improving my lot."

Whenever Santiago managed to rub together a few reals, he disappeared from Lima and went to live in the hills of Amancaes, San Jerónimo, or San Cristóbal, which are only a few miles from the city. There he spent his time contemplating the flight of birds, hunting them, and studying their anatomy. On this subject there are some very curious observations in his book.

After 12 years of climbing up and down hills and chasing condors and every sort of flying creature, not excepting even flies, Santiago thought that he had reached the end of his labors, and shouted: "Eureka!"

In November of 1761 he presented a petition to His Excellency the viceroy don Manuel de Amat y Juniet, in which he said that by means of an apparatus or flying machine that he had invented, but for whose construction he lacked monetary resources, flying was something easier than sucking a freshly laid egg, and less dangerous than crossing oneself. Furthermore, he asked the viceroy for an audience in order to explain his theory to him.

It is probable that His Excellency lent him an ear, and that after Santiago's explanations he remained as much in the dark as before. What definitely appears from the book is that Amat brought the request to the attention of the Royal Tribunal, as this decree proves:

"Lima, November 6, 1761.—Refer this matter to Dr. don Cosme Bueno, the holder of the chair in Mathematics, so that after hearing the petitioner the corresponding aid may be granted him."—Three signatures and a flourish.

While don Cosme Bueno, the most learned man in Peru at the time, was drawing up his report, the matter was the obligatory subject of conversation in Lima's literary circles, and on the morning of November 22 an idle and ill-intentioned mischief-maker spread the rumor that at four in the afternoon Cárdenas was going to fly, as a trial, from San Cristóbal hill to the main square.

Let us listen to Santiago himself relate the consequences of the trick played on him: "In the usual manner of the people of this country, so curious about new things and eager to see wonders, there was not a single noble or plebeian who did not move closer to the hill or occupy the balconies, rooftops of the houses, and church towers. When they realized that nobody had offered to fly, given such an opportunity, God unleashed his wrath, and people surrounded me in the porch of the cathedral, saying to me: Either you fly or we'll stone you to death. Advised as to what was happening, His Excellency the viceroy sent a military escort to defend me, and surrounded by it, I was taken to the palace, thus rescuing me from the insults of the crowd."

From that day forward, our man was the talk of the town. Everyone forgot that his name was Santiago de Cárdenas and called him Santiago the Flier, a nickname the poor man resignedly put up with, for had he become angry he would have risked bodily harm.

Even the Holy Office of the Inquisition had to publish decrees to protect Santiago, forbidding by edict the singing of the "Pava," an indecent popular song in which Cárdenas served as a pretext for offending the honor of one's fellow.

I excuse myself from copying the four verses of the song that have come into my hands, because they contain words and ideas that are extremely obscene. As a sample:

> Cuando voló una marquesa
> un fraile también voló,
> pues recibieron lecciones
> de Santiago el Volador.
> ¡Miren qué pava para el marqués!
> ¡Miren qué pava para los tres![3]

Don Cosme Bueno finally submitted his report with the title "Dissertation on the Art of Flying." He divided it into two parts. In the first he supports the possibility of flying, but in the second he destroys this position with serious arguments. Dr. Bueno's report reached print, and honors the erudition and talent of its author.

Despite the fact that the report was unfavorable, Santiago de Cárdenas did not admit defeat: "I let a year go by," he says, "and presented my second petition. The news of the war with the English and the news that was arriving from Buenos Aires seemed to me to be an opportunity to see my plan come to fruition."

---

[3] When a marquise flew, / A friar also flew, / For they received lessons / From Santiago the Flier. / What vulgar mockery of the marquis! / What vulgar mockery of the three!

Some tradesmen, perhaps to make fun of Santiago the Flier, offered him the necessary sum for him to build his machine, providing the government gave him permission to fly. Santiago undertook to serve as courier between Lima and Buenos Aires, and even to fly as far as Madrid, a journey that he calculated he would make in three days' flight, in this order: "One day to fly from Lima to Portobelo, another day from Portobelo to Havana, and the third from Havana to Madrid." He adds: "This still gives me a great deal of time, for if I succeed in flying as fast as a condor (80 leagues per hour), it will take me less than a day to reach Europe."

"This petition," Cárdenas says, "did not cause the same astonishment and uproar as the first one, and I confess that, with the astuteness with which heaven endowed me, I had aready found partners for my plan." Here it is relevant to say, along with the proverb: One madman creates a hundred more.

As for the viceroy Amat, he answered Cárdenas's petition with the following decree: "This is not the time."

A man less persevering than Santiago would have abandoned the project, but my countryman, who aspired to emulate the persistence of Columbus, then undertook to write a book with the intention of sending it to the king along with a petition, whose tenor he copies in the preface of his bulky manuscript.

It also appears the the duke of San Carlos had made himself the protector of the Icarus of Lima, and solemnly offered to put his book in the hands of the king, but by the time Cárdenas finished writing in 1766, the duke had left Peru.

A few months later, the soul of Santiago de Cárdenas took flight to the world where the mad and the sane are measured by the same rod.

The author of a curious work entitled *Viaje al globo de la luna*,[4] a book in the collection of the Biblioteca Nacional in Lima, which must have been written around the year 1790, says of Santiago de Cárdenas: "This good man, who in fact had great skill and discernment for mechanical work, was on the point of losing his senses over his theory of flying, and naturally his words were better than his deeds. He had had a portrait of himself made, standing at the door of his shop, in the public thoroughfare, dressed in feathers and with wings outspread in

---

[4] Voyage to the planet of the moon.

flight, illustrating his portrait with distichs in Latin and Spanish alluding to his genius and the art of flying which he boasted of possessing. I remember this inscription: '*Ingenio posem superas volitare per arces me nisi paupertas in vitas deprimeret.*'[5] He observed very closely the flight of birds and discoursed on gravity and their movements, often correctly. One afternoon the common people of the city had their curiosity aroused by the vague rumor that had it that a certain fellow was going to take flight from the top of San Cristóbal hill. And it happened that the so-called Flier (who, being ignorant of the rumor, casually left his house) found it necessary to take refuge in the sanctity of a church in order to free himself from a fierce crowd of youngsters who were following him and making a great racket. A certain wit kept the people scattered over the hillsides and the banks of the Rimac in suspense, for while climbing the hill on a mule that he covered with his cape, and with both his arms covered with feathers outstretched, he gave popular curiosity a fair idea of a bullfighter's pass, the way large birds flap their wings in order to take off. And so the crowd shouted: 'He's flying! He's flying! He's flying!'"

Mendiburu too, in his *Diccionario Histórico,*[6] devotes an article to don José Hurtado y Villafuerte, the owner of a hacienda in Arequipa, who around the year 1810 tamed a condor, which flew to the top of the highest hill of Uchumayo, carrying with it a boy, and then flew down with its rider. Hurtado y Villafuerte, in a letter he had published at the time in the *Minerva Pervana,* believes in the possibility of traveling by using a condor as a mount, and calculates that seven hours would be enough time to go from Arequipa to Cádiz.

Cárdenas's work is unquestionably ingenious, and contains observations that are surprising, in that they are the spontaneous fruits of an uncultivated intelligence. He employs few scientific terms, but he nonetheless makes himself understood.

After expounding his theory at length, he undertakes to answer 30 objections and has the naiveté to take seriously and answer many objections to his theory made with the obvious intention of ridiculing him.

---

[5] Possessed of genius, I can fly over the highest obstacles, unless a life of poverty weighs me down [Latin].
[6] See note 1, "Drink, Father, It Will Keep You Alive."—Ed.

I shall not attempt to offer an opinion as to whether aerial navigation is a paradox that occurs only to people not in their right mind, or whether it is feasible for a man to master the space traversed by birds. But what I do believe in all sincerity is that Santiago de Cárdenas was not a charlatan out to deceive, but a man of conviction and very great inventiveness.

If Santiago de Cárdenas were a madman we must agree that his madness was contagious. Even today, more than a century after his death, there exists in Lima a man who for 20 years has pursued the idea of competing with eagles. Don Pedro Ruiz is one of those beings who have the faith of which Christ spoke, a faith that moves mountains.[7]

An observation: Don Pedro Ruiz could not have known the manuscript with which I have been dealing, but—by an odd coincidence!—his point of departure and the specifications of his flying machine are, in the last analysis, the same as those imagined by the ill-starred protégé of the duke of San Carlos.

In conclusion: Santiago de Cárdenas aspired to immortalize himself, by perhaps realizing the most portentous of discoveries, and—human misfortune, his name lives only in the splendid puppet shows of Lima.

Even after death the boos and jeers of an audience pursue him.

Destiny has terrible ironies.

---

[7] Don Pedro Ruiz, a native of Eten, was a skillful mechanic. In May of 1880 he died in Callao, while trying out a torpedo that he had invented and that he proposed launching against the Chilean vessels that were blocking the port. In 1878 Ruiz published a short work, illustrated with 24 plates, on the art of flying [Author's note].

Fourth Series

Three Historical Questions Concerning Pizarro

Did He or Did He Not Know How to Write?

Was He or Was He Not

Marquis of Los Atavillos?

What Was His Battle Standard and

Where Is It?

I

Historical opinions as to whether Pizarro did or did not know how to write vary greatly, and some are contradictory. Intelligent and thorough chroniclers assert that he didn't even recognize the letter O by its being round. That is how one anecdote has become common currency. It tells how one of the soldiers who were keeping watch over Atahualpa in the prison of Cajamarca wrote the word *God* on the Inca's fingernail. The prisoner showed it to everyone who visited him, and once he discovered that all of them except Pizarro were able to read the word with no difficulty, he had nothing but scorn for the leader of the conquest and considered him the inferior of the least of the Spaniards. Malicious or biased writers deduce from this that don Francisco had his pride injured, and that it was for this childish trifle that he took his vengeance upon Atahualpa by having him beheaded.[1]

It is difficult for us to believe that a man who rubbed elbows with distinguished members of the Spanish nobility (for he fought bulls as a picador before Queen Juana, earning fame for his bravery and skill as undying as that that later he would gain for his exploits in Peru); it is difficult, we repeat, to imagine that he was so lazy as not to know his abc's, and all the more so in that, though a rough and ready soldier, Pizarro was quite capable of greatly respecting and bringing distinction to men of letters.

What is more, in the days of Emperor Charles V education was not neglected to the point that it was in previous times. It was no longer believed that knowing how to read and write befitted only second sons and friars, and people were beginning to laugh at the formula used by the Catholic Sovereigns in the document whereby they rewarded noblemen with the title of Gentleman of the Bedchamber, a title that was coveted as much as or more than the habit of the Orders of Santiago, Montesa, Alcántara, and Calatrava. One of the most curious phrases that, say what you will to the contrary, implies a great deal that is offensive to a man's dignity, reads as follows: "And inasmuch as you [here the name was inserted] have proved to us that you *know neither how to read nor how to write* and are handy with the needle, we have seen fit to name you Gentleman of our royal Bedchamber, etc."

Pedro Sancho and Francisco de Jerez, Pizarro's secretaries before Antonio Picado occupied this post, have left a number of accounts concerning their chief, and far from confirming a suspicion of such supreme ignorance, it appears from these accounts that the governor *read letters*.

Nonetheless, Montesinos asserts, in his *Anales del Peru,* that in 1525 Pizarro set out to learn how to read, that his persistence came to nothing, and that he was content merely to learn how to sign his name. Almagro laughed at this and added that signing one's name without knowing how to read was the same as receiving a wound without being able to give one.

---

[1] Atahualpa was garrotted, not decapitated. The belief that Atahualpa was decapitated is common in some Andean communities.—Ed.

As for Almagro the Elder,[2] it is proven historical fact that he did not know how to read.

What is beyond doubt to us, as is true as well for the learned scholar Quintana, is that don Francisco Pizarro did not know how to write, despite the fact that the opinion of his contemporaries is not unanimous in the regard. But it would be enough to substantiate our view to look for a moment at the contract concluded in Panama on March 10, 1525, between the cleric Luque, Pizarro, and Almagro, which ends with these exact words: "And because the aforementioned Captain Francisco Pizarro and Diego de Almagro do not know how to sign their names, Juan de Panés and Alvaro de Quiro signed for them in the registry containing this document."

A historian of the last century states:

"In the ecclesiastical archives of Lima I found various documents and instruments signed by the marquis (in an elegant hand), which I showed to several people, comparing certain signatures with others, amazed at the audacity of the calumny whereby his enemies sough to tarnish his reputation and belittle him, thereby taking out on that great captain their own passions and prejudices and those they inherited."

Contradicting this, Zárate and other chroniclers say that Pizarro knew how to write two signatures, and that between the two, his secretary set down these words: *El Marqués Francisco de Pizarro.*

The documents of Pizarro's that I have seen in the Lima Biblioteca, in the manuscript section, all have the two signatures. Some are signed *Franxº. de Piçarro,* and only a few *El marqués.* In the National Archives and in those of the town hall there are also several of these autograph signatures.

Putting an end to the question of whether Pizarro did or did not know how to sign his name, I opt for the latter, and here is the most telling reason that I have for so doing:

In the Archivo General de Indias, housed in what was the Casa de Contratación[3] in Seville, there are several letters in which, as in the

---

[2] Diego de Almagro (1480–1538), conquistador and rival of Francisco Pizarro for the control of Peru. Defeated at the Battle of Salinas, he was garrotted by order of Pizarro. For what happened afterwards, see "The Knights of the Cape."—Ed.

[3] The chamber of commerce set up in Seville by Ferdinand V and Isabel II.

documents we possess in Lima, it can be seen even by the amateur paleographer that the signature is at times written by the same hand as the body of the document written by the scribe or amanuensis. "But if there were any doubt remaining," a distinguished Buenos Aires writer, don Vicente Quesada, who visited the Archivo de Indias in 1874, affirms, "I have seen in a report, in which Pizarro makes a statement as a witness, that the notary certifies that, after the statement was drawn up, Pizarro signed it *with his usual signs,* while in other declarations the notary certifies that the witnesses *are affixing their signatures* to them before him."

II

Don Francisco Pizarro was neither the marquis of Los Atavillos nor the marquis of Los Charcas, as a great many writers have variously called him. There is not a single document whereby it can be proved that he held these titles, nor did Pizarro himself ever use in the heading of orders and decrees any other title than: *El marqués.*

In support of our belief, we shall cite Gonzalo Pizarro's words when, as a prisoner of La Gasca, the latter rebuked him for his rebelliousness and ingratitude toward the king, who had so greatly rewarded and honored him. "The favor that His Majesty bestowed on my brother was only the title and name of marquis, without giving him any estate, and if not tell me what it is."

The escutcheon and heraldic arms of Marquis Pizarro were these: shield, manteled: in the upper part, in gold, black eagle, columns, and water; and on a gules field, gold castle, orle of eight wolves, in gold; in the second part, mantled in red, castle of gold with a crown; and on a silver field, red lion with an F, and below, on a silver field, red lion; in the lower part, a silver field, eleven heads of Indians, that of the middle crowned; orle with chains and eight griffins, in gold; on seal, coronet of marquis.

A letter written by Charles V to Pizarro, dated October 10, 1537, states the following, which will substantiate our assertion: "Meanwhile you will call yourself marquis, as I here write it, for, inasmuch as the name of the land that will be given you as your share is not known, the aforementioned title is not being sent now." And since until the arrival of Vaca de Castro the crown had not determined what lands and vassals would constitute the marquisate, it is clear that don Francisco was a marquis in name only, or a marquis without a marquisate, as his brother Gonzalo said.

It is a known fact that by doña Angelina Pizarro he had a son who was baptized with the name of Francisco and died before he reached the age of 15. By doña Inés Huaylas or Yupanqui, the daughter of Manco-Capac, he had a daughter, doña Francisca, who married her uncle Hernando, and in a second marriage don Pedro Arias.

By royal warrant, and without his having contracted marriage to doña Angelina or doña Inés, Pizarro's children were declared to be legitimate. If Pizarro had had the title of marquis of Los Atavillos, they would have been his heirs. It was almost a century later, in 1628, that don Juan Fernando Pizarro, the grandson of doña Francisca, obtained from the king the title of Marquis of the Conquest.

Piferrer, in his *Nobiliario español,*[4] states that according to genealogists the lineage of the Pizarros was illustrious and went far back; that men with that name distinguished themselves with Pelayo's forces at Covadonga;[5] and that his descendants then settled in Aragon, Navarre, and Extremadura. And he concludes, writing for publication, that the arms of the Pizarros are: "gold shield and a pine with gold pine cones, two wolves rampant and two slates[6] at the foot of the trunk." There is no one like a genealogist when it comes to lineages and family trees. Only a fool would believe such liars!

III

There is also an error concerning Pizarro's standard that I propose to dispel.

When the Independence of Peru was declared in 1821, the town council of Lima sent Generalísimo José de San Martín[7] official notice

---

[4] *Nobiliario de los reinos y señoríos de España* (1857–1860) by Francisco Piferrer (1813–1863).—Ed.

[5] Pelayo was an eighth-century ruler from the Spanish state of Asturias who achieved fame in the early Christian resistance to the Moors.—Ed.

[6] In Spanish, *pizarras.*

[7] José de San Martín (1778–1850), Argentinian soldier who led the liberation of Chile and Perú, also known as "The Protector." After meeting with Bolívar in 1822, San Martín withdrew from the theater of war.—Ed.

to the effect that the city was making him a gift of *Pizarro's standard*. Shortly before his death in Bologna, this leader of the South American revolution made a will, with a clause returning to Lima the standard offered him as a gift. In fact, the executors of his estate formally presented the precious relic to our representative in Paris, who took care to send it to the government of Peru in a box appropriately fitted out. This was in the days of the temporary administration of General Pezet, and at that time we had the opportunity to see the classic standard on view in one of the reception rooms of the Ministry of Foreign Relations. On the fall of this government, on November 6, 1865, the mob sacked several of the offices in the presidential palace, and the standard disappeared, after having been perhaps torn to shreds by some rabid demagogue who imagined that he saw in it the proof of the calumnies that the spirit of partisanship invented at the time in order to overthrow President Pezet, the victor on the battlefields of Junín and Ayacucho, whom his enemies accused of criminal connivance with Spain, aimed at subjecting the country once again to the yoke of what had been the mother country.

Mobs do not reason or discuss, and the more absurd the matter may be the more easily it is accepted.

The standard that we saw had not the armorial bearings of Spain but those that Charles V accorded the city by royal warrant on December 7, 1537. The bearings of Lima were: a shield on an azure field with three royal crowns in a triangle, and above them a gold star, points touching the crowns. As an orle, in a red field, was the motto in gold letters: *Hoc signum vere regum est.*[8] As a seal and device were two black eagles with a crown of gold, a J and a K (the initials of Karolus and Juana, the sovereigns) and above these letters a gold star. This flag was the one that the royal standard-bearer, by the law of inheritance, carried on January 5 in the processions of Corpus and Saint Rose, along with a proclamation of the sovereign and other acts of equal solemnity.

The people of Lima persisted in wrongly calling this standard Pizarro's flag, and accepted without question that this was the war pennon that the Spaniards carried for the conquest. And as it persisted without being refuted from generation to generation, the error became traditional and historical.

[8] Truly, this is the sign of the kingdom [Latin].

Let us now take up the matter of Pizarro's real standard.

After the execution of Atahualpa, don Francisco made his way to Cuzco, and we believe that it was on November 16, 1533, that he made his triumphal entry into the illustrious capital of the Incas.

The banner that on this occasion was carried by his standard-bearer Jerónimo de Aliaga was what churchmen call a gonfalon. On one of its sides, of scarlet damask, the armorial bearings of Charles V were embroidered; and on the other side, which was white according to some, or yellow according to others, Saint James the apostle was depicted in the attitude of a warrior, on a white horse, with a shield, cuirass, and a helmet with a panache or crest, displaying a red cross on his chest and a sword in his right hand.

When Pizarro left Cuzco (proceeding to the Jauja valley and the founding of the city of Lima) he did not do so in order to wage war and left his battle standard or gonfalon in the Temple of the Sun, already converted into a Christian cathedral. During the civil war between the conquistadors, neither the Almagrists, nor the Gonzalists, nor the Gironists, nor the Royalists dared take it into combat, and it remained as a sacred object on one of the altars. There, in 1825, after the battle of Ayacucho, General Sucre found it;[9] he sent it to Bogotá, and the government immediately sent it to Bolívar, who gave it as a gift to the city of Caracas, where it is preserved today. We do not know whether three centuries and a half are enough to have reduced this martial emblem of the conquest to tatters.

[9] Antonio José de Sucre Alcalá (1795–1830), one of Bolívar's most trusted and celebrated lieutenants, who led patriot forces to victory at the Battle of Ayacucho in 1824, sealing Latin American independence.—Ed.

The Scapegoat[1]

I

The Inca Titu-Atauchi, the brother of Atahualpa, was on his way to Cajamarca with a large retinue of Indians loaded down with gold and silver to add to the treasure for their sovereign's ransom when he received the news that on August 29, 1533, the Spaniards had put Atahualpa to death. Titu-Atauchi hid the riches that he was bringing, and gathering warriors together, he went to join forces with Quizquiz, the bravest and most experienced of the generals of the Inca empire who was the head of an army harassing the conquistadors.

The latter had begun their march on Cuzco, doing battle each day against Quizquiz's troops. Fifty Spaniards, led by Francisco de Chaves, covered Pizarro's rear guard, and one afternoon, held up by a storm, they set up camp five leagues away from the main body of their comrades. Suddenly they found themselves under attack by six thousand Indians. The Spaniards fought with their usual bravery, but because they did not act in concert and were pursued by an enemy that outnumbered them, they were forced to flee, with disastrous results, leaving behind seven dead and thirteen prisoners.

Among the latter were the gallant captain Francisco de Chaves, the man who died defending Pizarro on the day of the conspiracy of the

---

[1] Spanish: *"el que pagó el pato."* Literally, the one who paid for the duck. According to Umphrey the expression comes, perhaps, from an old custom of having a duck killed at a wedding; the one who is left to pay the bill is, therefore, *"el pato de la boda,"* 7.

Almagrists, Alonso de Ojeda, another valiant warrior who went mad a year later, and Hernando de Haro, no less notable for his courage and chivalry.

History says that in the mockery of a trial, set up to condemn Atahualpa to death, which began and ended in a single day, the Inca had many who pleaded for his life, and it is the unanimous opinion that if the illustrious Hernando de Soto had been present in Cajamarca, the conquest would not have borne the stain of this crime, as iniquitous as it was useless. Of the 24 judges of Atahualpa, only 13 sentenced him to death. The 11 who refused to sign the death sentence deserve that we note their names, in homage to their upright conduct. Their names were Juan de Rada (who later was the leader of the Almagrists who murdered Pizarro), Diego de Mora, Blas de Atienza, Francisco de Chaves, Pedro de Mendoza, Hernando de Haro, Francisco de Fuentes, Diego de Chaves, Francisco Moscoso, Alfonso Dávila, and Pedro de Ayala. As the proverb has it, there was everything on the vine: wine grapes, vine leaves, and verjuice grapes.

Titu-Atauchi knew not only the names of those who had authorized the death of the Inca, but also those who, like Juan de Rada, had defended him, thereby risking falling into disgrace with Pizarro. Francisco de Chaves and Hernando de Haro were among this number.

Titu-Atauchi had sworn to take vengeance for the blood of his brother on the first of his executioners who had taken him prisoner. Moreover, he had offered great rewards to anyone who handed over to him the person of Felipillo, the traitorous Indian who served the Spaniards as interpreter, and who, to avenge himself for the contempt shown him by one of the wives of Atahualpa, used bits of gossip he had gathered to exert his influence with the principal conquistadors to have the Inca condemned. But even though Titu-Atauchi did not have the joy of taking his vengeance, don Diego de Almagro took it upon himself to condemn Felipillo to death and ordered him quartered for another act of treason in which he had caught him. Titu-Atauchi found out the names of the prisoners, spoke warmly with the most notable of them, had the wounded among them carefully cared for, and when they were out of danger, had the nobility to set them free, giving them an escort of Indians who took them, on their shoulders, to the environs of Cuzco. In addition he gave precious emeralds to those captains who had been opposed to the execution of Atahualpa, thus giving them a proof of his gratitude for their honorable but fruitless efforts in favor of the monarch.

As they bade the young Inca farewell, Francisco de Chaves noted that one of the 13 prisoners was missing. Titu-Atauchi gave a sardonic smile, and they say that he answered with a phrase in Quechua that, though the translation of it may not be literal, at least embodies the idea:

"Ah! The one that is left is going to be the scapegoat!"

And then there are those who claim that 13 isn't a number that brings misfortune!

II

Titu-Atauchi betook himself to Cajamarca, and shut the prisoner up in the same room that Atahualpa had occupied during his captivity.

Who was that Spaniard chosen to be the scapegoat? Why would the Inca, who had shown himself to be so generous toward the vanquished, wish to display such cruelty toward this man?

Sancho de Cuéllar had the misfortune to spend his early years as the amanuensis of a notary in Spain, and we say misfortune because this circumstance was enough to cause his companions, taking him to be clever at using the jargon of the courtroom, to name him court clerk for Atahualpa's trial.

Sancho de Cuéllar was a favorite, and deservedly so, of don Francisco Pizarro. He was one of the 13 famous companions of Pizarro's on the island of El Gallo, to whose heroism the success of the conquest was owed.[2]

Again the fateful 13!

Sancho de Cuéllar acted craftily as a court clerk during the trial, for he not only set down words that worsened the sad position of the captive Inca, but on notifying him of the sentence and accompanying him to the jail, treated him with disrespect and mocked him.

Titu-Atauchi had him brought to the same site where Atahualpa

[2] In 1527, Francisco Pizarro and his men found themselves stranded on the island of El Gallo. When the desperate men were rescued, and offered the option of returning to Panama, Pizarro exhorted them to follow him to Peru. Only 13 agreed.—Ed.

had met his death, accompanied by a crier who proclaimed: "Pacha-camac[3] orders this tyrant killed because he killed the Inca Atahualpa."

The Indians had kept the garrote that served for the execution of their monarch, giving it the name of "the accursed pole." They used it to kill Sancho de Cuéllar, whose corpse remained in the square for an entire day, where the crowd desecrated it.

This may well be the only time in the history of humanity that a clerk of the court has paid the court costs and served as a scapegoat.

---

[3] Pachacamac is both a powerful Inca deity as well as a famous shrine built in his honor.—Ed.

Friars' Work!

Until a little more than twenty years ago, two wooden crosses set into a wall could be seen in the Plaza Mayor of Lima. One of them was above the arch of the gate leading to the callejón de Petateros. Opposite it were the scaffold and the post for victims' heads. It is thus our Christian supposition that the object of the aforementioned cross was to console those condemned to death with the sight in the last moments of the emblem of our redemption.[1]

The other cross was located where Palacio and Correo Streets meet, and below the balconies of the house of Nicolás de Ribera the Elder, the first mayor and member of the town council after Pizarro founded the city. When and why was that cross placed there?

Here, kind reader, is what I have discovered thanks to extensive historical research.

I

After the battle of Iñaquito, in which the first viceroy of Peru came to such a disastrous end,[2] don Hernando Vela Núñez, the brother of that ill-starred governor, fell prisoner in the port of San Buenaventura.

---

[1] This cross is now in the Museo Nacional and is known as the cross of those who died on the scaffold. It was previously preserved in the Biblioteca de Lima [Author's note].

[2] Angered by the curtailment of the privileges of the conquistadors, Gonzalo Pizarro revolted against the crown. In 1546, Pizarro defeated Blasco Núñez de Vela, Peru's first viceroy, at the Battle of Iñaquito, and ordered the viceroy's execution.—Ed.

The wrath of the victor had somewhat abated, and when the prisoner was brought to Lima and taken before His Most Magnificent Lordship don Gonzalo Pizarro, the latter asked him:

"Does Your Grace pledge and promise, according to the practice and custom of the knights of Castile in bygone days, to remain under arrest in the house of Hernando Montenegro, not to leave it except to hear Mass on the days of obligation, not to quarrel or cause trouble over past matters of government, and not to encourage disturbances or discord?"

Let us agree that this was a great deal to ask, but General Vela Núñez, who was not very sure of keeping his head on his shoulders, knelt before a crucifix, and holding out his right hand, replied:

"Yes, I promise and pledge to do what is asked."

And so months went by without his failing to keep his promise for one moment.

There finally came news that La Gasca, the king's envoy, had arrived in Panama with full powers of the monarch to bring into line the troublemakers of these realms. At that point Vela Núñez decided not to take up arms against Gonzalo, but to get around the latter's vigilance and escape to Spain, for the general had wearied of adventures, dangers, and disappointments. The caretaker of the monastery of San Francisco took it upon himself to make the arrangements for Vela Núñez's escape, and very cautiously hired the skipper of a brigantine, anchored for the moment in Callao and about to sail to Nicaragua.

Captain Bernardino de Loayza was to leave with Vela Núñez, for he had tried to raise men for the king in Huánuco and when his efforts came to naught, he had no other recourse save to take refuge in the Franciscan monastery. In those days there was no beating around the bush, and anyone who became involved in politics knew that he was risking his neck by so doing.

Everything was now ready for the escape, but on the morning of the appointed day Gonzalo learned of all the details of their plan, and ... farewell money paid for the escape! The two had fallen out of the frying pan into the fire.

II

Captain Juan de Latorre y Villegas, known by his nickname of El Madrileño,[3] was one of those heartless victors who had desecrated the dead body of the viceroy. In his ferocity, El Madrileño went so far as to pull hairs out of the dead man's beard and mustache and adorn the upturned brim of his hat with them. Thus bedecked, he swaggered through the streets of Quito, and later on the streets of Lima.

This scoundrel had had the good luck to discover a rich *huaca*[4] in the ruins of Pachacamac, from which he extracted a treasure in gold and silver and precious stones, estimated to be worth 80,000 duros. In the name of the crown, Gonzalo Pizarro claimed one-fifth of that sum, but El Madrileño refused to pay up, and brought suit before the pretense of a Tribunal that was sitting at the time. As the saying goes, everything whets the whale's appetite but nothing satisfies it.

Captain Villegas was a good friend of the caretaker of San Francisco, and went to him one day to ask his advice on how to flee Lima and take his treasure with him. The Reverend Father, after making him swear to keep it secret, told him of Vela Núñez's plan, adding that there couldn't be a better opportunity for him, since in Vela Núñez he would have someone at the royal court to speak on his behalf so that the monarch would not punish him for his rebellion and his desecration of the dead body of the viceroy.

But when the Franciscan met with Vela Núñez and proposed that El Madrileño escape with him, the general exclaimed, in proud indignation:

"Joining up with a traitor of his sort! Before I'd do a thing like that I'd call for the executioner to come and behead me!"

This Juan de Latorre y Villegas was the son of one of the thirteen famous comrades of Pizarro's on the Isla del Gallo, on whom Queen Juana bestowed the title of Knights of the Golden Spur. Four months after Gonzalo Pizarro met his death, Latorre was found hiding in a cave, and La Gasca ordered him hanged. On receiving the news of the unfortunate end of the young rebel, his father, the elderly man from

---

[3] The man from Madrid.
[4] In native Andean belief, a sacred site or object, natural or man-made. In this context, a sacred burial site containing treasure.—Ed.

the Isla del Gallo, celebrated his death by appearing in the streets of Arequipa muffled in a red cape. For the men of that century, that is what was meant by loyalty to their king.

III

However much the caretaker tried to sugarcoat the pill, Villegas realized that Vela Núñez refused to be associated with him, so he went to the palace and betrayed the latter's plan to escape, blaming his own complicity on the fact that, in the interest of the revolutionary cause, he had laid a trap for the prisoner to see how well he was keeping his promise. It is undoubtedly true that he who isn't up to playing the part of Saint Michael can play the devil at the saint's feet instead.

Cepeda the judge, Gaspar Mejía, a captain, and Antonio de Robles, the chief bailiff, were with Gonzalo when he heard the news. Pizarro was furious, and turning to Cepeda he said to him:

"Go to Montenegro's house and seize that villainous Vela Núñez and throw him in the royal jail."

The infamous Cepeda, that man who was like a coin with two sides, both of them false, didn't wait to have the order repeated, and hurried out of the room, followed by Robles.

Gonzalo then turned to Mejía:

"Don Gaspar, take the men of my guard, and go to San Francisco. If the friars resist arrest, have them hanged and bring me Loayza."

The captain left the palace, followed by pikemen and harquebusiers, when at that moment a cleric appeared, mounted on a fine mule.

It was Baltasar de Loayza, who had been an enthusiastic supporter of the viceroy and had always occupied himself with mundane affairs and politics rather than with his churchly duties. The captain did not know the other Loayza, and since by a fateful coincidence the cleric also lived in a cell of San Francisco, Mejía thought that the order to imprison Loayza referred to this cleric. So it was that when he spied him coming from around a corner he exclaimed:

"What a piece of luck! We've saved ourselves time and trouble."

And taking hold of the mule's bride to halt it, he said to the cleric:

"Dismount this minute, even if it means using your mule's ears to do so, you sly fox, and give yourself up."

Baltasar de Loayza, who did not have a very clear conscience, tried to resist, but the men of the guard fell upon him, and threw him to the ground just under the balconies of the house of Ribera the Elder.

A crowd of onlookers milled about in defense of the priest, rocks were thrown, and one of them broke Father Baltasar's head open.

Pizarro, who had witnessed this event from a balcony, dispatched one of his officials to the scene, who approached don Gaspar and said to him:

"His Lordship the governor says that your grace is clumsier than a hand without fingers, because you've got the order all wrong. It isn't this man, but Bernardino de Loayza that you're to nab."

"I'm sorry," Mejía murmured, "because this man is also a trouble-maker who's just begging to be hanged."

Having been set free, Father Loayza was washing his head wound in a basin, and as Mejía was withdrawing with the men of the guard, he shouted prophetically:

"You captain of bandits! My blood has flowed here, and so will yours."

"I'm laughing at your prophesying! That's friar's work!" the captain answered scornfully.

And he went on his way to San Francisco.

IV

Naturally, what with the delay and the threat of an uprising, Bernardino de Loayza had time to make his escape.

Three or four days later, on November 19, 1546, General Hernando Vela Núñez, as a man unfaithful to his word and a rebel of these realms, was brought to the Plaza Mayor, where his head was cut off and placed on the post.

As the hapless man was kneeling before he was executed, there entered the plaza, mounted on a spirited horse, the chief bailiff Antonio de Robles, one of Gonzalo's favorites, who, perhaps to gain favor with him, made his mount caracole and knocked the doomed man over.

Fray Tomás de San Martín, a worthy officiant at the altar who was offering the last rites to the man about to be executed, was angered by such dastardly behavior, and said in a loud voice:

"You heartless wretch! I hope in God's name that you'll find yourself in the same spot some day."

But that blackguard let out an insolent guffaw and wheeled his horse around, murmuring:

"Bah! Who pays attention to sermons? They're friars' work!"

V

But the truth is, and the chroniclers all tell the same story, that both prophecies were fulfilled to the letter.

On the eve of Corpus Christi in the year 1547, Diego Centeno appeared with his army just a mile away from Cuzco. The city was defended by double the usual force, headed by Antonio de Robles, whom Gonzalo Pizarro had sent from Lima to lead it.

On the stroke of midnight, Centeno proclaimed to his men and swore that the next day he would either oblige them to bury him or else he would carry one of the poles of the baldachin in the Corpus procession.

And he mounted such a bold attack that as day dawned victory was his.

At eight that morning the body of Robles was swaying back and forth on the gallows, and four hours later Diego Centeno—despite the fact that he had received two wounds in the battle—carried one of the poles of the baldachin in the procession of the Most Holy.

Some will say that in those days when tigers and wolves mercilessly devoured each other it was not difficult to predict to a warrior that he would come to a disastrous end, for such was the fate of at least two-thirds of the conquistadors. But what was really surprising was the death of Captain Gaspar Mejía.

A few minutes after Vela Núñez had been executed, don Gaspar was heading for the palace when, on passing below the balconies of Ribera the Elder, his horse reared and threw its carefree rider against a corner of the house.

By the time people ran to help him to his feet he was dead.

It was then that the cross we have referred to was set in place, following which some architect or mason of this progressive century that dislikes stale stories, being ignorant of the history related to this cross, was responsible for its disappearance. As we all know, we are not living in the year 1631, when, as Calancha[5] relates, the Inquisition of Lima punished Sebastián Bogado for the crime of having removed several crosses in the calle de Malambo.

[5] Friar Antonio de la Calancha (1584–1654) was born in Chuquisaca (Bolivia) and wrote the *Crónica moralizada del Orden de San Agustín en el Perú, con sucesos egemplares en esta Monarquía.* (1638).—Ed.

Saint Thomas's Sandal

If you take to reading Brazilian chroniclers and historians, you can't help firmly believing that Saint Thomas traveled all over South America preaching the gospel. The facts and documents on which these gentlemen base their belief are so authentic that there is no weak point into which to sink one's teeth.

In Ceará, in San Luis de Maranhao in Pernambuco, and in other provinces of the empire next to us a number of proofs of the apostolic visit exist.

In Belén del Pará the one who is writing these lines was shown a boulder, highly venerated, on which the disciple of Christ had stood. Whether this is true or not requires verification that I want nothing to do with, for God did not make me to be an investigating magistrate.

The matter, moreover, is not a dogma to be taken on faith nor has anyone put my neck in a noose to make me believe or burst.

We Peruvians could not be left behind when it came to the evangelical visit. It would have been all we needed if, had Saint Thomas attended a social gathering in the vicinity, he had turned up his nose at cutting loose in the house that is his[1] in Peru or affected reluctance to do so!

In Calango, 16 leagues from Lima and near Mala, there exists on a hillside a very smooth, polished white boulder. I have not laid eyes on it, but someone who has seen it and run his hand over it told me about

---

[1] A traditional welcoming greeting.

it. On it, as though imprinted in soft wax, there can be seen the outline of a size 14 foot, and around it Greek and Hebrew characters. In his *Crónica Agustina* Father Calancha[2] says that he examined this rock in 1615, and that ten years later the bachelor-at-law Duarte Fernández, touring the diocese on a mission from the Archbishop don Gonzalo de Ocampo, ordered the letters destroyed, because the idolatrous Indians attributed a diabolical meaning to them. A great shame, say I!

Since it is but a short distance from Calango to Lima and the road not at all rough, it is safe to say that one day we had as our guest who drank water from the Rimac[3] one of the 12 beloved disciples of the Savior. And if this is not a great honor for Lima, as were the recent visits of the duke of Genoa and don Carlos de Borbón, never mind.

"But, señor collector of traditions, how did Saint Thomas get from Galilee to Lima?"

"How should I know? Go to heaven and ask him. It might have been by hot air balloon, by swimming, or *pedibus andando.*[4] What I assert, and along with me eminent writers, both sacred and profane, is that His Grace turned up in these parts. That's all there is to it, and there's no use pestering me with impertinent questions."

But there is something more to say. Other towns in Peru lay claim to the same good fortune.

In Frías, in the district of Piura, there is a rock on which there is preserved the outline of the apostle's foot. In Cajatambo another like it came be seen, and when Saint Toribio visited Chachapoyas His Grace granted indulgences to those who prayed before a certain boulder, for he was convinced that this distinguished personage had stood on top of it to preach.

Many people marveled at how gigantic the footprint was, for the foot of the sinning sons of Adam isn't 14 inches long or, in other words, a size 14. But a religious chronicler sententiously replies that a size 14 isn't all that large for such a great man.

I'll be damned! And what a foot!

But since the apostle left traces even in Bolivia and Tucumán, as is proved by a book in which there is a lengthy discussion of the cross of

---

[2] See "Friars' Work!" note 5.—Ed.
[3] The river that traverses Lima.—Ed.
[4] By walking [Latin].

Carabuco venerated as an object belonging to the blessed traveler, we Peruvians wanted something more; and when the volcano of Omate or Huaina-Putina felt like playing one of its tricks, the Dominican fathers of a monastery in Parinacochas found, among the ashes or lava, nothing less than one of Saint Thomas's sandals.

The chronicles did not say whether it was for a right foot or a left, an unforgivable oversight on the part of such intelligent writers.

The sandal was made of a material never used by either Indians or Spaniards, which proves that it came directly from the shop of Ashaverus or Juan Waiting-for-God (the Wandering Jew), a famous shoemaker in Jerusalem, the Fasinetti of our day, so to speak.

Friar Alonso de Ovalle, the superior of the monastery, placed it with great ceremony in a rosewood box with gold fittings, and around the year 1603, approximately, brought it to Lima, where it was received in procession beneath a canopy and with great festivities attended by the Viceroy Marqués de Salinas.

Erudite authors of that century say that the blessed sandal wrought many, a great many, miracles in Lima, and that it was highly revered by the Dominicans.

Calancha states that, once the curiosity of the inhabitants of Lima was satisfied, Father Ovalle returned to Parinacochas with the relic, but others maintain that the sandal never left Lima.

The truth remains in the place where it belongs. I neither add nor subtract, neither alter nor comment, neither deny or assert.

I simply note down the tradition, taking the matter under advisement, with some saying white and others red.

The Black Mass

One of Granny's Stories

(To My Children Clemente and Angélica Palma)

Go buy me a handkerchief
to drool into.
In the shop opposite
they sell them by the yard.[1]

(POPULAR REFRAIN)

Once upon a time. The air for the birds, the water for fish, the fire for the wicked, the earth for the good, and heaven for the best; and the best are the two of you, little angels of my choir, and may His Divine Majesty make you saints and watch over you by night as by day.

Well, children, in 1802, under the rule of Aviles,[2] who was a viceroy as good as hot buns, I made the acquaintance of ña San Diego. I met

---

[1] Ve y compráme un pañuelo / para la baba: / en la tienda del frente / los hay de a vara.
[2] Gabriel de Aviles, 37th viceroy of Peru, 1801–1806.

her many times at nine o'clock Mass, in the church of Santo Domingo, and it warmed my heart to see her so contrite, and how she went to the altar to take communion, so carried away that her feet never appeared to touch the floor. I thought of her as blessed, but as you will see in a moment, it was all nothing but cunning and the devil's tricks and lies.

Mother San Diego was probably around 50 then. She would go from house to house curing the sick, and receiving alms in return for this act of charity. She did not use the sorts of remedies to be found in an apothecary's shop, but rather, relics and prayers, and by putting the cord of her habit over the stomach of a sick person, she could make the most stubborn cramps go away, as though she could touch their insides with her hand. She cured me of a toothache just by praying by herself for an hour and holding a little bone to my jaw. I don't know whether it was a bone of Saint Fausto, Saint Saturnino, Saint Theophilus, Saint Julian, Saint Adrian, or Saint Sebastian, for the Pope sent a shipment of the bones of all these saints as a gift to the Lima Cathedral. Ask His Reverence the archbishop or the canon Cucaracha when you've grown up, and they'll tell you I'm not making it up. It was not, then, the pious ña San Diego who cured me, but the Devil, God forgive me, for if I sinned it was out of ignorance. Make a nice sign of the cross, without curling your fingers, and then cross yourselves again, little angels of the Lord.

She lived—it's as though I can still see her—in a little room on the callejón de la Toma, on the way to La Luna baths, turning off to your right.

At the point when the people of Lima were most taken in by ña San Diego's piety, the Inquisition began to keep an eye on her and trail her. An inquisitor, a godfearing man as gentle as a dove, with whom I was on as familiar terms as I am with my hands, was given orders to keep watch on her one Saturday night, and what do you think he saw on the stroke of midnight? He saw ña San Diego, who had turned into an owl, children, and was flying out the window of her room.

When she went to Santo Domingo the next day, very self-satisfied and as if butter wouldn't melt in her mouth, to try to explain to Father Bustamante, a silver-tongue preacher, the little green carriage of the Inquisition was already waiting in the square for her. God save us and defend us!

I was a youngster who lived nearby, and I will swear till the hour of my death that when the Holy Office searched ña San Diego's room, they found in a cupboard a blind rabbit, a magnet covered with blond hairs, a doll with pins stuck in it, a dried-up scorpion, a lizard's tail, an old shoe they said had once belonged to the queen of Sheba, and Jesus safeguard me, a pot full of oil of earthworms with which to to anoint her body and grow feathers, allowing her to take flight after saying, as is customary among that riffraff: "With no help from God or the Virgin!" Please accompany me as I recite a *salve* to seek forgiveness for the involuntary heresy I have just committed.

The crafty sorceress remained in prison for something like a year without being willing to confess to a single thing; but where would she have ended up with Father Pardiñas, a priest of great shrewdness who was my confessor and told me everything in confidence? Children, recite an Our Father and a Hail Mary for the soul of Father Pardiñas.

As I was saying, like it or not, the witch was forced to drink down a mugful of blessed oil, whereupon she began to make faces like a monkey and vomit it all up, that is to say, she confessed everything. The Devil can hold out against anything that is done to him, except making him drink holy oil, which is the blessed remedy to make him talk more than a barber or a leader of a political club at election time. Then ña San Diego declared that for about ten years she had lived (Jesus, Mary, and Joseph!) as the Devil's concubine. You girls don't know what concubinage is, and may you never find out. For my insouciance and for having allowed that bad word to escape me, recite a *credo* as you cross yourselves.

She also declared that every Saturday night on the stroke of 12, she anointed her body with a witch's concoction and flew and flew through the air until she reached the top of Ramas hill, where she met other witches and warlocks to dance indecently and hear a Black Mass. Do the two of you not know what a Black Mass is? I've never heard one myself, believe me, but Father Pardiñas, may he rest in peace, told me that a Black Mass is one celebrated by the Devil, in the form of a he-goat, with horns three feet long and tips sharper than a mattress maker's needle. The Host they use is a bit of decaying Christian flesh, which he gives to the others as a communion wafer. Don't forget, you sleepy-heads, to pray tonight to the blessed souls in Purgatory and your guardian angel to keep you safe and defend you from witches who suck the blood of children and make them scrawny.

I remember it as though it were yesterday. Christ be with me! On Sunday, August 27, 1803, they brought ña San Diego out, riding a donkey and dressed as an *obispa,* or woman bishop. But since you haven't seen this costume, I'll tell you that it was a hat in the shape of a miter and a long sackcloth garment called a *sanbenito,* on which were painted, amid the fires of Hell, devils, female devils, and large snakes. Gently beat your breast three times.

Along with ña San Diego there came out another sly wretch of the same breed, as much a witch as she and a woman also sentenced by the Inquisition. Her name was ña Ribero, an old woman skinnier than a tithed hen with the pip. They reached the church of Santo Domingo, and from there were transported to the Beguine convent in Copacabana. The two of them died in that house before their heresy could contaminate the country. May God have forgiven them.

And I came and went, and they gave me. . . . nothing, save for some calfskin slippers, others of lead, and others of caramel: I put on the calf skin ones, gave the lead ones to Big Foot,[3] and those of caramel I kept for you, Clemente, and for you, Angélica.

And now, you two youngsters, recite with me a rosary of the fifteen mysteries, and then to sleep with you, after kissing mama's and papa's hand, and may God help you and make you saints. Amen, amen, amen.

[3] The devil.

Bolívar's Justice

(To Ricardo Bustamante)

In June of 1824 the liberating army was spread out in the adminis-trative department of Ancachs, preparing to undertake the opera-tions of the campaign that, in August of that year, resulted in the battle of Junín, and four months later the splendid triumph of Ayacucho.[1]

Bolívar was residing in Caraz with his staff, the cavalry led by Ne-cochea, the Peruvian division of La Mar, and the battalions Bogotá, Caracas, Pichincha, and Voltíjeros, that had fought so bravely under the courageous Córdova.

The Lara division, formed by the Vargas, Rifles, and Vendedores battalions, occupied quarters in the city of Huaraz. The officers of these corps were a group of young gallants, as invincibly victorious in the combats of Mars as in those of Venus. Just as they had enlisted to fight heroically against the large and experienced royalist army, so in their life in the barracks they besieged with no less courage and boldness the female descendants of the greedy exiles from Paradise.

The Colombian officers[2] were, then, a reason for heart pangs for the

---

[1] Bolívar led patriot armies to victory at the Battle of Junín (August 6, 1824), as did Field Marshal José Antonio de Sucre at the decisive Battle of Ayacucho (December 9, 1824). Ayacucho is considered to be the final battle of the Wars of Independence.—Ed.

[2] "Colombian" in this context refers to soldiers of the Republic of Gran Colombia, which comprised the Audiencia of Quito, the Viceroyalty of New Granada and Captaincy

young ladies, for distress to their mothers, and for worry to their husbands since those confounded soldiers couldn't come across a little face that was halfway appetizing without saying, as did the valiant Córdova later: "Advance at the pace of a victor," and without taking certain familiarities capable of giving stomach aches to the least suspicious and touchy husband. How confident those liberators were!

The doors of all the houses were open to them, and it was useless for any of them to be closed, for the officers always had their own way of skinning a cat and entering a house as though it were a conquered fortress. Furthermore, no one dared to treat them coldly, first because they were the latest fashion; and second, because it would have been most ungrateful to turn our noses up at those who came from the banks of the Cauca and the Apure to help us break the siege and share our reverses and our victories; and third, because in the homeland of those days nobody wanted to be taken for a lukewarm patriot.

Since the Lara division had a regular military band, the officers, who, as we have said, loved partying, went with the band after retreat at eight to whatever house they pleased, and improvised a ball to which the mistress of the house invited her friends in the neighborhood.

A lady, whom we shall call señora de Munar, the widow of a rich Spaniard, lived in one of the houses near the main square with two daughters and two nieces, all of them girls with reason to aspire to an immediate marriage, for they were good looking, rich, well brought up, and of the old aristocracy of the town. They had what in those days was called salt, pepper, oregano, and cumin, that is to say, the four things that men who came from Spain looked for in the women of the New World.

Although the señora de Munar, doubtless out of loyalty to the memory of her deceased husband, was a royalist, and a royalist to her fingertips, she was unable to excuse herself one night from receiving in her drawing room the dashing Colombian officers, who at the sound of music gave evidence of wanting to kick up their heels in the aristocratic drawing room.

As for the young ladies, it is a well-known fact that their hearts leap

---

General of Venezuela. After the Wars of Independence, Gran Colombia broke apart into Ecuador, Colombia, and Venezuela.—Ed.

when there is a prospect of swaying provocatively with a dancing partner.

The señora de Munar swallowed hard at each flirtatious compliment that the officers addressed to the young ladies of her household, now pinching the niece who was misbehaving by encouraging an officer's attentions, now calling to order in a low voice the daughter who was paying more attention to the compliments of a liberator than good upbringing requires.

It was already past midnight when one of the girls, whose charms had aroused the senses of the captain of the fourth company of the Vargas battalion, retired to her room feeling indisposed. The libertine and love-smitten captain, thinking that he was fooling the girl's Argos of a mother, went to look for the dove in her nest. She resisted the importunities of the don Juan, which were probably on the way to going too far, when a hand swiftly seized the sword that the officer was wearing at his waist and sank the blade in his side.

The one who thus castigated the man who had tried to bring dishonor to a family was the elderly señora de Munar.

The captain rushed into the drawing room, covering the wound with his hands. His comrades, who were devoted to him, made a great commotion, and after surrounding the house with soldiers and putting everyone with skirts under arrest, took the dying man to the garrison.

Bolívar was just finishing lunch when the news of this scandal reached him. He immediately mounted his horse and in only a few hours made the journey from Caraz to Huaraz.

That day his army received the following:

General Order

His Excellency the Liberator has learned with indignation that the glorious flag of Colombia, whose safekeeping he entrusted to the Vargas battalion, has been sullied by its members, who should have been more watchful of its honor and splendor, and as a consequence, as an exemplary punishment of the offense, he issues the following orders:

1. The Vargas battalion will occupy the last place in the line, and its flag shall remain in the hands of the general in command until, by a victory over the enemy, the aforementioned corps erases the infamy that has befallen it.

2. The body of the offender shall be buried without the prescribed honors, and the blade of the sword that Colombia gave the battalion for the defense of freedom and morality, shall be broken by the quartermaster in the presence of the company.

Such a general order is worthy of the great Bolívar. Only thanks to it could the cause of independence maintain its prestige and military discipline be reestablished.

Sucre, Córdova, Lara, and all the Colombian leaders intervened with Bolívar to have him rescind the article whereby the Vargas battalion was disgraced through the fault of one of its officers. The Liberator did not yield for three days, at the end of which he deemed it wisest to give in. The moral lesson had been given, and the continued existence of the first article meant little now. The battalion had effaced the stain of Huaraz by the courage it displayed at Mataré and in the battle of Ayacucho.

After the Colombian captain had been buried, Bolívar made his way to the house of the señora de Munar and said to her:

"I salute the worthy matron with all the respect that is deserved by the woman who, in the midst of her frailty, succeeded in finding the strength to save her honor and that of her family."

The señora de Munar ceased at that instant to be a royalist, and answered with enthusiasm:

"Long live the Liberator! Long live the homeland!"

Fifth Series

Don Alonso the Brawny

The story is told of the Venezuela general Páez,[1] the hero of the plains, that in the days of the war to the death with Spain, he took captive a stout Spanish soldier who enjoyed the reputation of being a man of herculean strength. The leader of the patriots said to him:

"Listen, you clumsy fellow: I'll spare your life if you succeed in throwing me to the ground." The prisoner smiled and accepted the challenge, believing victory was certain, but Páez, who for this sort of fight had more cunning and agility than physical strength, managed after two minutes to pin the Spaniard to the ground.

Then the victor said to him:

"All right, you tottering wreck, get ready to be shot!"

To which the soldier replied without turning a hair:

"That's to be expected, general: you've played with me like a cat with a mouse. So gobble me up now."

My readers may guess that Páez found the reply amusing and pardoned the prisoner.

The royalist army also had a strong man, Major Santalla, whom people say took an ordinary deck of 40 cards, tore it through the middle and said:

"Many can do that."

---

[1] José Antonio Páez (1790–1873) was Venezuela's most successful liberator after Bolívar, under whose authority he served until 1830. Páez was a gregarious *llanero* (plainsman).— Ed.

Then he did exactly the same thing with the 80 bits of bristol board left, saying:

"Few can do that."

And he ended by suddenly tearing in 2 the 160 bits of cards left, exclaiming with a triumphant air: "Only I, Major Santalla, can do that!"

But when it comes to strong men, Páez, Santalla, and all modern Samsons are suckling babes compared to my don Alonso, about whom a chronicler recounts that when his horse tired, he threw it over his shoulder, without taking off its trappings, and went on his way as though it were nothing.

*   *   *

THE CONQUISTADORS CALLED Captain Alonso Díaz, a relative of the governor of Panama don Pedro Arias Dávila, don Alonso the Brawny.

A resident of Cuzco when the rebellion in support of Almagro the Younger broke out, and very devoted to Marquis Pizarro, don Alonso did not want to leave the city, and remained hidden there conspiring for the cause of the Licentiate Vaca de Castro, sent by the king to put an end to the disturbances in Peru.

On receiving the news that the royal troops, numbering 800 soldiers, were leaving Guamanga to fight 600 of Almagro's, don Alonso decided to leave his hiding place and headed for the camp in Chupas, anxious to arrive in time to take part in the battle that took place there on September 16, 1542.

He had only a few leagues to go to arrive in Vaca de Castro's camp, when he saw horsemen on spirited steeds coming at full gallop. They were three soldiers that the victor was sending to Cuzco with the news of the defeat of Almagro's troops.

Alonso Díaz stopped one of the emissaries, and the latter, on recognizing him as one of the loyal supporters of Pizarro and one of the first conquistadors to come with him to these realms, dismounted, exclaiming:

"Good news, captain! Long live the king! The tyrant is vanquished."

Don Alonso was so overjoyed on learning the happy news that he threw himself into the soldier's arms, saying to him:

"Long live the king! Hug me tight, valiant soldier, hug me tight!"

And so close was the embrace and so great the strength with which don Alonso the Brawny hugged him that the soldier cried out and fell dead with a torrent of blood spurting from his mouth.

Alonso Díaz, who in the battles of the conquest killed not with the sword but by smothering Indians with his strong arms, forgot, in his keen joy at the victory, that his embraces dealt death to the enemy.

When the involuntary murderer was put on trial, Vaca de Castro found him not guilty, but forbade him in the future, under penalty of death, to embrace anyone, friend or enemy, man or woman.

Señor de Mendiburu, in the article that he devotes to Alonso Díaz in his *Diccionário histórico del Perú,* says that a royal decree came from Spain taking away from the braggart the right to embrace. I presume that this royal decree meant the approval of the sentence handed down by Vaca de Castro.

*   *   *

THAT CUNNING COUNTS more than strength, as the proverb has it, is proved by the result of a sword duel between Alonso Díaz and Francisco de Villacastín. The latter was one of the companions of Marquis Pizarro, who professed great affection for him, to the point that he made him one of the first potentates of Cuzco by giving him as a wife a *ñusta,*[2] the daughter of Huayna-Capac, called doña Leonor. Through this marriage he came to be Villacastín, lord of Ayaviri, an encomienda that gave him more than 8,000 Indians as vassals.

Villacastín was a person held in ridicule because of his loyalty. His front teeth were missing, and what caused this imperfection was, in all truth, just cause for laughter. It so happened that one day don Francisco was wandering through a woods in Panama when a monkey fetched him such a fierce blow with a stone from the top of a tree that it made him spit out four teeth. Villacastín recovered in a moment, drew his crossbow, and managed to kill the monkey that had left him so badly disfigured for life. Ours is a lucky day in which not only false teeth, but even false jaws, abound! If memory serves me well, Garcilaso the historian,[3] who knew Villacastín and associated with him, recounts the story of the stoning.

---

[2] Princess.

[3] The Inca Garcilaso de la Vega (1539–1616), product of the union between a Spanish soldier and the granddaughter of Inca Tupac-Yupanqui (See "Palla Huarcuna," note 1), was the author of a history of the Incas titled *Comentarios reales, que tratan del origen de los Incas* (1606–1617).—Ed.

Alonso Díaz, who was a great joker, making fun of Villacastín on one occasion, said to him:

"Your grace has only the guts to challenging a braggart of a monkey, and came out with teeth lost *in eternum.*"

Villacastín was piqued and unsheathed his sword. Don Alonso put himself on guard, and they crossed swords. But don Francisco, though he had less strength and vigor than his adversary, was lighter than he, and after fencing for only a short while, dealt don Alonso Díaz such a fierce blow with his sword that he lay for a week between life and death.

*   *   *

ALONSO DÍAZ HAD BEEN implicated as a member of Girón's faction[4] and once that leader had been vanquished and executed, he welcomed the pardon that the Royal Audience had proclaimed in 1554, and thereupon retired to live peacefully in Cuzco, where he was one of the wealthiest residents. But in 1556 the viceroy and marquis of Cañete, fearing new uprisings with Captain Díaz as an agitator, ordered him to be garroted in secret.

His curiosity aroused, a great friend of His Excellency asked him one day why he had ordered such an outstanding Spaniard killed, and the viceroy answered with a smile:

"I did it to cure that madman of his mania for embracing, for since his embraces are dangerous and were forbidden him, he went against the royal will, and at a ball was seen, as ten of the most notable residents of Cuzco testify, to embrace a lady who had stood as cosponsor with him at a baptism.

Let the truth be what it may, for I neither affirm it nor deny it, and I am not in a mood to argue as to whether his bear hugs were well- or ill-considered. Whether a man who gave embraces or a revolutionary, the fact is that don Alonso the Brawny died an unfortunate death.

---

[4] See "The Knights of the Cape," note 7.—Ed.

Margarita's Wedding Dress

It is likely that some of my readers have heard old women of Lima remark, when they wanted to think over how much the price of something had gone up:

"Good heavens! Why, that's more expensive than Margarita's wedding chemise."

I would have been left with a lingering curiosity as to who that Margarita was whose wedding dress was the talk of the town, had I not come across, in the Madrid newspaper *La América*, an article signed by don Ildefonso Antonio Bermejo (the author of a noteworthy book on Peru), who, although he touches only lightly on the girl and her wedding dress, put me on the right path to disentangling the skein and getting the story that you are about to read straight.

I

Margarita Pareja was (around the year 1765) the most pampered daughter of don Raimundo Pareja, a Knight of the Order of Santiago and collector general of taxes in Cuzco.

The girl was one of those Lima beauties who captivate the devil himself and make him cross himself and throw stones. She had a pair of black eyes that were like two torpedos loaded with dynamite that caused an explosion in the depths of the soul of Lima's dashing young men.

There arrived from Spain around that time a bold young man, the son of the crowned city of the bear and the madrone tree[1] named don Luis Alcázar. He had an uncle in Lima, a rich bachelor of old highborn Aragonese stock, and prouder than the sons of King Fruela.[2]

It was only natural that as he waited for the time to come when he would inherit his uncle's fortune, our don Luis should be as poor as a church mouse and be going through the pains of hell. When I say that even his love-adventures were on credit, to be paid for when his fortunes took a turn for the better, I need say no more.

Alcázar met the lovely Margarita in the procession of Saint Rose. The girl's eyes sent their darts staight to his heart and inspired his love at first sight. He paid her courtly compliments, and though she answered neither yes nor no, she made it clear with little smiles and other arms of the feminine arsenal that the handsome young man was a dish very much to her liking. The truth is, as if I were in the confessional, that the two of them fell in love to the roots of their hair.

Since lovers forget that arithmetic exists, don Luis believed that his current poverty would not be an obstacle to the prospering of his love, and so he went to Margarita's father, and without further ado asked him for the hand of his daughter.

The petition was not to don Raimundo's liking, and he courteously dismissed the petitioner, telling him that Margarita was too young to marry, for despite her 18 Mays, she still played with dolls.

But this was not the heart of the matter. The negative answer stemmed from the fact that don Raimundo did not wish to be the father-in-law of a poor devil, as he told his friends in confidence, and one of them went with this bit of gossip to don Honorato, which was the name of the uncle from Aragón. The latter, who was prouder than the Cid,[3] fumed with rage and said:

"What's this I hear! Snubbing my nephew! There are many who would give anything to be related by marriage to that young man, than whom there is none more gallant in all of Lima. Who has ever seen such insolence! How far will that petty tax collector go with me?"

---

[1] Madrid.

[2] The medieval King of Asturias, known in legend, like his offspring, for his inordinate pride.

[3] Ruy Díaz de Vivar (1043–1099) is a legendary Spanish hero known as "El Cid" (from the Arabic meaning "lord") who was immortalized in the thirteenth century epic *El cantar de mío Cid.*—Ed.

Margarita, who was ahead of her time, for she was as nervous as one of today's damsels, wept and wailed and tore her hair and had tantrums, and if she did not threaten to poison herself it was only because sulfur matches had not yet been invented.

She lost color and weight, her health quite visibly declined, she spoke of becoming a nun, and no one could do a thing with her.

"Either Luis's bride or a nun!"[4] she cried each time her nerves were upset, something that happened from one hour to the next.

The Knight of the Order of Santiago grew alarmed and called in doctors and healers, all of whom declared that the girl was well on her way to becoming consumptive and that the only *melecina*[5] to save her wasn't sold in an apothecary's shop.

Either marry her to the young man of her choice, or soon lay her out in a coffin with a palm frond and crown. Such was the ultimatum from the doctors.

Don Raimundo (finally acting as a father!), forgetting in his concern to take his cape and cane, rushed like a madman to don Honorato's house and said to him:

"I have come to ask you to consent to your nephew's marrying Margarita tomorrow, because if not the girl will go to her last resting place very soon."

"That can't be," the uncle answered rudely. "My nephew is a 'poor wretch' as you put it, and what you ought to seek for your daughter is a man rolling in money."

The altercation was stormy. The more don Raimundo pleaded, the more the Aragonese hit the roof, and don Raimundo was about to depart dejected when don Luis, intervening in the matter, said:

"But uncle, it is not Christian behavior to cause the death of someone who is not to blame."

"Do you declare yourself willing to marry her?"

"With all my heart, my uncle and master."

"Well then, my boy. I agree to do as you wish, but on one condition, which is this: Don Raimundo is to swear to me before the consecrated Host that he will not give an *ochavo* to his daughter, nor will he leave her a *real* as her inheritance."

---

[4] Umphrey's translation, 127. The original reads: "¡O de Luis o de Dios!"
[5] A corruption of *medicina,* medicine.

At this point another even stormier dispute ensued.

"But my dear fellow," don Raimundo argued, "my daughter has a dowry worth 20,000 duros."

"We give up any claim to the dowry. The girl will come to her husband's house with nothing more than what she is wearing."

"Allow me to give her furniture as a wedding gift and her bride's trousseau."

"Not so much as a pin. If that doesn't suit you, leave matters as they are and let the girl die."

"Be reasonable, don Honorato. My daughter needs to have at least a wedding chemise to replace the clothes she is wearing."

"Very well. I agree to her having such a garment so that you won't accuse me of being obstinate. I consent to your giving her a bridal chemise, and that's the end of it."

On the following day don Raimundo and don Honorato went to the church of San Francisco very early in the morning, knelt to hear Mass, and according to their agreement, at the moment that the priest elevated the divine Host, Margarita's father said:

"I swear not to give my daughter anything but her wedding chemise. May God condemn me if I swear falsely."

And don Raimundo fulfilled *ad pedem litterae*[6] what he had sworn to, for neither in life nor in death did he later give to his daughter anything worth so much as a *maravedi*.[7]

The Flanders lace trimming the bride's wedding chemise cost 2,700 duros, according to Bermejo,[8] who appears to have copied this detail from the *Relaciones secretas* of Ulloa and don Jorge Juan.[9]

---

[6] To the letter [Latin].

[7] Any number of medieval Spanish silver coins, used in the thirteenth to fifteenth centuries to value silver and base silver coins, in the fifteenth to eighteenth centuries to value copper coins; a Spanish copper coin of small value used in the seventeenth to eighteenth centuries, frequently used as a type of worthless or valueless object.

[8] Ildefonso Antonio Bermejo (1820–1892), author of the *Repúblicas americanas: episodios de la vida en la República del Paraguay* (1873).—Ed.

[9] Antonio de Ulloa (1716–1795) and Jorge Juan (1713–1773) coauthored the *Noticias secretas de América sobre el estado naval, militar y político de los Reynos del Perú y provincias de Quito, costa de Nueva Granada y Chile: gobierno y régimen particular de los pueblos de Indias, etc., etc.* (1826).—Ed.

Furthermore, the drawstring at her neck was a diamond chain worth 30,000 pesos.

The newlyweds made the Aragonese uncle believe that the bridal chemise was worth a doubloon at best, because don Honorato was so stubborn that had he discovered the truth he would have made his nephew divorce Margarita.

Let us agree that the fame that Margarita Pareja's bridal chemise came to have was highly deserved.

Abascal's Clever Trick

I

That His Excellency Viceroy don Fernando de Abascal y Souza, Knight of the Order of Santiago and marquis of Concordia,[1] was a man of great skill is a point on which friends and enemies who managed to meet him are in accord. And in case a contemporary of mine should question the fact, in order to oblige him to strike his flag it will suffice for me to tell of an incident that happened in Lima at the end of 1808, that is to say, when Abascal had been viceroy for scarcely a year and a half.

The senior member of the town council of this City of Kings[2] was . . . who? I do not record the name for fear of finding myself involved in another dog and cat fight of a lawsuit. Let us call him señor de H. . . .

His Lordship the town councilor belonged to the scallion species. His head was white and the rest was green; that is to say that despite his white hair and his complaints he still showed off like a peacock and feasted his eyes on the great-great-grandnieces of Adam. He lived the life of a bachelor, treated himself like a prince, had a sizeable fortune,

[1] José Fernando de Abascal y Souza (1743–1821) was the 38th viceroy of Peru, 1806–1816.—Ed.

[2] Lima was founded on the Feast of the Epiphany by Francisco Pizarro, hence the phrase "City of Kings."

and his house and person were in the care of a housekeeper and a legion of slaves.

One morning as señor de H . . . was finishing his cup of delicious Cuzco chocolate with cinnamon and vanilla, a poor devil, a vendor of jewels, appeared with a little box that contained a brooch, a pair of earrings and three diamond rings. Señor de H . . . remembered that Easter was coming, and that for the occasion he had promised to present such a trinket as a gift to a girl who had coaxed him into making that promise. A duro more, a duro less, and the deal was closed for 100 doubloons. He kept the little box and bade the peddler goodbye with these words:

"Very well, my friend, come back in a week for your money."

The appointed day arrived, and after that another and another, and the creditor never managed to speak with his debtor: at times because señor de H . . . was out, at others because he was visiting prominent citizens of the town, and finally because the black doorkeeper refused to let him past the entryway. The vendor caught up with His Lordship late one afternoon in the doorway of the town hall, and in the presence of several of the latter's colleagues said to him:

"Forgive me, sir, if I turn up here because I was unable to find you at home, for we poor devils must importune our debtors."

"And what it is you want, my good man? Alms? Here you are, brother, and go with God."

And señor de H . . . took a peseta out of his pocket.

"What do you mean, alms?" the creditor answered indignantly. "Pay me the 100 doubloons you owe me."

"Has anyone ever seen such a shameless rogue!" the town councilor cried. "Come, constable. To jail with this man."

And there was no way out. The hapless vendor protested, but since protests of the weak against the strong are mallow water, our man went, protest and all, to jail for 24 hours for lack of respect for the person of a man known to be a town councilor or *municipillo*.

Once he was set free the poor wretch went from Caiaphas to Pilate with his complaint, but inasmuch as he presented neither witnesses nor documents the one called him a madman and the other a rogue.

The case reached the ears of the viceroy, who summoned the victim to his palace in secret, questioned him in detail, and said to him:

"Put your mind at rest and tell no one that we have seen each other. I promise you that by tomorrow morning you will either have recovered your jewelry or have gone to jail for six months as a slanderer."

II

Except for nights at the theater, which Viceroy Abascal failed to attend only if he was ill or for some other grave reason, he received his aristocratic friends from seven to ten. The lovely Ramona, though barely 14, did the honors of the drawing room with great grace, except when she saw a little mouse run across the rug. Abascal's pampered daughter was so high-strung that her father forbade the lighting of skyrockets in the vicinity because when they went off they caused the girl to have nervous convulsions. Affectations of a spoiled girl! As the years went by, she was not frightened by the mustachio sported by Pereira, a fine lad whom the king had sent to make war on the insurgents. He had only just arrived in Peru when he kissed Ramona, winning by so doing her hand and her heart, and returning with his new wife to Spain. A fateful blow to all the young marquises and counts of Lima who had been eager to please the girl.

That night señor de H . . . attended, as usual, the gathering of the viceroy's intimates in his palace. The viceroy, while deep in conversation with him, asked him for a pinch of snuff, and señor de H . . . passed him his gold box with his monogram in rubies. Abascal sniffed a noseful, and out of distraction, doubtless, put the other man's little box away in the pocket of his dress coat.

Suddenly Ramona began to scream. A tiny little spider was climbing up and down the white satin with which the walls of the drawing room were hung, and Abascal, on the pretext of going off to fetch lemon balm water or the little bottle of vinegar of the seven thieves, a hallowed remedy against nerves, slipped off through a side door, called the captain of the guard of halberdiers, and said to him:

"Go to señor de H . . . 's house and tell Conce, his housekeeper that, using as a sign this snuffbox, which you will leave with her, her master is sending for the little box of jewels that he bought two weeks ago, because he wants to show the jewelry to Ramoncita, who is the most curious young lady that ever was."

III

Señor de H . . . returned home that night at ten o'clock, and the house-keeper served him his supper. As His Lordship was savoring a Creole stew, doña Conce, with all the confident informality of an old servant, asked him:

"And how was the gathering, sir?"

"So-so. The innocent Ramona threw a tantrum, and that was the last straw. That young lady is a Doña Affectations and needs a hard-hearted husband like myself, who would give her a timely thrashing that would be sure to cure her of her fears. And the worst of it is that her father is a brazen old man who sponged a pinch of snuff from me and made off with my holiday snuff box."

"That's not so, sir. Here is the box. One of the palace officers brought it."

"When was that, Conce?"

"The church bell at the church of Las Nazarenas had just struck eight, and obeying the message you sent me, I gave the officer the little box."

"You're tipsy, Conce. What little box are you talking about?"

"The one with the jewels that you bought the other day."

A few days later señor de H . . . set out on a trip to the North, where he owned a valuable country estate, and no more was seen of him in Lima.

Naturally he enjoined his steward to pay his creditor before he left.

The gentlemanly Abascal advised the captain of halberdiers and the owner of the jewelry to keep the whole matter a deep secret, but the story in all its details came to light, seeing as how a secret shared by three is one shouted from the rooftops.

Sixth Series

The Demon of the Andes

(To Ricardo Becerra)

Historical Notes on the Field Marshal
Francisco de Carbajal

Arévalo, a little city in Old Castile, gave birth to the soldier who by his indomitable valor, his military gifts, his exploits that border on the fantastic, his rare good fortune in combat, and his sarcastic and cruel temperament was known, in the first days of the colonial period, by the name of The Demon of the Andes.

Who were his parents? Was he born on the wrong side of the blanket or the fruit of an honorable marriage? History maintains a profound silence on these points, although we have read a book in which it is stated that he was the natural son of the terrible Cesare Borgia, duke of Valentinois.[1]

After having been a soldier for more than 30 years in Europe under the grand captain Gonzalo de Córdoba, and having fought with the rank of lieutenant in the famous battles of Ravenna and Pavia, Francisco de Carbajal came to Peru to lend powerful aid with his sword to the marquis don Francisco Pizarro. He received handsome rewards from Pizarro, and soon he was the possesser of a fat fortune.

After the tragic end met with in Lima by the daring conqueror of

---

[1] Cesare Borgia, duke of Valentinois (1476–1507) held a Spanish archibishopric and cardinalate before embarking on bloody military campaigns in central Italy.—Ed.

Peru, Carbajal fought stubbornly against the faction of the young Almagro. In the bloody battle of Chupas, as the battle was favoring the Almagrists, Francisco de Carbajal, who commanded a regiment of the royal infantry that had lost heart, threw his helmet and cuirass down and stepping before his men, exclaimed: "Demotion and disgrace to the one of you who retreats! I am twice the target for the enemy that you are!" The troops fervently followed the lead of their robust, brawny captain and captured Almagro's artillery. Historians agree that this heroic act of bravery decided the battle.

The day came when the apostle of the Indies, Bartolomé de las Casas, succeeded in obtaining from Charles V the fiercely opposed Ordinances in favor of the Indians, and the execution of the Ordinances was entrusted to the man least suited to introduce reforms. We are referring to the first viceroy of Peru, Blasco Núñez de Vela. It is a well-known fact that the lack of common sense of the king's representative caused him to praise to the skies the interests that the reform was aimed at, thus encouraging the great rebellion of Gonzalo Pizarro.

Carbajal, who foresaw the turn that events would take, hastened to realize his assets in order to return to Spain. As luck would have it, at the time there was not a single ship ready to set out on an ocean crossing as risky as it was long. The dominant qualities in the soul of our hero were gratitude and loyalty. Many ties united him to the Pizarros, and they conspired to give him the second most important role in the rebel ranks.

Gonzalo Pizarro, who always greatly esteemed the valor and experience of the veteran soldier, immediately appointed him field marshal of the army.

Carbajal, who was not only a valiant soldier but a man who knew his way around politically, gave Pizarro at that juncture the most timely advice imaginable in view of his compromised situation: "Since things are going extremely well for you," he wrote him, "take over the government once and for all, and after that matters will proceed as you please. Since God has not given us the power of divination, the real way of succeeding is to be stout hearted and be ready for anything that happens, for great things are not undertaken without great risk. The best thing to do is to entrust your justification to the lancers and harquebusiers, for you have gone too far to hope for favor from the crown." But Pizarro's upbringing and his habits of respect for the sovereign limited his ambition, and he never dared to be seen to be in open rebellion against the king. Carbajal's bold counsel frightened him. Politically speaking, the field marshal was a man who was ahead of his time and who set forth what was gospel in the nineteenth century: A revolution defeated is called an uprising; a triumphant rebellion is called a revolution. Success dictates the name.

It is not our intention to recount the history of the long and wearying campaign that, with the death of the viceroy in the battle of Iñaquito on January 18, 1546, placed the country, though only for a short time, in the power of the Most Magnificent don Gonzalo Pizarro. We summarize the great services of Carbajal in this campaign in the following lines of a historian:

"The octogenarian warrior annihilated or demolished the royalists of the South. At an age in which few men still have the fire of their passions and the vigor of their limbs, he crossed the Andes six times without tiring. From Quito to San Miguel, from Lima to Guamanga, from Guamanga to Lima, from Lucanas to Cuzco, from Callao to Arequipa, and from Arequipa to Charcas. Eating and sleeping on horseback, he was insensible to the chills of the highlands, to the blinding glint of the sun on the desert sands, and to the privations and fatigues of forced marches. The superstitious common people said that Carbajal and his horse flew through the air. Only thus could they explain such tireless activity."

After the victory of Iñaquito, Pizarro's power seemed indestructible. Everything appeared to conspire to have the victorious governor make Peru independent. His tempter The Demon of the Andes wrote him from Andahuailas, urging him to make himself king: "You must declare yourself king of this land conquered by your arms and those of your brothers. Your claims are far greater than those of the kings of Spain. In what clause of his will did Adam bequeath the empire of the Incas to them? Don't be intimidated because vulgar gossip accuses you of disloyalty. No one who has made himself king has ever had the name of traitor. Those governments that force created time makes legitimate. Reign and you will be honored. In any event you are the de facto king and you must die on the throne. France and Rome will aid you if you have the will and the cunning to win their protection for yourself. Count on me in life and in death, and when troubled times come, I have a neck as big around for the gallows as the next man."

Among the paintings that adorned the walls of the Museo Nacional until 1860 and later were transferred to the Palacio de la Exposición, we remember having seen a portrait of The Demon of the Andes,[2] beneath there could be read these words:

> Del Peru la suprema independencia
> Carbajal ha tres siglos quería
> Y quererla costóle la existencia.[3]

But it was written in the stars that Pizarro was not the man chosen by God to create the Peruvian nation. By crowning himself he would have created special interests in the country, and people would have made their destiny as one with his. Therefore, on the arrival of the bachelor-at-law La Gasca with plenipotentiary powers from Philip II to proceed with matters pending in America and to be lavish with exemptions, honors, and rewards, treason began to bear very bitter fruits in Pizarro's ranks. His friends scattered to swell the ranks of La Gasca's supporters. Only Carbajal's harshness kept the traitors in line. So great was the terror inspired by the name of the veteran soldier that on a certain occasion Pizarro said to Pedro Paniagua, Gasca's emissary:

"Wait until Field Marshal Carbajal comes and you'll get to see him and know him."

"That, sir, is something that I have no desire to wait for," the emissary answered; "I'll annotate the marshal as 'seen and known'[4] here and now."

In Lima the rebellion against Pizarro had reached the boiling point. The people who at an open meeting of the city council had proclaimed him liberator, who had called him "Most Magnificent" and obliged him to continue in the post of governor since he disdained the throne that they had offered him, that same people a year later denied him all possibility of their sympathies. The love of the people is a sad, very sad thing!

[2] The portrait of Carbajal is now in the Palacio de la Exposición. Don Mateo Paz Soldán in his *Geografía del Perú*, a book printed in Paris in 1862, also has these words [Author's note].

[3] Peru's supreme independence / Carbajal wanted three centuries ago / and wanting it cost him his life.

[4] The usual phrase acknowledging the review of official documents.

In order not to be overcome in Lima, Pizarro found himself obliged to withdraw to the South and wage the battle of Huarina. The loyal men who accompanied him numbered no more than 500. Diego Centeno, in command of a 1,200 men, attacked the limited revolutionary forces; but the strategic cunning and the heroic valor of the aged field marshal won for so desperate a cause the last of its victories.

The great figure of the victor of Huarina has its frighteningly dark side: his cruelty. Carbajal barely gave quarter to those who surrendered, and more than 300 deserters or soldiers suspected of treason were executed.

The story has it that in Cuzco doña María Calderón, the wife of a captain of Centeno's troops, allowed herself with womanly indiscretion to call Pizarro a tyrant, and repeated in public that the king would soon triumph over the rebels.

"Comadre,"[5] Carbajal said to her on three different occasions, "swallow your words, because if you don't contain your accursed tongue I'll have you killed, as sure as there is a God. The spiritual kinship that you have with me will be of no use to you."

As soon as he saw the futility of his third warning, the marshal appeared at the lady's house, saying to her: "I'll have you know, señora comadre, that I've come to garrote you." And after having exposed her dead body in the window, he exclaimed: "Accursed body of yours, comadre chatterbox, if you don't learn your lesson from this I don't know what else to do!"

Finally, on April 9, 1548, the battle of Saxsahuamán began. Fearing that Carbajal's impetuousness would be fatal for him, Gonzalo Pizarro made the infamous Cepeda second in rank, leaving the field marshal to resign himself to fighting as a mere soldier of the line. The first shots had barely been fired when Cepeda, the second in command, and Captain Garcilaso, the father of the historian,[6] went over to La Gasca's side. Their treason was contagious, and La Gasca, with no other arms save his breviary and his council of chaplains won cheap and bloodless laurels at Saxsahuamán. It was neither valor nor military science, but ingratitude and treachery that defeated the generous brother of Marquis Pizarro.

[5] A fellow sponsor of a child at baptism.
[6] Father of Inca Garcilaso de la Vega, see "Don Alonso the Brawny," note 3.—Ed.

When Carbajal saw the traitorous desertion of his comrades, he put one leg over the saddletree and began to sing the song that became so popular later:

> Los mis cabellicos, maire,
> uno a uno se los llevó el aire.
> ¡Ay pobrecicos,
> los mis cabellicos![7]

When the horse he was riding fell, the field marshal found himself surrounded by enemies resolved to kill him, but a timely intervention by Centeno saved him. Some historians say that the prisoner asked him:

"Who is your grace who is granting me such mercy?"

"Doesn't your grace recognize me?" the other answered affably. "I am Diego Centeno."

"By my holy patron saint!" the veteran soldier answered, and then said, alluding to the retreat from Charcas and the battle of Huarina: "Since I always saw your grace from the back, I didn't recognize you from the front."

Gonzalo Pizarro and Francisco de Carbajal were immediately put on trial and condemned to death. As a knight of a religious order, the governor was sentenced to decapitation. The field marshal, who was a commoner, was to be drawn and quartered. When this sentence was read to him, he answered:

"It suffices to kill me."

A captain, who on one occasion don Francisco wanted to hang because he suspected him of being a traitor, approached him:

"Although your grace intended to finish me off, I would be pleased to serve you in any way you might choose."

"When I wanted to hang you I could do so, and if I didn't hang you it was because I never liked killing such despicable men as you."

A soldier who had been an aide of the marshal's but had passed over to the enemy, said to him in tears:

"My captain! May it please God to let your grace live and kill me!

[7] O the hairs on my head, marshal / The wind blew away one by one. / O the hairs on my head, / Poor things!

If your grace had fled at the same time as I did, you wouldn't be in the trouble you're in today."

"Brother Pedro de Tapia," Carbajal answered him with his usual sarcasm, "since we were such great friends, why did you sin against friendship and not notify me so that we could flee together?"

A merchant who complained of having been ruined by don Francisco, began to insult him:

"And by what sum am I indebted to you?"

"It surely adds up to a thousand ducets."

Carbajal calmly took from his waist the scabbard of his sword (having presented the sword itself to Pedro Valdivia on surrendering to him), and handing it to the merchant said to him:

"Well, little brother, put this scabbard on my account and don't come complaining again about debts I owe you, for in the bottom of my heart I do not recall having any other debt save five maravedis I owe to a witch who kept a tavern in Seville, and if I didn't pay it was because she baptized the wine with water, and thus exposed me to an attack of stomach cramps and diarrhea."

When he was put in a basket drawn by two mules to take him to the place where he would be put to death, he let out a guffaw and began to sing:

¡Qué fortuna! Niño en cuna,
Viejo en cuna. ¡Qué fortuna![8]

On the way, the crowd tried to seize the condemned man and tear him to pieces. Making a show of valor and self-possession, Carbajal said:

"I say, sirs, clear the way! There is no reason to mill about. Let justice be done."

And at the moment that the executioner Juan Enríquez was preparing to dispatch the victim, the latter said to him with a smile:

"Brother Juan, treat me as one tailor to another."

Carbajal was executed on the battlefield itself on April 10, at the age of 84. On the following day La Gasca made his triumphal entry into Cuzco.

[8] What luck! As a child, in a cradle, / As an old man, in a cradle. What luck!

Here is the moral portrait that a historian draws of the unfortunate field marshal:

"Among the soldiers of the New World, Carbajal was doubtless the one possessed of the most military gifts. A strict disciplinarian, active and persevering, he knew neither danger nor fatigue, and such were his sagacity and the resourcefulness that he displayed in action that the common people believed that he had a familiar devil. With such an extraordinary character, with strength that lasted much longer than it does in most men, and with the good fortune of never having known defeat save at Saxsahuamán in the 65 years that he lived the military life in Europe and in America, it is not surprising that fabulous things were recounted of him, or that his soldiers, taking him to be a supernatural being, should call him The Demon of the Andes. He had a gift for talk, if it can be called that, and gave free rein to his loquacity on any occasion. He looked on life as a comedy, although more than once he made it a tragedy. His ferocity was proverbial, but even his enemies recognized in him a great virtue: fidelity. For that reason he was not tolerant of the perfidy of others; for this reason he never showed compassion toward traitors. This constant loyalty, in times when such a virtue was a rarity, surrounds with respect the great figure of Field Marshal Francisco de Carbajal." But the vengeance of the crown did not end for Carbajal with his being put to death.

His estate, or house and grounds in Lima, was formed where the streets that today are known as Pelota and Los Gallos met. The grounds were sown with salt, the inside walls were demolished, and on the corner of the latter street a bronze tablet was placed, with an infamous inscription in memory of the owner. The street was given the name of Mármol de Carbajal.

But among the soldiery the field marshal had left many passionate followers, and as soon as La Gasca returned to Spain they removed the ignominious tablet one night. The Royal Tribunal made a number of arrests but they proved fruitless, for the thieves were never found.

Shortly thereafter there took place the famous rebellion of Captain don Francisco Girón, who, by proclaiming the same cause as was defeated at Saxsahuamán, endangered the power of the Royal Audience for 13 months.

Having been defeated, Girón was taken prisoner, brought to Lima, and his bloody head placed on a post in the main square between two posts with the heads of Gonzalo Pizarro and Francisco de Carbajal.

About 60 years had gone by since the horrible drama of Saxsahuamán. A descendant of Saint Francis Borja, duke of Gandía, the viceroy poet-prince of Esquilache, was governing Peru in the name of Philip III. We do not know whether it was because of strict orders or in order to surround the monarchical principle with an aura of terrifying power that on January 1, 1617, with great ceremony a memorial tablet was placed in the house of the field marshal.

The tablet reads:

IN THE NAME OF HIS MAGNIFICENCE PHILIP
III OUR LORD ANNO DOMINI 1617 HIS EXCEL-
LENCY DON FRANCISCO DE BORJA, PRINCE OF
ESQUILACHE, VICEROY OF THESE REALMS, OR-
DERED THE RESTORATION OF THIS TABLET
THAT IS THE MEMORIAL OF THE PUNISHMENT
METED OUT TO FRANCISCO DE CARBAJAL,
FIELD MARSHAL OF GONZALO PIZARRO, IN
WHOSE COMPANY HE WAS PERFIDIOUS AND A
TRAITOR TO HIS KING AND NATURAL LORD,
HIS HOUSES BEING DEMOLISHED AND THE
LAND SOWN WITH SALT IN THE YEAR 1538.
THIS IS WHERE HIS TOWN HOUSE STOOD.

This tablet may be seen today, set in one of the walls of the reception room of the Biblioteca Nacional.[9] But some years later a relative of Carbajal's was responsible for its disappearance from the corner of Los Gallos, as is proved by the following lines that complete the tablet in the reception room of the library:

[9] In 1906 this tablet was transferred to the Historical Museum installed in the Palacio de la Exposición [Author's note].

> IN THE REIGN OF HIS MAGNIFICENCE PHILIP
> IV OUR LORD HIS EXCELLENCY DON PEDRO DE
> TOLEDO Y LEYVA, MARQUIS OF MANCERA,
> VICEROY OF THESE REALMS, GENTLEMAN OF
> THE BEDCHAMBER AND MEMBER OF HIS WAR
> COUNCIL, THIS TABLET BEING AGAIN LOST,
> ORDERED IT RESTORED ANNO DOMINI 1645.

When Peru won its independence, the calle del Mármol de Carbajal lost its name. We sons of the Republic could not, in all propriety, share in a mercilessness that did not respect even the sanctity of the tomb.

The Judge's Three Reasons

O n October 27, 1544, the residents of Lima were terrified. And with good reason, I assure you.

On getting up out of bed and opening their doors wide to allow God's grace free passage, they were confronted with the heartstopping news that Francisco de Carbajal, without being heard by a soul, had slipped into the city with 50 of his men, imprisoned a number of the leading citizens said to be friends of Viceroy Blasco Núñez, and hanged, not a couple of poor devils as would have been desirable, but Pedro del Barco and Machín de Florencia, men of great importance because they had been among the first conquistadors, that is to say, those who captured Atahualpa in the main square of Cajamarca.

Carbajal charitably warned the inhabitants of Lima that he was determined to go on hanging its residents and sacking the city if it did not accept Gonzalo Pizarro as governor of Peru; the latter, with the greater part of his army, was just two leagues away, awaiting their reply.

The Royal Tribunal was composed at the time of the bachelors-at-law Cepeda, Tejado, and Zárate, for the bachelor-at-law Alvarez had gotten out of a tight spot by declaring himself to be on the side of the viceroy. The judges, frightened by Carbajal's threat, summoned the notables to a meeting of the town council. The matter was discussed only superficially, for there was no time to lose in long speeches or flowers of rhetoric, and a document was drawn up recognizing Gonzalo as governor.

When it came the turn of Judge Zárate (a doddering old man,

according to Palentino) to sign, he began by drawing a cross and underneath it, before setting down his scribble of a signature, he wrote: "I swear by God and by this cross and the words of Holy Scripture that I am signing for three reasons: out of fear, out of fear, and out of fear."

*   *   *

JUDGE ZÁRATE LIVED with a daughter, doña Teresa, a girl of 20 fresh years of age, pretty from her shoes to her tortoise shell comb, who bore in her veins all the ardor of her Andalusian blood, a cause more than sufficient to surmise that she was tiring of her condition as an unmarried young lady. The girl, as was natural at her age, had a heart-throb, Blasco de Soto, a lieutenant in Carbajal's regiment, who had asked her father for her hand and found his request refused, for His Honor wanted a man with an assured fortune as the husband for his daughter. Her suitor was not discouraged at the refusal, and acquainted Carbajal with his predicament.

"What's this I hear!" Francisco shouted in a rage. "A farcical judge turning down my lieutenant, who is a lad without peer! The old gaffer will have me to deal with. Come, my boy, don't worry, either I am not Francisco de Carbajal or tomorrow will be your wedding day. I will be sponsor at your wedding and that's all there is to it. I regret that you're really in love, because you should know, my boy, that love is the wine that most quickly turns to vinegar; however, that's not my concern but yours, and you're certain to be a winner. What I must do is see you married, and I shall do so as surely as there are grapevines in Jerez, and between you and Teresa you will multiply until the blackboard is full."

And the field marshal went to the judge's house, and without further ado asked for the girl's hand for his godson. Poor Zárate was filled with remorse, stammered a thousand excuses, and finally gave in. But when the notary required him to sign the document giving his consent, the good oldster took the goose quill and wrote: "Let this sign of the cross indicate that I consent for three reasons: out of fear, out of fear, and out of fear."

*   *   *

THUS THE PHRASE "the judge's three reasons" became proverbial in Lima. We have heard it from the mouth of many oldsters and it is as useful as the phrase about the 99 reasons the artilleryman gave for not having fired a salvo: "Reason number one: Having no powder. There is no need to mention the 98 other reasons."

Shortly after his daughter's marriage, Zárate fell gravely ill of dysentery, and on the night that he received Extreme Unction Carbajal came to visit him and said to him:

"Your grace is dying because he wishes to. Never mind the doctors; drink a pinch of powdered unicorn's horn in some herb tea, for it is as efficacious for your illness as a saint's bone."

"No, señor don Francisco," the sick man answered. "I am dying, not because I so willed, but for three reasons."

"Don't say them, for I know what they are," Carbajal interrupted him, and left the dying man's room laughing.

The Witches of Ica

I

Limeños of old called Ica a land of good grapes and renowned witches. In our day it was the scene of the miracles of the venerable Friar Ramón Rojas, widely known as Father Guatemala, whose canonization is being carefully considered by Rome.

I do not believe in any magic charms save those that a pretty girl's face naturally comes by. Every good-looking woman has a pair of familiar little devils in her eyes that make us men fall into more than one temptation, followed later by heavy-caliber renunciations.

But the people of Ica are given to believing in the supernatural, and they cannot be made to understand even if they were tortured on the wheel that it is not true that witches travel through the air mounted on broomsticks, that they cast evil spells, and that they can read the book of the future without spelling out each word, just as I read a bulky manuscript of another century.

It is true that the Inquisition of Lima helped to enhance the reputation of witches that the women of Ica enjoyed. At hand are my collection of *Anales,*[1] in which there figure among the women condemned many from the town of Valverde, whose artifices I do not wish to take up in this article so that you won't say that I repeat myself like a bishop giving his benediction.

[1] A reference to Palma's *Anales de la Inquisición de Lima* (1863), a series of chronicles about the Spanish Inquisition in Lima.—Ed.

II

The first sorcerer who prospered in Ica (around the year 1611) deserved to be called an astrologer instead. He was white, of medium height, with dark hair and a well-shaped nose, who spoke very slowly and sententiously, and whose occupation was that of a healer.

He was the Falb[2] of his century, a great prognosticator of earthquakes and very skillful at reading omens.

It would appear that he even tried to write a book, to judge from the following lines taken from a letter he sent to a friend:

"The way of knowing when a year will have abundant water. The look of the sky on the afternoon of the first of January is observed, and if it is yellowish green it will be a good year for water."

What is more, he explains the abundance of water, when that particular circumstance does not occur, as characteristic of leap years.

He also characterizes years as solar or lunar, according to the greater or lesser influence of the sun and moon.

"How can it be known when it is time to declare that there is an epidemic? For this, the only thing that need be done is to pay attention to whether whirlwinds form or not during the month of February. In the first case there is certain to be a plague; it may by noted that pock marks, for example, first appear on leaves of grape vines."

The theory of the astrologer from Ica concerning rains is also curious. "Clouds," he states, "are nothing but spongelike masses that have the quality of absorbing water. These sponges come into contact with the sea, and once their thirst is quenched, they mount to the upper regions of the atmosphere, where the winds wring them out, and the water in them falls to the ground." As for the large number of *sapitos* (frogs) that appear in Ica after a downpour, he said that they were due to the fact that the germs of them contained in the clouds develop before reaching the ground. He named any piling up of clouds a "double plume," and the ensuing flood was given the name of "male swelling."

The fact is that, as happens to all charlatans when they set out to explain natural phenomena, he neither understood himself nor did anyone else understand him, conditions more than sufficient for him to become a man of great prestige.

---

[2] Rudolf Falb (1838–1903), Austrian astronomer and meteorologist.—Ed.

"Only a mortal who has a pact with the devil can know so much," the people of Ica said, and for all their complaints everyone went to him to buy medicinal herbs.

III

Witches did not disappear from Ica in view of the fact that the Cortes of Cadiz did away with the tribunal of the Inquisition in 1813. Evidence in support of this:

Until a few years ago, Mama Justa was still alive, a most repugnant black, a fence for stolen goods, and a crafty woman, very skillful at preparing love potions and sticking dolls with pins, and (God save us!) mending maidenheads. The sloven lived into old age. The only persons to have formally accused her successor, ña[3] Manonga Lévano, were several neighbor women who swore, by the consecrated Host, that they had seen her turn into an owl and fly.

Ña Lévano's occupation was that of midwife. She would arrive at the home of the woman in childbirth, place on the woman's head a wide-brimmed straw hat that she maintained had belonged to Archbishop Perlempimpim, and before five minutes had gone by an offspring would come into the world. There was no tale to the effect that the magic had ever failed.

Ña Dominguita from the convent of Socorro is still alive, and all of Ica calls her a witch without it making her angry. She is an old woman bent over with age, the hobgoblin of the children because she wears a sort of turban. In the little garden of her house there is a small tree, planted by Father Guatemala, which bears little gold-colored flowers that according to ña Dominguita fall off on Cuasimodo's Day, little flowers that possess miraculous virtues. She was educated in the Beguine convent of Socorro, founded in the previous century by the Dominican friar Manuel Cordero, whose portrait is preserved behind the door to the chapel. Ña Dominguita hates everything that smacks of progress, and predicts that the iron horse will bring many misfortunes to Ica. On the eve of the battle of Saraja she not only predicted the winning side, though to do so she had no need to be a witch, but also designated by name those men of Ica who would die in it. Her words

---

[3] See "Santiago the Flier," note 1.

always have a double meaning, and the quick thinking that gets her out of tight spots is amazing.

Don Jerónimo Illescas, who was born in Ica and lived there, an obese man and a great wit, was what is meant by an aristocratic sorcerer. He knew as much about reading cards as a French trickster. Ño Chombo Illescas, as the townspeople called him, ran, until his death a few years ago, a tavern on the corner of San Francisco and sold tasty sausages made by Tiburcio, a black tosspot employed by don Jerónimo in the kitchen. This Tiburcio was also a character, for he had found a way to make excuses for his constant drinking.

"Black boy! Why are you always drunk?" a local gentleman would ask him.

"Master, how do you expect me not to get drunk out of satisfaction if my sausages turned out to be delicious?" Tiburcio would answer.

If he was again reproached on the following day, he would answer:

"Ay, master! Why wouldn't I get drunk out of disappointment if my sausages were a failure and tasted really bad?"

Don Jerónimo's fame as a seer had spread from the city to the country. Indian women, above all, came from afar and paid him a peso per consultation. There are fools in Lima who, in order to be like Napoleon the Great, pay four sols to a fortune teller who reads cards.

IV

Like the witches of Mahudes and Zugarramurdi in Spain, those in Cachiche, a barony, countship, or seigneury of a friend of mine, are famous. Being from Cachiche and being a witch are synonymous. No one can go to Cachiche in search of the delicious figs that that place produces without returning bewitched.

The excellent figs of its gardens also contribute to Cachiche's renown. These figs are like those of Biscay, about which it is said that in order to be good, they must have the neck of a hanged man, the clothes of a poor man, and the eye of a widow; that is to say, one end dry, a wrinkled skin, and the other end oozing tears.

Let us pursue the subject of the witches of Cachiche.

In order not to be tedious, we are going to speak only of Melchorita Zugaray, the most famous sorceress that Cachiche has had in our day.

The laboratory or workroom of this woman with many tricks up her sleeve was a room closed off with a hide over the door, and at the dark bottom of the walls there stood out a white linen cloth, onto which holes in the ceiling made for the purpose cast beams of light.

The person who came to consult with Melchora concerning an illness were taken to the laboratory, where, after certain cabalistic rituals, the witch placed him in front of the brightly lit cloth and craftily interrogated him concerning his life and habits, paying careful attention to what he had to say about his friends and enemies. She then snipped off a bit of his clothing or a lock of his hair and set a meeting time for the next day in order to *sacar muñeco.*[4] The patient would come, Melchora would take him to a field or to an animal pen and unearth a little rag doll pierced with pins. The victim would pay a goodly sum, and if he wasn't cured it was because he had had recourse to the sorceress's fund of knowledge too late.

Others, above all jealous women and scorned suitors, sought Melchora out to have her put them in close touch with the devil. The witch would dress in men's clothing, and accompanied by the person requesting her services, would make her way to a mountaintop where, among other incantations to summon the Evil One (Jesus three times!), she used the following one:

> Patatín, patatín, patatín,
> calabruz, calabruz, calabruz,
> no hay mal que no tenga fin,
> si reniego de la cruz.[5]

The devil would naturally turn a deaf ear, and the witch, who had received her pittance beforehand, would put an end to the magic spell, saying that if Bigfoot failed to appear it was because the victim was afraid or lacked faith in him.

V

Four years have not yet gone by since the tribunals of the Republic found a number of unfortunates of the province of Tarapacá guilty of

---

[4]To cast a spell by placing pins in a doll.

[5]Patatín, patatín, patatín, / calabruz, calabruz, calabruz, / there is no ill without an end, / if I deny the cross.

having burned a witch to death, and I believe that the act of burning a victim at the stake has more recently been repeated in other towns in the South.

As for Ica, one of the issues of *El Imparcial,* a newspaper published in that city in 1873, states that a poor woman of Pueblo Nuevo was tied to a tree by a man who gave her a terrible flogging as punishment for having cast a spell over him. The very same thing had happened in 1860 to Jesús Valle, an 80-year-old black slave of the former marquis and marquise of Campoameno, who had her hands full keeping the peons of a hacienda from turning her into toast.

VI

And to end my account of the witches of Ica, for this article is already longer than it should be, I shall tell why José Cabrera, known as el Chirote, won fame in Ica as a past master of sorcery.

It so happened that the spouse of a friend of his felt the first labor pains, and as the husband went in search of the midwife, el Chirote stayed behind to look after the woman. She screamed and made such a fuss that Cabrera, annoyed no end by her carrying on, gave her such a hard slap that it made her head spin round. Getting slapped and giving birth to a boy was a matter of two minutes.

The husband, the new mother, and the neighbor women called ño Cabrera a sorcerer, and even today no one calls him by his nickname of Chirote the sorcerer without his answering calmly:

"I deserve it. I got that nickname for having taken it upon myself to do a good deed."

The Royalist Smells of Death to Me

I have often heard, from the mouth of old ladies, the following catch phrase: "The royalist smells of death to me," and as I was investigating its origin I was given the following account by a respectable elderly man who had been a lieutenant in the Alejandro Imperial Regiment number 45. I need only add that a large part of his account is consistent with the historical documents that I have been able to consult.

The schoolmaster in the town of Pichigua, in the province of Aymaraes, was, in 1823, an eccentric old man who had lived in the town for almost 20 years. No one knew where he came from, for he had appeared in the town as though fallen from heaven, and obtained from the authorities ten pesos' salary a month for teaching the youngsters their abc's and Christian doctrine.

In 1823 Pichigua was a small town inhabited by 800 Indians. Today its population is barely half that. Around that time, Colonel don Tomás Barandalla appeared in the town one morning with two companies of the Alejandro Imperial Regiment, and the Indians of Pichigua, who were diehard royalists, welcomed him with enthusiastic acclaim.

Barandalla had come to Peru in 1815 as captain of the Extremadura Regiment, which at the end of that year rebelled in Lima over a question of pay, with order being restored thanks to the energy of Viceroy Abascal.[1] The viceroy punished the rebels and to restore discipline dissolved the corps, leaving only two remaining companies that served as

[1] See "Abascal's Clever Trick," note 1.—Ed.

a base for the formation of the Alejandro Imperial, of which by 1823 Barandalla was the colonel.

The latter, showing off his Burgundian-style mustachio and wearing his dress uniform, was receiving the congratulations of the principal dignitaries of Pichigua in the corridor of the house of the parish priest, don Isidro Segovia, when an old man in a threadbare cape of thick Cuzco wool halted in the doorway. Near him was a group of Indians, with their heads bared, contemplating the valiant colonel in bewilderment.

The old man stood there without doffing his hat, and looking at Barandalla with a scornful air, said to those in the group of Indians:

"The royalist smells of death to me."

And alluding to the close friendship that appeared to exist between Segovia the priest and the Spanish officer, he added:

"An abbot and a crossbowman bode ill for the Moors."

One of the colonel's spies heard him, and going over to the colonel told him of this remark. Barandalla looked toward the door, his eyes fixed on the old man, still with his hat pulled down and smiling disdainfully.

"Who is that man in the cape?" the colonel asked one of the townspeople.

"A poor devil, sir: he's the schoolmaster."

"He looks like an insurgent," Barandalla said, and turning to one of his officers he added: "Take him out and shoot him."

The priest and several dignitaries dared to unbutton their lips, pleading on behalf of the man condemned, but Barandalla stood firm. The schoolmaster put up not the slightest resistance, and allowed himself to be tied up, still murmuring:

"The royalist smells of death to me."

"The one who smells of death is this insolent old man, so much so that I'm going to have him shot," the officer interrupted him.

"Well and good!" the old man answered without batting an eye. "The fact that I smell of death doesn't keep another man from smelling too. And turning to the group of townspeople, he said in a loud voice: "My sons, it's not Barandalla who is killing me; it's the justice of God. Twenty years ago today I stabbed my wife, my mother-in-law, and my children to death in Huaylas. Let the one who is guilty pay the price, and God have mercy on my soul."

A month later in Cuzco Viceroy La Serna signed a number of promotions, and Barandalla received the rank of brigadier, perhaps as a reward for his cruel deeds. Barandalla was the one responsible for the shooting of the parish priest of the town of Reyes, in Junín. The brigadier was about to pay the devil tenfold for it.

From the day that the schoolmaster had informed him that he smelled of death, Barandalla began to suffer a strange illness that took him to his grave in 1824, shortly before the battle of Ayacucho, just a year to the day after the old man was shot.

Seventh Series

Friar Gómez's Scorpion

(To Casimiro Prieto Valdés)

> *Beginning at the beginning,*
> *I wish to begin.*
> *To see if by beginning*
> *I can begin.*[1]

In diebus illis,[2] I mean to say when I was a boy, I often heard old women exclaim, on pondering the beauty and price of a piece of jewelry:

"That's worth as much as Father Gómez's scorpion!"

I have a young daughter, as good as they come, a flower of grace and the salty froth of wit, with eyes saucier and more mischievous than a couple of notaries:

> chica que se parece
> al lucero del alba
> cuando amanece[3]

---

[1] Principio principiando; / principiar quiero / por versi si principiando / principiar puedo.
[2] In bygone days [Latin].
[3] a girl who is like / the morning star / as dawn breaks

In my paternal dotage I have nicknamed this attractive youngster of mine "Friar Gómez's little scorpion." And what I propose to do in this Tradition, my friend and comrade Prieto, is to explain the saying of the old women and the meaning of this compliment that I offer my Angélica. The tailor pays his debts with stitches, and I have no other way of satisfying the literary debt that I have contracted with you save to dedicate to you the following handwriting exercises.

I

Friar Gómez was a lay brother who was the contemporary of don Juan de la Pipirindica, he of the silver tongue, and of Saint Francis Solano. This brother lived in the monastery of the Franciscans, where he was in charge of the refectory in the infirmary or hospital. The people called him Friar Gómez, and the chronicles of the monastery and tradition know him as Friar Gómez. I believe that even in the petition for his beatification and canonization that was sent to Rome he is not given any other name.

Friar Gómez wrought miracles wholesale in my country, seemingly offhandedly and without realizing that he was performing them. He was a born miracle worker, like the man who spoke in prose without being aware that he did.

It happened that one day the lay brother was walking along the bridge when a runaway horse threw its rider to the flagstone pavement. The unfortunate man lay there senseless, with his head turned into a sieve and blood gushing from his mouth and nostrils.

"Could be a fatal blow to his head!" the crowd cried. "Somebody go to San Lázaro for the holy oils!"

And everything was confusion and a great to-do.

Friar Gómez calmly went over to the man who was lying on the ground, placed the cord of his habit on his mouth, gave him three blessings, and with no more of a doctor and nothing from an apothecary shop the man with the head injury rose to his feet as good as new.

"A miracle! A miracle! Long live Friar Gómez!" the crowd of spectators exclaimed.

And in their enthusiasm they tried to carry the lay brother off in triumph. To avoid this show of their admiration, Friar Gómez ran to his monastery and shut himself up in his cell.

The Franciscan chronicle tells of this last differently. It says that in order to escape those applauding him, Friar Gómez took to the air and flew from the bridge to the bell tower of his monastery. I neither deny this nor affirm it. It may be true and it may not. When it comes to miracles, I waste ink neither on defending them nor on refuting them.

Friar Gómez was in the mood to work miracles that day, for when he emerged from his cell he made his way to the infirmary, where he found the priest who was later to be canonized as Saint Francis Solano lying on a mat, the victim of a terrible headache. The lay brother felt his pulse and said to him:

"You are very weak, Your Paternity, and had best eat."

"Brother," the future saint answered, "I have no appetite."

"Do try, Reverend Father, to swallow just a mouthful."

And the lay brother was so insistent that in order to be free of his unreasonable demands, the sick man thought of something that would have been impossible even for the viceroy to get, since it was not the right season.

"Look here, little brother, the only thing I'd like to eat is a couple of mackerel."

Friar Gómez put his right hand up his left sleeve and took out a pair of mackerel so nice and fresh that they seemed to have just come out of the sea.

"Here they are, Your Paternity, and may they make you feel better. I'm going to cook them this minute for you."

And the fact is that with the blessed mackerel Saint Francis Solano was cured as if by magic.

It seems to me that these two little miracles with which I have incidentally occupied myself are not mere trifles. I leave in my inkwell many others wrought by our lay brother, because I don't propose to relate the story of his life and miracles.

Nonetheless, in order to satisfy curiosities that demand as much, I shall mention that over the door of the first cell of the little cloister, which even today serves as an infirmary, there is an oil painting depicting these two miracles, with the following inscription:

"The Venerable Friar Gómez.—Born in Extremadura in 1560. Took the habit in Chuquisaca in 1580.—Came to Lima in 1587.—Was a nurse for forty years, practicing all the virtues, endowed with heaven's gifts and favors. His life was a continual miracle. Died on May 2, 1631, and was reputed to be a saint. The following year his body was placed in the chapel of Aranzazú, and on October 13, 1810, was transferred to lie beneath the high altar, in the vault in which the priors of the monastery are buried. Dr. don Bartolomé de las Heras was a witness to this transfer. This venerable portrait was restored on November 30, 1882, by Master Zamudio."

II

One morning Friar Gómez was in his cell absorbed in meditation when there were discreet little taps on the door, and a plaintive voice said:

"*Deo gratias.*[4] Praised be the Lord!"

"Forever and ever, amen. Come in, little brother," Friar Gómez answered.

And there entered the most humble cell an individual dressed in tatters, the *vera efigies*[5] of a man made miserable by poverty, but in whose face there could be read the proverbial uprightness of an old Castilian.

The only pieces of furniture in the cell were four leather chairs, a grimy table, and a wooden platform with no mattress, sheets, or blankets, with a stone for a headrest or pillow.

"Be seated, brother, and tell me straightaway what brings you here," Friar Gómez said.

"It so happens, Father, that I am a good man through and through."

"So it appears, and may you continue to be one, for it will bring you peace in this life and blessedness in the next."

"And it so happens that I am a peddler, that I am burdened by a family, and that my peddling does not prosper, on account of my lack of means and not on account of any laziness or lack of effort on my part."

"I am glad, brother, for God will help a man who works honorably."

"But it so happens, Father, that up until now God has turned a deaf ear to me, and He is slow in coming to my aid."

"Don't despair, brother, don't despair."

"Well, it so happens that I have knocked on many doors asking for

[4] Thanks be to God [Latin].
[5] True figure [Latin].

500 duros, and I have found all of them locked and barred. And it so happens that last night as I was mulling things over, I said to myself: Come, Jeromo, cheer up and go ask Friar Gómez for the money, for if he so desires, a mendicant friar and poor though he is, he will find a way to get you out of the straits you're in. And so here I am because I've come, and I beg you, Your Paternity, to lend me that small amount for six months, and you may be certain that no one will say about me:

> In the world there are those who revere
>   certain saints,
> But their gratitude ends
>   along with the miracle,
> for a charitable deed
>   always brings to life
>   unknown ingrates.[6]

"How could you have imagined, my son, that you would find such a large sum in this poor cell?"

"It so happens, Father, that I wouldn't know how to answer that, but I have faith that you will not let me go off empty-handed."

"Faith will save you, brother. Wait a moment."

And looking up and down the bare whitewashed walls of the cell, Friar Gómez spied a scorpion that was walking calmly along the window frame. He thereupon tore a page out of an old book, went over to the window, carefully picked up the bug, wrapped it in the paper, and turning toward the elderly Castilian, said to him:

"Here, my good man, go pawn this little jewel, but see that you return it to me within six months."

The peddler outdid himself in expressing his thanks, took his leave of Friar Gómez, and made his way to a pawnshop as fast as his legs could carry him.

The piece of jewelry was splendid, truly fit for a Moorish queen, to say the least. It was a brooch in the shape of a scorpion. The body was formed by a magnificent emerald in a gold setting, and the head by a large diamond with two rubies for eyes.

---

[6] En el mundo hay devotos / de ciertos santos / la gratitud les dura / lo que el milagro; / que un beneficio / da siempre vida a ingratos / desconocidos.

The pawnbroker, a man who knew his business, looked covetously at the piece of jewelry, and offered to advance the man in need 2,000 duros for it, but our Spaniard insisted that he would accept only a loan for 500 duros for six months, with a usurer's rate of interest, naturally. They shook hands and the pertinent papers were signed, with the moneylender harboring the hope that later on the owner of the piece of jewelry would come back for more money, for the exorbitant interest he charged would make it impossible for the peddler to redeem the piece of jewelry and thus make him the owner of a jewel that was precious both for its intrinsic value and for its artistic worth.

And with this bit of capital the peddler's trade prospered to the point that at the end of the six months he was able to redeem the piece and returned it to Friar Gómez, wrapped in the same paper in which he had received it.

Friar Gómez took it, set it on the window sill, and gave it his blessing, saying:

"Little creature of God, go on your way."

And the scorpion proceeded to walk freely about the walls of the cell.

> Y vieja, pelleja,
> aquí dió fin la conseja.[7]

---

[7] And an old one, a bag of bones, / Here ends the tale.

Canterac's Bugler

(To Lastenia Larriva de Llona)

The battle waged by the patriot and royalist cavalries at Junín was a hard-fought one.

A single pistol shot (for at Junín no powder was wasted) and a half hour of brandishing lance and saber. A combat of centaurs more than of men.

Canterac, followed by his bugler, scoured the camp, and the bugler incessantly sounded the order to put the enemy to the sword.

That bugler seemed to have the gift of ubiquity. His bugle resounded everywhere; it was like the symbolic trumpet of the last judgment. "To the right, to the left, in the center, in the rear guard, yet again the bugle. As long as it sounded, victory was not possible. The Spanish bugler, the only one, kept victory in the balance."[1] Necochea and Miller sent several aides in different directions, their only mission being to silence that damnable bugler.

A fruitless mission. The fateful bugle sounded tirelessly, and its echoes were more and more ominous for the patriot cavalry, in whose ranks disorder was beginning to spread.

---

[1] In the original Spanish text, Palma inserts a parenthetical reference after this passage containing the name Capella Toledo. Luis Capella Toledo (1838–1896), Colombian author of *Leyendas históricas* (1879), a collection of historical legends.—Ed.

Riddled with bullet holes, Necochea fell from his horse as he said to Captain Herrán:

"Captain, let me die; but do silence that bugler first."

The royalist cavalry was gaining ground, and a sergeant Soto (a native of Lima who died in 1882 with the rank of major), took Necochea prisoner, slinging him across the rump of his charger.

It can be said that defeat was a *fait accompli*. The sun of the Incas was being eclipsed and Bolívar's star was fading.

A recently formed squadron of recruits was relegated by the general to leading a valiant charge on one flank and in the rear guard against the prideful near-winners, and the fighting was renewed. The troops, close to defeat, regrouped and mounted a spirited attack on the Spanish squadrons.

General Necochea sat up.

"Victory for the homeland!" he shouted to the platoon of royalist soldiers that was leading him away as a prisoner.

"Victory for the king!" Sergeant Soto answered.

"No!" insisted the brave Argentine. "Canterac's bugler can no longer be heard. You are defeated."

And this was in fact the case. The ever-shifting victory went to Peru, and Necochea was rescued.

"Long live the hussars of Colombia!" a leader shouted as he approached Bolívar.

"Balls!" was the answer of the liberator, who had witnessed all the events that took place during combat. "Long live the hussars of Peru!"

Captain Herrán had succeeded in taking Canterac's tireless bugler prisoner, and right there on the battlefield he presented him to Necochea as a prisoner who had surrendered. The latter, still irked by the memory of the recent vicissitudes on the battlefield or by the pain of his wounds, said laconically:

"Have him shot."

"General," Herrán remarked, interrupting him.

"Or let him become a friar," Necochea said, as though finishing the sentence.

"I'll become a friar, sir," the prisoner hastened to answer.

"Do you give me your word?" Necochea persisted.

"I do, sir."

"Well, you are free to go. Make your cape into a cassock."

Once the War of Independence was ended, Canterac's bugler took the habit of friar in Bogotá, in the convent of San Diego.

History knows him by the name of Father Tena.

The Protectress and the Liberatrix

(Historical Monographs)

I

Doña Rosa Campusano

I, the collector of traditions, must have been 13 or 14 years old, and a pupil in a preparatory school.

Among my schoolmates was a boy of the same age, the only son of don Juan Weniger, the owner of two valuable shoe stores in the calle de Plateros de San Agustín. Alejandro, for that was the name of my schoolmate, a fine young fellow who some years later died with the rank of captain in one of our disastrous civil wars, hit it off with me, and on holidays we used to get into mischief together.

Alejandro was a boarding pupil and spent Sundays at home with his father, an unsociable German in whose house, which I came by often in search of my companion, I never saw so much as the shadow of a lady's skirt. In my mind, Alejandro's mother had died.

Since no school lacks precocious sorts given to slander, in one of those set-tos frequent among schoolboys, Alejandro exchanged words with another boy, and the latter, with the air of someone hurling a crushing insult, shouted at him:

"Shut up, protector!"

Alejandro, who was a rather spirited youngster, sealed the mouth of his adversary with such a strong punch that he broke one of his teeth.

I confess that, in my semi-infantile frivolity, I didn't pay attention to the word or think it an insult. I also confess that I didn't know its meaning or import, and I even suspect that the same was true of my comrades.

"Protector! Protector!" we murmured. "Why could that have made that boy get so worked up?"

The truth was that none of us would have made a comrade spit blood over one little word. When all is said and done, each of us has the intelligence that God has given him.

One afternoon Alejandro said to me:

"Come with me, I want to introduce you to my mother."

And that was what happened. He took me to the top floor of the building in which the Biblioteca Nacional is located, the director of which, who at the time was the eminent Vigil, gave free lodging to three or four families who had fallen on hard times.

My friend's mother lived there in a two-room apartment. She was a lady nearing 50, with a very pleasant face, thin, of medium height, with an almost alabaster complexion, expressive blue eyes, a small mouth and delicate hands. Twenty years before, her beauty and grace must have made her a captivating woman who addled the brain of many a young man attempting to demonstrate his masculine charms. To walk she leaned on a crutch, hoping it would pass for a cane, and had a slight limp.

Her conversation was amusing and full of jokes popular with Limeñans, so that her way of sometimes searching for refined words struck me as affected.

Such was, in 1846 or 1847, the years when I knew her, the woman who in everyday chronicles of the era of Independence was given the nickname of the Protectress, a monograph on whom I am going to set down briefly.

*   *   *

ROSITA CAMPUSANO WAS BORN in Guayaquil in 1798. Although the daughter of a family of modest social station, her parents saw to it that she had a good education, and at 15 she danced like an Arab *almeh*, sang like a siren, and played on the harpsichord and vihuela all the songs of the musical repertory then in fashion. With these social graces, along with her personal beauty and youth, it is clear that the number of her suitors had to be like that of the stars: infinite.

The young lady was ambitious and a dreamer, which is to say that on reaching her 18 spring, rather than being the wife of a poor man who cherished her with his most heartfelt love, she preferred to be the beloved of a rich man who, out of vanity, would consider her his valuable jewel. She did not want to wear percale and a flower in her comb but instead be dressed in silk and velvet and wear a dazzling diadem of pearls and diamonds.

In 1817 Rosita arrived in Lima in the company of her lover, a wealthy Spaniard almost half a century old, whose pleasure it was to surround his beloved in all the splendors money can buy and satisfy her caprices and fancies.

Within a short time Rosita's elegant salon, on the calle de San Marcelo, was the center of gilded youth. The counts of La Vega del Ren and of San Juan de Lurigancho, the marquis of Villafuerte, the viscount of Dan Donás and other titled supporters of the revolution; Boqui, the Caracan Cortínez, Sánchez Carrión, Mariátegui, and many outstanding conspirators in favor of the cause of Independence formed Rosita's circle of intimates, and she, with the fervent enthusiasm with which women conceive a passion for any grandiose idea, became an ardent supporter of the patriots.

After San Martín[1] disembarked in Pisco, doña Rosa, who at the time had as her official lover General Domingo Tristán, began an active correspondence with the illustrious Argentine. Tristán and La Mar, who was another of the passionate lovers of the gentle lady, were still serving under the king's banner, and perhaps in the presence of the young lady they gave away political secrets that she in turn used for the benefit of the cause with which she sympathized. It was also said that Viceroy La Serna burned the incense of gallantry before the pretty young woman from Guayaquil, and that not a few secret plans of the royalists thus passed from the house of doña Rosa to the patriots' camp in Huaura.

Don Tomás Heres, the prestigious captain of the Numancia battalion, urged on by two of his friends, Oratorian priests, to join the good

---

[1] See "Three Historical Questions Concerning Pizarro," note 7.—Ed.

cause, could not make up his mind to do so. Doña Rosa's charms finally made him decide, and the Numancia, 900 troops strong, passed over to the Republican side. The cause of Spain in Peru suffered a mortal blow from that moment on.

In a revolution that, at the beginning of 1821, was to be headed by the commandant of the Cantabria battalion in the fortress of Callao, it was doña Rosa who was entrusted with placing this leader in contact with the patriots. But Santalla,[2] a brute of such herculean strength that he could bend a gold peso in two with only three fingers, repented at that very moment and broke with his friends, giving the plot away to the viceroy, although he was chivalrous enough not to betray any of those involved.

San Martín, in this respect unlike his minister Monteagudo and Bolívar the Liberator, gave no cause for scandal in Lima because of his love-adventures.[3] His relations with Rosita remained a secret. He was never seen in public with his beloved, but since nothing under the sun remains hidden, something must have gotten out, and the heroine was known by the nickname of the Protectress.[4]

The Order of the Sun[5] having already been organized, San Martín, by a decree of January 11, 1822, created 112 secular dames of honor and 32 who were nuns, chosen from among the most notable of the 13 monasteries of Lima. Among the former were the countesses of San Isidro and La Vega and the marquises of Torre-Tagle, Casa-Boza, Castellón, and Casa Muñoz.

The traveler Stevenson, the secretary of Lord Cochrane who as such shared the ill will of his chief against San Martín, criticizes in Volume III of his curious and entertaining work, printed in London in 1829, *Historical and descriptive narrative of twenty years' residence in South America,* the fact that the protector had invested his favorite, doña Rosita, with the bicolor sash (white and red), the emblem of the dames of honor. This sash bore the following inscription in gold letters: *To the*

---

[2] Santalla also appears in "Don Alonso the Brawny."—Ed.

[3] For an account of Bolívar's "love-adventures," see "The Liberator's Three Etceteras."—Ed.

[4] After seizing Lima in 1821 in the War of Independence, San Martín became Protector of Peru.—Ed.

[5] An award for patriotism instituted by San Martín during his Peruvian government.—Ed.

patriotism of the most sensitive of ladies. It seems to me that in the early days of Independence sensitivity was very much in fashion.

Without discoursing on the suitability or unsuitability of the creation of an antidemocratic Order, and keeping solely to the known facts, I find Stevenson's criticism unfair. It is certain that to no other of the dames of honor did the cause of Independence owe services of such magnitude as those lent it by doña Rosa. In the hour of recompense and honors it was impermissible to wrong her by ungrateful oblivion.

With the withdrawal of San Martín from public life doña Rosa Campusano's star was also eclipsed. With Bolívar another feminine star was to shine brightly.

Later on, when the years and perhaps disappointments as well had faded the woman's charms and caused her to live in straitened circumstances, the Congress of Peru awarded the dame of honor of the Order of the Sun a modest pension.

The Protectress died, in Lima, somewhere between the years 1858 and 1860.

II

Doña Manuela Saenz

The port of Paita, around the year 1859, when I was paymaster aboard the corvette *Loa,* was not, despite the gentleness of the waters of its bay and excellent sanitary conditions, a very promising station for navy officers. There was very little chance to form decorous ties with families. On the other hand, for the rough sailor, Paita, with its barrio of Maintope, with every other doorway frequented by female providers of hospitality (cheap at the moment, very expensive later on because of the consequences), was another paradise of Mohammed, complemented by the nauseatingly bad stews of the inn or cheap eating house of don José Chepito, a personage of immortal renown in Paita.

I can say about myself that I seldom disembarked, preferring to remain aboard ship with a book or the jovial chat of my shipmates for diversion.

One afternoon, in the company of a young Frenchman who was a shop assistant, I went for a stroll along streets that were veritable sand pits. My companion halted near the church and said to me:

"Would you like, don Ricardo, to make the acquaintance of the very best thing there is in Paita? I take it upon myself to present you and I assure you that you'll be well received."

It occurred to me that he was going to introduce me to a pretty girl, and since at 23[6] the soul is frolicsome and the body asks for nothing better than a good time, I answered without hesitating:

"Blessings be on such as we, Frenchie. Come what may, let's not stray."

"Well then, *en route, mon cher.*"

We went on for half a block, and my *cicerone* stopped at the door of a modest-looking little house. Once inside, the pieces of furniture in the parlor were all equally shabby. They consisted of a broad leather chair with wheels and a push bar, and next to it an oak bench with cushions upholstered in linen, a large square table in the middle of the room, a dozen chairs with rush seats, some of which cried out for immediate replacement, and at one end, a rough sideboard with dishes and eating utensils, and at the other a comfortable hammock from Guayaquil.

In the wheelchair, with the majesty of a queen on her throne, was an elderly lady who seemed to me to be 60 at most. She was dressed poorly but neatly, and one could easily guess that that body had worn grosgrain, satin, and velvet in better days.

She was a plump woman, with very lively black eyes, in which the remains of the vital fire still left to her seemed concentrated, a round face and aristocratic hands.

"Doña Manuela, I would like to introduce to you this young man, a sailor and a poet, because I know that you will be pleased to speak with him of poetry."

"Welcome, señor poet, to this poor house of yours," the elderly lady replied, addressing me in a distinguished tone of voice that caused me to surmise that the lady had lived in a high social sphere.

And with a gesture full of a politeness that came naturally, she bade me be seated.

Our conversation on that afternoon was strictly formal. In the lady's accent there was a trace of the superior woman accustomed to take command and impose her will. She was a perfect example of the

[6] In 1859, Palma was 26, not 23.—Ed.

haughty woman. Her speech was fluent, correct, and not at all presumptuous, with irony the dominant note in it.

From that afternoon on, I found in Paita an attraction, and I never left ship without spending an enjoyable hour of delightful conversation with doña Manuela Sáenz. I remember too that almost always she served me sweets, made herself in a little iron brazier that she had placed next to her wheelchair.

The poor lady had been crippled for many years. A faithful servant dressed and undressed her, seated her in the wheelchair, and brought her to the little parlor.

When I led the conversation around to historical reminiscences, when I tried to obtain from doña Manuela confidences about Bolívar and Sucre, San Martín and Monteagudo, or other personages whom she had known and dealt with on equal terms, she cleverly avoided answering. Looking backward was not to her liking, and I even suspect that she deliberately shied away from ever talking about the past.

Ever since doña Manuela had settled in Paita, in 1850 if memory serves me, every passenger of some note or importance who was traveling by steamship, either heading for Europe or coming from it, disembarked motivated by the desire to know the lady who had managed to capture the heart of Bolívar.[7] In the beginning doña Manuela was pleased to welcome visitors, but she soon realized that she was the object of impertinent curiosity and resolved to receive only those persons who were introduced to her by her close friends.

Let us sketch now the biography of our friend.

Doña Manuela Sáenz, a member of a prominent family, was born in Quito in the final years of the last century, and was educated in a convent of nuns in her native city. She was two or three years older than her compatriot, Rosita Campusano, a native of Guayaquil. In 1817 she married don Jaime Thorne, an English physician, who a few years later came with his wife to live in Lima.

I cannot specify the exact date when, after the marriage ties were broken for reasons that I have not endeavored to ascertain, doña Man-

---

[7] Manuela Sáenz's visitors at Paita included Simón Rodríguez, the Jacobin pedagogue who had been Bolívar's childhood tutor, the North American novelist Herman Melville, and Guiseppe Garibaldi (for the latter, see "Between Garibaldi . . . and Me").—Ed.

uela returned to Quito, but it must have been toward the end of 1822, for among the 12 dames of the Order of the Sun was señora Sáenz de Thorne, who undoubtedly was one of the most impassioned patriots, figures on the list.

After the victory of Pichincha, won by Sucre in May of 1822, the Liberator arrived in Quito, and at this time there began his amorous relations with the beautiful Manuelita, the only woman who, after becoming his lover, managed to dominate the sensual and fickle Bolívar.

During the Liberator's first year in Peru, doña Manuela remained in Ecuador, completely involved in politics. It was then that, lance at the ready and at the head of a cavalry squad, she put down an uprising in the main square and streets of Quito.

Shortly before the battle of Ayacucho doña Manuela joined the Liberator, who was in Huaura.

All the generals of the army, including Sucre, and the most prominent men of the era honored Manuela with the same attentions that they would have paid the lawfully married wife of the Liberator. The ladies were unanimously disdainful of the favorite, and she, for her part, did nothing to win the sympathies of the creatures of her sex.

When Bolívar returned to Colombia doña Manuela remained behind in Lima, but when the revolution headed by Bustamante to protest against awarding Bolívar the presidency for life broke out in the Colombia division, a revolution that echoed throughout Peru, doña Manuela made her way inside one of the barracks disguised as a man, with the aim of getting a battalion to fight back. When her attempt failed, the new government notified her to leave the country, and doña Manuela set out to join Bolívar in Bogota. There Bolívar and his favorite lived together as though they were man and wife, and Bogota society had to turn a blind eye to this scandalous behavior. The lady from Quito lived in the governor's palace with her lover.

Providence reserved for her the role of savior of the life of the Liberator, for on the night when the Septembrists stormed the place,[8] she obliged Bolívar to escape by letting himself down from a balcony, and

---

[8] On September 25, 1828, in Bogotá, Bolívar narrowly escaped an assassination attempt by conspirators who considered him a tyrant. Manuela Sáenz delayed the would-be assassins in their bedroom.—Ed.

seeing him safe in the street, confronted the would-be murderers, detaining them and putting them on the wrong track in order to gain time and allow her lover to leave the scene of the encounter.[9]

Generous-hearted in the extreme, doña Manuela persuaded Bolívar to commute to exile the death sentence that had been imposed by the court-martial on, among other revolutionaries, two that had heaped the most insults on her. Bolívar resisted doing as she wished, but his beloved adamantly insisted and two lives were pardoned. Never did a favorite better use her influence to further a most noble action!

Many years after the death of Bolívar in December of 1830, the Congress of Peru (and by that I also mean one of the three governments of Colombia at the time) awarded a life pension to the Liberatrix, a nickname by which doña Manuela is known even in contemporary history. What is more, even in her old age she did not take offense at being called that, and on several occasions I saw arrive at her house people who, like a person asking the most natural and simple question, said: "Does the Liberatrix live here?" Doña Manuela would smile faintly and answer: "Come in. What do you want of the Liberatrix?"

What reasons did Bolívar's beloved have for coming to settle and to die in one of what was at the time one of the most dismal places in Peru? The poor cripple said to me, one day when I ventured to put the question to her, that she had chosen Paita on the advice of a doctor, who was of the opinion that with sand baths the sick woman's nerves would recover the pliancy they had lost. Someone has written that it was out of pride that doña Manuela refused to live in large cities where she had been admired as a dazzling star: She was afraid of leaving herself open to vengeful snubs.

When doña Manuela came to live in Paita, her husband, doctor Jaime Thorne, had died an unfortunate death. Thorne, the associate of a certain señor Escobar, worked on the hacienda of Huayto, over the ownership of which he had a stormy running legal battle with Colonel Justo Hercelles, who also claimed rights to the property as part of his

---

[9] Don Florentino González, one of the leaders of the conspirators writes: "There came out to meet us a beautiful lady, sword in hand, and with admirable presence of mind asked me what we wanted. One of our men made threats against the lady, and I refused to carry them out." [Author's note.]

inheritance from his mother. One afternoon in 1840 or 1841 when Thorne, arm in arm with a pretty girl who may have been consoling him for doña Manuela's infidelities, not long past, was strolling along one of the paths on the hacienda, three masked men flung themselves on him and stabbed him to death. Rumor (that often is wrong) held Hercelles guilty of having been behind the unknown assassins. Hercelles also met a tragic end a year or two later, for as the leader of a revolution against the government of President General Vidal, he was shot by a firing squad in Huaraz.

III

The Protectress and the Liberatrix

I, who had the good fortune to know and spend time with both San Martín's favorite and Bolívar's, can testify to major differences between the two. Physically and temperamentally they were opposites.

In doña Rosa I saw woman in all her delicacy of feeling and the weaknesses typical of her sex. In Rosa's heart there was a store of tears and tender affections, and God allowed her to know the joy of motherhood, which He denied to Manuela.

Doña Manuela was a mistake of nature, for in sculpturally feminine lineaments she embodied a masculine spirit and aspirations. It was not her way to shed tears; instead she flew into a rage like a hard-hearted man.

The Protectress loved her home and the luxurious life of the city, and the Liberatrix found herself at ease in the midst of the turbulence of the barracks and the camp. The former never went for outings except in a calash. The latter was seen in the streets of Quito and Lima mounted like a man on a spirited steed, escorted by two Colombian lancers and wearing a red dolman with gold frogs and white cotton balloon pants.

Doña Manuela denied her sex, whereas doña Rosa was proud to be a woman. The latter took care to dress in fashion and the other dressed in the taste of her dressmaker. Doña Manuela always wore two gold or coral hoops as earrings, and doña Rosa was dazzling in her profusion of fine jewels.

The first, educated by nuns amid the austerity of a cloister, was a free thinker. The second, who spent her childhood amid social agitation, was a devout believer.

Doña Manuela kept her nerves under control, remaining calm and energetic in the midst of bullets and at the head of lancers and swordsmen bathed in blood or facing the sharp dagger of assassins. Doña Rosa knew how to faint or swoon, like all those precious and vain creatures of the fair sex who dress from the head down,[10] when confronted with the hooting of an owl or the scurrying of a frightened mouse.

Doña Rosa perfumed her handkerchief with the most exquisite English fragrances. Doña Manuela used mannish verbena water.

Even in their literary taste they were total opposites.

When absolutism was restored and with it the Inquisition, because stupid drunken mobs in Madrid surrounded the carriage in which Ferdinand VII was parading, shouting "Long live the King!" "Long live chains!" whereupon the monarch sarcastically answered them: "Do you want chains, sons? Well, don't worry, they'll be yours for the asking," the name of doña Rosa Campusano figured in the secret registry of the Holy Office of Lima as a reader of Heloise and Abelard and of pornographic books. There was a flood of such books in Lima around that year, and the persecution that the fathers of families undertook so that they would not be introduced into the home caused even religious bigots to overindulge in reading so as to have something to tell their confessor during Lent.

The courtly Arriaza and the gentle Meléndez were the poets that Rosita read.[11]

What a contrast to the tastes of Manuela! She read Tacitus and Plutarch; she studied the history of the Peninsula by Father Mariana and that of America by Solís and Garcilaso; she was a passionate admirer of Cervantes, and for her there were no poets outside of Cienfuegos, Quintana, and Olmedo.[12] She knew by heart the *Canto a*

---

[10] As opposed to men (except for clerics), who dress by pulling their trousers up over their feet.

[11] Juan Bautista Arriaza (1770–1837) and Juan Meléndez Valdés (1754–1817).—Ed.

[12] Juan de Mariana (1536–1624); Antonio de Solís (1610–1686); El Inca Garcilaso de la Vega (see "Don Alonso the Brawny," note 3); Nicasio Alvarez Cienfuegos (1764–1809);

Junín[13] and whole parliamentary speeches of Pelayo, and her eyes, a bit puffy from the weight of the years now, sparkled with enthusiasm on reciting the verses of her favorite poets. In the days when I knew her, one of her favorite readings was the fine poetic translation of the Psalms by the Peruvian Valdés.[14] Doña Manuela was beginning to experience flashes of asceticism, and her earlier traces of rationalism had evaporated.

Rosa Campusano was decidedly a woman through and through, and without scruples; had I been young in her days of graciousness and elegance, I would have enrolled in the list of her . . . platonic lovers. Doña Manuela, even in the days when she was a beauty, would have inspired in me only the respectful feeling of friendship that I professed for her in her old age.

Doña Rosa was a womanly woman.

Doña Manuela was a manly woman.

Manuel José Quintana (1772–1857); José Joaquín Olmedo (see "The Christ in Agony," note 3).—Ed.

[13] See "The Christ in Agony," note 3.—Ed.

[14] José Manuel Valdés (1767–1843), author of *Salterio peruano o parafrasis de los ciento cincuenta Salmos de David, y de algunos cánticos sagrados en verso castellano: para instrucción y piadoso ejercicio de todos los fieles y principalmente de los peruanos* (1833).—Ed.

The King of the Camanejos[1]

(To José María Zuviria, in Buenos Aires)

The sacristy of the church of La Merced, in Arequipa, has two rooms: one in which the friars don vestments to celebrate Mass, which differs little or not at all from that of any monastery in Christendom; and the other, which might be called the antesacristy and is the only passageway between the church and the monastery.

Like the rest of the building, the sacristy is made of stone masonry. In the center of its vault there is a clerestory, identical to the one in the Penitentiary of San Pedro in Lima, and near it a hole through which there passes the rope of the church bell by which the faithful are summoned to Mass.

The furniture is scarcely deserving of notice, since it is limited to a rough wooden bench and two confessionals of the same sort.

Hanging on the walls are several oil paintings, but so old and so badly preserved that anyone who proposed to describe what they represent would have a hard time of it.

One of these paintings, which hangs over the door leading down to the monastery, and the only one halfway preserved, represents a friar dressed in the liturgical garments for saying Mass, with his arms outstretched as though pleading for help. On the crown of his head he

---

[1] A play on words. He is not only the king of Camaná, but the king of fools.

has a wound from which blood is pouring, and there are bloodstains from it on his chasuble and on the floor. It would appear that the scene began on an altar that can be seen on the right, on which there can be discerned an open missal on a lectern, a paten, a communion cloth, and a candle, which indicate that the friar had been celebrating the Holy Sacrifice when he was attacked by another person who can be seen a short distance away, dealing the friar blows with a chalice that he is holding in his hand. This individual is a gentleman dressed in calf-length breeches, clocked hose, shoes with steel buckles, and a flowing cape of Segovia worsted.

Having concluded this indispensable preamble, we proceed to the Tradition that explains this emblematic canvas. Onward to the sea, water!

I

Until the year 1823 there ate bread in the city of Misti a hidalgo named don Pedro Pablo Rosel, born in Arequipa and the son of a Spaniard of high social standing and a woman of the Arequipan aristocracy.

This fellow, who had received the sort of careful education that in those days was given to a boy of good lineage, and who could discourse with sound reasoning on any subject, would have passed for a man of outstanding ability and good sense had not the following foolishness escaped him from time to time:

"I am not a nobody, do all of you agree?"

"Who doubts it, señor Rosel?" one of the members of his social circle would answer.

"I'll have you know, my friend," don Pablo continued, "that you are speaking to no less a personage than the prince who is heir to the throne of Camaná; but those crafty Rosel *zambos*[2] (which is how he described his relatives) stole me from the palace when I was a baby, bribing the matrons of honor, the ladies-in-waiting, and the maids of honor of my mother the queen, and brought me to Arequipa."

"And how did Your Majesty come to discover such a villainous act?"

"Through a revelation from the archangel Saint Michael, who on

---

[2] Individuals of mixed black and Indian blood.

three occasions appeared to me and told me all the details, from A to Z. But I shall soon drive the usurper from the throne, and those Rosel *zambos* will see what's what."

We have said that aside from his madness don Pedro Pablo acted with good sense that sane men would envy, for he had good ideas when it came to his business undertakings and agriculture, and his hacienda fared wondrously well.

In order not to lower himself by rubbing elbows with anybody and everybody to the detriment of his royal dignity, don Pedro Pablo allowed himself to be seen only rarely in the streets of Arequipa. In his home and in his intimate circle he received only half a dozen friends, to whom he had given his word that they would be future ministers of his kingdom, and Friar Francisco Virrueta, of the Mercedarian order, the presumptive archbishop of Camaná. All of them agreed with everything the gentle madman said, discussed with him a plan for his hacienda by virtue of which the olives of Camaná would be worth their weight in silver, and talked neither more nor less nonsense than if they had been in congress drafting laws or members of the real Council of Ministers.

Regina, for that was the name of don Pedro Pablo's only daughter, a girl so sober and serious minded that she seemed to have an old woman inside her, received the members of His Majesty's nighttime circle of friends with delicious cups of chocolate and buns. The young princess knew how to do the honors of a palace.

Father Virrueta was in the habit of saying Mass at five in the morning in the church of La Merced, and among the few who attended it don Pedro Pablo was often to be found; on various occasions he served as acolyte, for His Majesty of Camaná was a devout man and one respectful of the Church, even though, like Louis XI and Philip II, he maintained that monarchs, while greatly respecting the Pontiff, ought not to give an inch where matters of patronage were concerned.

On one of those mornings the gentle madman had awakened in a bad mood.

Biting his lips to contain his anger, he put up with the priest's consuming the Host without asking his permission when, in his opinion, this was absolutely necessary when the Eucharist was celebrated in the presence of the monarch; but on seeing that the officiant was about to drink the *sanguis*,[3] with the same lack of respect and to the detriment of royal prerogatives, he snatched the chalice from Father Virrueta, and fetching him such a tremendous blow on his head that he almost split it in two, shouted at him in a rage:

"I will not tolerate this from you, you ill-bred friar! I allowed you to consume the Host without my leave, believing that you didn't ask for my permission because you were absent minded; but you wickedly drank the *sanguis* as well, and so I am punishing you. Take this, you dolt of a friar!"

And overcome with rage, the madman went on dealing the friar more blows, which the latter had no way of escaping save to take to his heels. Fortunately for him, his pursuer became entangled in the chain dangling from the bell of an altar and fell down, a circumstance that the other priests assisting at Mass took advantage of to overpower His Camanejan Majesty and tie him up with his two elbows behind his back.

As was only natural, what had happened caused a great stir in Arequipa, not only because of the Mercedarian friar's bashed head but also because of the irregularity into which the church had fallen because of the *sanguis* spilled on the floor. As theologians and canon lawyers were reaching an agreement with the ecclesiastic authority for the ritual rehabilitation of the church, it remained closed for several months. After the requisite sprinklings of holy water, the Latin phrases and plain song, the ringing and pealing of bells that followed, everything that had previously taken place inside the church was pronounced null and void and the floor of the desecrated church clean and purified.

Once there was an end to these purification rites, in which Father Virrueta was the principal figure, the community of monks agreed, by unanimous vote, to have a picture painted to commemorate what had happened and and have it hung near the altar. But Father Virrueta took more of a dislike for the above-mentioned painting than Sancho Panza for the blanket he was tossed in, and ordered it to be moved to the sacristy, where it doubtless will hang for a long time still, since it has now resisted more than half a century without suffering damage from

[3] The blood of Christ when the Eucharist is celebrated.

earthquakes, fires, and cloudbursts. Even the moths and mice are afraid of it and won't come near it.

II

As is only to be expected, Rosel's madness obliged the family to take measures, not only to avoid conflicts later on, but also to cure him, if there existed such a possibility within the powers of science. But despite the doctors, the madman went from bad to worse, his violence becoming a permanent danger to neighbors and kinfolk. Only his daughter Regina, who was not a high-strung young lady who was easily frightened, had some control over him.

As a last resort, the family decided to take don Pedro Pablo to a little country house that the madman owned in the vicinity of San Isidro, a mile from the city. But inasmuch as Regina refused to have her father transported there in a cage, authorities, relatives, and doctors had to plot together to come up with a scheme in which violence, severity, or a straitjacket played no part.

One morning a lieutenant of royal musketeers, accompanied by six splendidly mounted soldiers in full parade dress, came to Rosel's house. Once ceremonious genuflections and the proffering of polite phrases were over, the soldier said to Pedro Pablo:

"Your Majesty, I come as an envoy from your loyal vassals of Camaná to call to your august attention the fact that the throne is vacant, and that all of them are moaning and sighing for you to appear as soon as possible and free the land from ambitious men and usurpers who are fighting over the crown. If it should be your sacred and royal will to set out this minute, I offer you a magnificent, gallant escort."

Offering his hand for the emissary to kiss, the king answered:

"Arise, Marquis of Good News, for I wish to reward you for your fidelity to your sovereign. My kingdom summons me, and I will swiftly answer its call. We will set out after delighting our stomachs. Regina, lunch."

At the table the brand-new marquis had a good deal to say as he told of the enthusasm of the Camanejos for their monarch, a description that the latter listened to with an air of "it is only my just due."

"We shall see how to make those poor devils happy," the good-natured smile of His Majesty don Pedro Pablo I seemed to say.

On leaving the patio, one of the soldiers, kneeling ceremoniously, presented him with a horse in splendid trappings. As he placed the royal foot in the stirrup, the monarch asked him:

"What is your name?"

"Marcos Quispe Condorí *taitay*,"[4] answered the soldier, an uneducated Indian from the highlands.

"Well, you shall share in the distribution of my royal rewards, Marcos Quispe Condorí. I make you from today on a Knight of the Golden Spur, free of all tribute and tax."

"May God repay you, *taitay*."

And the retinue set out on the Way of the Cross to Calvary.

They were within a block of reaching the little country house when some 20 men armed with shotguns and rusty sabers suddenly appeared, shouting "Death to the king!"

The Marquis of Good News and his six horsemen flung themselves on the rebels with the battle cry "Long live the king!" and the latter answered with shotgun fire. The scuffle appeared to be in earnest.

And what do you think His Majesty did? Well, sirs, he had the good sense and the nobleness of spirit (that sane leaders of old never had) to take out his white handkerchief and cry out in a voice fraught with emotion:

"I surrender, my sons, let blood not be spilled on my account."

Decidedly, only a madman is capable of such self-sacrifice.

The victors seized don Pedro Pablo and shut him up in a room after tethering him by the right leg by means of a chain fastened to an iron ring in the wall.

Regina accompanied her poor father in his captivity. Probably the loss of the battle (and along with it dethronement and imprisonment) had a favorable effect on Rosel's nervous system, for his fits of rage abated, his inoffensive madness again demanding nothing save that he be treated with the consideration owed a king in disgrace. One thing more: Seated in his leather armchair, he received his tenants, with whom, after settling accounts, he spoke sensibly about irrigation and sowing. His friends the former ministers also came to visit him in their spare time, a marvel that no man fallen from power can boast of. In

---

[4] Variant of *taitai*. See note 6 "A Letter Sings."

the season for ripe figs friends abound, but in rough times they never come round.

Only Father Virrueta bore the madman who had almost beat his brains out an ill will that was permanent. His Paternity was hard hearted.

It was believed that in his last illness Rosel had come to his senses once more, for he no longer insisted that he be addressed as Your Majesty and protested against such madness. His doctor and his confessor, convinced that the dying man was in his right mind, agreed that the Viaticum, a sacrament that don Pedro Pablo urgently requested, be administered. So they brought the holy oils, accompanied by half of Arequipa, for don Pedro was obliging, honored, and much loved. But on hearing the music and the little bell, the sick man asked what the noise was, and the confessor answered that it was the Divine Majesty, coming to see him off to eternity. Rosel remained lost in thought for a time, and then, in a voice already muffled by his approaching death, he murmured, as though to himself:

"Very well! Show Him in. Two Majesties will meet."

With such clear proof that Rosel's madness persisted, the reader will not be surprised to learn that the parish priest left without administering the last rites.

Since neither *El Comercio* nor any other newspaper existed as yet in 1823, I have not been able to find out whether the king of the Camanejos rightfully received funeral honors from his subjects.

Eighth Series

Friar Martín's Mice

> *Y comieron en un plato*
> *perro, pericote y gato.*[1]

With this couplet there ends an account of virtues and miracles that circulated as a broadsheet in Lima around the year 1840, on the occasion of the celebration, in our capital of religion and culture, of solemn ceremonies honoring the beatification of Friar Martín de Porres.

This holy man was born in Lima on December 9, 1579, the natural son of the Spaniard don Juan de Porres, a knight of the Order of Alcántara, and a slave woman from Panama. While Martincito was still a youngster, his father took him to Guayaquil, where he learned to read and write in a school whose schoolmaster made liberal use of the rod. Two or three years later his father returned with him to Lima and set him to learning the useful occupation of barber and bloodletter, in the shop of a barber on the calle de Malambo.

Martín disliked using the razor and the lancet, although he eventually became skilled at handling them, and chose instead the career of saint, which in those days was a profession like any other. At the age of 21 he took the habit of lay brother or *donado* in the monastery of the

[1] And there ate out of the same dish / dog, mouse and cat.

Dominicans, where he died on November 3, 1639, in the odor of sanctity.

Our countryman Martín de Porres, during his life and after his death, wrought miracles wholesale. He worked miracles with the same ease as others write verses. One of his biographers (I don't recall whether it was Father Manrique or Dr. Valdés) says that the prior of the Dominicans had to order him to stop "miracling" (forgive me for this verb). And as proof of how deeply rooted the spirit of obedience was in this servant of God, he tells how, just at the moment that Friar Martín was walking past a scaffolding, a bricklayer fell from a height of some 25 or 30 feet, and our lay brother stopped him halfway down, shouting: "Wait there a minute, brother!" And the bricklayer hung suspended in midair until Martín returned, with the superior's permission. Quite a good miracle, wouldn't you say? Well, where there's a good one, there's one better.

The prior ordered the miracle-working lay brother to buy a sugarloaf for the infirmary. Perhaps he did not give him the money needed to procure a loaf of white, refined sugar, and Fray Martín came back with a loaf of unrefined.

"Don't you have eyes, brother?" the superior said to him. "Didn't you see by the color of it that it looks more like brown sugar than refined?"

"Don't be vexed, Your Paternity," the lay brother in charge of the infirmary answered imperturbably. "I'll wash it this minute and everything will be put right."

And without giving the prior time to argue with him, he placed the sugarloaf in the water of the baptismal font and it came out white and dry.

So then! Don't make me laugh, for I've one lip that's cracked.

Believe it or not. But let it be clearly understood that I am not putting a dagger to my reader's breast to make him believe. Freedom has to be free, as a journalist from my country once said. And I note here that I intended only to speak of the mice under Friar Martín's jurisdiction, so the saint is escaping me and is on his way to heaven. An end to this introduction and on to the point of the story, the mice I mean.

Friar Martín de Porres had a special liking for mice, bothersome guests that came to us almost at the same time as the conquest, for up until the year 1552 these beasties were unknown in Peru. They arrived from Spain in one of the ships that a certain don Gutierre, bishop of Palencia, sent to our ports with a shipload of cod. Our Indians baptized the mice with the name of *hucuchas,* which means "come from the sea."

In Martín's barbering days, a mouse was still almost a curiosity, for relatively speaking, the rodent family had only just begun to multiply. Perhaps it was from that time on that he grew fond of the little rodents, seeing in them the handiwork of the Lord, and it may be imagined that, making a comparison between his person and that of these little creatures, he said what a poet has said:

> El mismo tiempo malgastó en mí Dios
> que en hacer un ratón, o lo más dos.[2]

When our Martín was fulfilling the functions of lay brother in charge of the infirmary, the mice made camp like Moors without an overlord in cells, kitchen, and refectory. Cats, which had been introduced into Peru in 1537, were rare in the city. It is a proven historical fact that the first cats were brought to Peru by a Spanish soldier named Montenegro, who sold one in Cuzco to don Diego de Almagro the elder for 200 pesos.

Growing tired of the invasion of mice, the friars invented different sorts of traps to catch them, with little success. Friar Martín too placed a mouse trap in the infirmary, and an inexperienced little mouse, attracted by the smell of the cheese, got itself caught in it. Friar Martín freed it, and placing it in the palm of his hand, said to it:

"Be off with you, little brother, and tell your comrades not to be a bother or do harm in the cells. Tell them to go live in the kitchen garden, and I will take care to bring them food each day."

The mouse ambassador fulfilled its mission, and from that moment on the mouse population abandoned the cloister and moved out to the garden. Martín naturally visited them every morning, taking them a basketful of kitchen scraps or leftovers, and the mice came running as though they had been summoned by a bell.

Our good Fray Martín kept a dog and a cat in his cell, and had managed to make both animals live in brotherly harmony, to the point that they ate out of the same bowl or dish.

---

[2] God wasted the same time in making me / as in making a mouse, or at most two.

He was watching them eat in peaceful concord one afternoon, when suddenly the dog growled and the cat bristled. This was because a mouse, attracted by the odor of the meat in the dish, had dared poke its nose out of its hole. Fray Martín spied it, and turning toward the dog and cat, said to them:

"Calm yourselves, you creatures of the Lord, calm yourselves."

He immediately went over to the hole in the wall and said:

"It is safe to come out, brother mouse. It appears that you'd like to eat. Come closer, they won't harm you."

And turning to the other two animals he added:

"Come, you two, leave a place for a guest, for God will provide for the three of you."

And the mouse, without being asked twice, accepted the invitation, and from that day on ate in the love and fellowship of dog and cat.

And ... and ... and ... isn't this story all stuff and nonsense? No, of course not!

Two Excommunications

B lessed be the nineteenth century, in which the principle of equality before the law is dogma, with no talk of laws or privileges.

The fact that dogma is frequently proven false in practice is none of my business. It is always a consolation to know that it exists in written form and that we are exercising our right when we loudly protest against the arbitrary acts of those in power.

This nonsense has come to mind and to my pen on taking as my subject the conflicts in which, in the middle of the last century don Nicolás de Boza y Solís, the mayor of Huamanga, found himself involved. I shall proceed to tell of them.

Next door to the residence of the bishop don Alfonso López Roldán, who was a dissenter without equal, was a tavern with a private door leading to the courtyard of His Reverence. The owner of the tavern was a Catalan, who answered to Cachufeiro, his name or his nickname of Fierceface, I don't know which, an ill-tempered man if ever there was one.

The occupation of tavern keeper, in which one easily made money, was a privilege; according to a royal warrant issued in Peru in the era of the viceroy and count of Chinchón, only Spaniards from Spain were allowed to run a tavern. Furthermore, the number of them was limited to 1 per block in Lima, to 30 in Arequipa and Cuzco, to 15 in Trujillo, and to 12 in towns like Huamanga. A tavern keeper was thus almost a dignitary.

As a measure to keep the peace, the mayor had ordered that no tavern be open after curfew, because when those fond of the juice of the vine congregated they caused scandal and a commotion, upsetting the peace-loving neighborhood. Cachufeiro paid no attention whatsoever to the edict nor to the repeated warnings of the constables, and kept his establishment open until whatever hour he felt like closing. His Lordship's temper finally reached the boiling point, for he made the rounds of the town after ten at night, and the insolent tavern keeper was taken to jail.

On being notified of the jailing of his neighbor, the bishop called for him to be set free, for the tavern, as he understood the law to read, enjoyed the same exemption from curfew as the episcopal residence. The mayor answered the note the bishop sent him by refusing, in respectful terms, to accede, arguing that a tavern with a door to the street was under the immediate jurisdiction of the civil authority, without the private door that led to or communicated with the bishop's courtyard and diocesan residence being taken into consideration. And to show his respect for His Reverence, the mayor had the scribe of the town council go in person to deliver his note and also give the bishop other satisfactory explanations verbally.

Don López Roldán had, as we have said, a hot temper, and after reading the note, he said in a rage to the scribe:

"Go back, you rotter of a rogue, and tell that bamboozling mayor that if he hasn't freed my neighbor within an hour, I shall proclaim him to be under major excommunication. Go."

It burned the scribe like Spanish fly, though he had neither eaten it or drunk it, to hear himself called not simply a rogue, but a rotter of a rogue, which is the worst of insults, and he answered:

"Allow me to say to Your Reverence that I haven't given him any reason to insult me."

"Be quiet, you heretical scoundrel, and clear out of here"—the bishop interrupted him, raising his fists—"before I excommunicate you too for talking back to me."

And the scribe turned on his heels and made his escape.

Can you believe that the mayor of Huamanga, don Nicolás de Boza y Solís, trembled like a leaf as he let the prisoner go? Well, it happened just that way.

The worst of it was that he was fool enough to write to Lima, passing on all the details of the affair to the marquis of Castellfuerte,[1] the hard-hearted and touchy viceroy.

"What! An exemption for taverns? Do we have such a thing? We must keep a tight rein on that bishop and give that half-witted mayor a severe reprimand," the viceroy exclaimed.

And convoking the Royal Tribunal, the case of Bishop Roldán was tried. The trial lasted two years and ended with the bishop losing out to the civil authority.

When Boza y Solís read the dressing down the viceroy had sent him in answer to his report, he murmured:

"Now I've gone and done it! It was damned if I do and damned if I don't."

II

As for tight spots, that is what, around the year 1640, the grandson of the conquistador Jerónimo de Aliaga found himself in.

It so happened that having married doña Juana de Esquivel, the latter brought him as her dowry 50,000 good hard pesos, not to mention valuable properties, in the city and in the countryside, that she would no doubt inherit as the only daughter of parents who were both old and rich. After 12 years of marriage, doña Juana died without offspring, and in her will she bequeathed her entire fortune to her husband, with no further encumbrances than that of establishing, with the 50,000 pesos of her dowry, a benefice for a dignitary of the canons of the archbishopric of Lima.

But months and months went by without don Juan giving a thought to the matter of the benefice, until those interested in it had recourse to the will, convinced that on their own they would get nothing. And it came down to a lawsuit, whereupon don Juan looked for a lawyer who was a past master at legal chicanery. Years and years went by and the benefice was still not funded. And even to this day it would not have been funded had the matter been left to scheming pettifoggers and notaries.

[1] José de Armendáriz, marquis of Castellfuerte, was Peru's eighth viceroy, 1724–1736.

But one day the archbishop had a fit of temper, and said: "Enough red tape."

And without further ado, he ordered that the priest of the parish of San Sebastián proclaim, at High Mass on the following Sunday, a major excommunication of the lawbreaker.

In those days an excommunication weighed not drams, as excommunications do today, but many tons. Excommunications nowadays are like operettas, in which they're a joke and make the excommunicated person a popular figure. They cause people to lose neither sleep nor their appetite. I know people who are dying to have themselves excommunicated.

It is also true that in those times, Rome abused its omnipotence with actions that today, certainly, it would not dare to carry out for fear of ridicule. It not only promoted whomever it pleased to the dignity of a saint, thereby doing no little injustice to living humanity, but also distributed high positions in the Church as it saw fit, and flattered kings to smooth the way for them. Thus in 1619, Paul V gave a cardinal's hat and named as archbishop of Toledo the infante don Fernando, the son of Philip III, a child ten years old, heeding the signs of virtue he gave, signs that when he was a grown man turned out to be meaningless. Clement XII, in the following century, that is to say yesterday morning, promoted a child nine years old, the infante don Luis Antonio, the son of Philip V, who was as much a cardinal and archbishop as the next person, and who also belied the signs of his promotion. And who excommunicated those simoniacal popes: Who? Let us turn the page.

At the time, don Juan was about to enter into a second marriage with doña María Bravo y Maza, an aristocratic and surpassingly beautiful Limeñan, permanently ready for love, who had the luxury of having a spiritual director, with the result that she went to confession only during Lent, and that for the sake of appearances. For the sins she took aboard the ship of her life, it was enough to confess one petty theft a year.

That Sunday, unaware that that morning he had been proclaimed outside the communion of the Church, he went at two in the afternoon to make the usual Sunday visit to doña María. A maid was waiting for him in the doorway overlooking the street, and without allowing him to cross the threshold said to him:

"My mistress asks that you do her to the favor of not disgracing her house by setting foot in it, sir."

That was the source of don Juan's troubles. According to his friends he couldn't have cared less about being excommunicated, but he wasn't about to give up his lady love. He wrote, and his letter was returned without having been opened; he sent go-betweens and they were not received. The lady in question stubbornly refused to so much as acknowledge the greetings of her excommunicated lover.

What was the poor suitor to do? There was nothing for it but to strike his flag and discreetly give in, and that is precisely what he did.

Even Henry IV, a person of more importance than the Aliagas of my country, said: "Paris is well worth a Mass."

And Mariquita, for don Juan, was worth more than Paris.

And so the benefice was funded, and there was a quiet wedding. Since little commemorative medals were not in use in that backward century, you will please excuse me if I fail to tell you the exact date of the wedding ceremony

The Major's Calf[1]

I

*Fragment of a Letter from the Third in Command of
the "Alejandro" Imperial Regiment to the Second in
Command of the "Gerona" Battalion*

Cuzco, December 3, 1822

My dear fellow countryman and comrade: I am taking the opportunity to write to you afforded me by the departure of Pedro Uriondo with letters from the viceroy to General Valdés.

Uriondo is the most entertaining native of Málaga that an Andalusian mother has ever brought into the world. I recommend him most highly to you. He has a mania for betting on anything and everything. In heaven's name, brother, don't give in to the weakness of accepting any bet with him, and for charity's sake pass this warning on to your friends. Uriondo boasts of never having lost a bet, and he is telling the truth. So, then, keep your eyes open and don't allow yourself to be trapped.

Ever yours,

JUAN ECHERRY

---

[1] A pun. The word *pantorrilla* in the Spanish title also means gullibility.

II

Letter from the Second in Command of the "Gerona" to
His Friend in the "Alejandro Imperial"

Sama, December 28, 1822

My unforgettable comrade and kinsman: I am writing to you on a drumhead as the battalion makes ready to march on Tacna, where I consider it a sure thing that we are going to nab Martínez the gaucho before he joins up with Alvarado's[2] troops, following which we propose to make him dance the *zorongo*.[3] From this day on the devil is going to carry off the insurgents. It is now time for Satan to take care of his own, and time that a colonel's epaulettes gleam on the shoulders of this your ever-faithful friend.

I thank you for having brought me the friendship of Captain Uriondo. He is a young man worth his weight in gold, and in the few days that we have had him at headquarters he has been the darling of the officers. How well the devil of a lad sings! And how he knows how to make the strings of a guitar speak!

He will leave tomorrow on his way back to Cuzco with the general's communications for the viceroy.

I regret to tell you that his laurels as the winner of wagers are fading. This morning he maintained that the appearance of hesitation that I have when I walk is due, not to the bullet wound I received in Upper Peru during the Guaqui campaign, but rather to a mole, the size of a grain of rice, which, according to what he stated as though he had examined me and palpated me, must be in the lower part of my left leg. He added, with an aplomb worthy of the doctor of my battalion, that that mole was the head of a vein, and that as time went by, if I didn't get it burned off with lunar caustic, I would suffer mortal heart attacks. I am intimately acquainted with the complaints of my bullet-ridden body and know that I am not covered with moles, so I burst out laughing. Uriondo was a bit piqued, and bet six doubloons that he

---

[2] Rudecindo Alvarado (1792–1872), a high-ranking member of José de San Martín's expeditionary force that liberated Chile and declared Peru's independence.—Ed.
[3] The *zorongo* is a dance of Andalusian origin.—Ed.

would convince me of the existence of the mole. To accept was equivalent to robbing him of his money, and I refused; but he stubbornly stuck to his assertion, and Captain Murrieta, who was a second lieutenant of Dismounted Cossacks in Callao, our fellow countryman Goytisolo, who is now captain of conscripts, Lieutent Sagado, who was with the Hussars and is now serving with the Dragoons; Father Marieluz, who is the men's chaplain, and other officers intervened, all of them telling me:

"Come, major, win those doubloons that are falling to you from the heavens."

Put yourself in my shoes. What would you have done? What I did, surely, showing my bare leg so that one and all might see that there was not even the shadow of a mole. Uriondo turned redder than a parboiled shrimp, and was obliged to confess that he was mistaken. And he handed the six doubloons over to me, which hurt my conscience, but in the end I was obliged to pocket them, for he insisted that he had lost them fair and square.

Against your advice, I was weak enough (as you put it) to agree to a bet between me and the unfortunate Malagan, and I was left, not only with my winnings of six doubloons, but also with the glory of having been the first to best the man you considered invincible.

At this moment, the bugler is blowing assembly. God keep you from a treacherous bullet, and for myself . . . the same.

DOMINGO ECHIZARRAGA

III

Letter from the Third in Command of the "Alejandro Imperial" to the Second in Command of the "Gerona"

Cuzco, January 10, 1823

Comrade: You . . . confounded me.

Captain Uriondo had bet me 30 doubloons that he would make you show your calf on the feast day of the Innocents.

Since yesterday, through your fault, there are 30 big gold cartwheels fewer in the meager purse of your friend, who pardons you for your naiveté and absolves you of having gone against his advice.

JUAN ECHERRY

IV

I the undersigned, guarantee, with all the gravity incumbent upon a collector of Traditions, the authenticity of the signatures of Echerry and Echizarraga.

Ninth Series

The Liberator's Three Etceteras

I

At the end of May 1824, don Pablo Guzmán, the governor of what was then the small town of San Ildefonso de Caraz, received an official letter from the chief of staff of the Army of Independence, written in Huaylas, in which he was advised that since one of the divisions would be arriving two days later, he should ready, without delay, cattle for the troops' mess and forage for the horses. He was further ordered to make ready for His Excellency the Liberator comfortable and decent lodging, with good food, a good bed, etc., etc., etc.

That Bolívar had such sybaritic predilections is no longer a subject for discussion, and Menéndez y Pelayo puts it very well when he says that history takes advantage of everything, and that it is not rare to find in the small the revelation of the large. Many times, without giving it a second thought, I heard soldiers of the generation now passed on that gave us a Homeland and Independence say, when they had incurred expenses by consuming a certain article that there was no imperious need for and tried to exaggerate the figure:

"My dear fellow! You spend more on cigars (for example) than the Liberator spends on cologne."

No one ought to be surprised that don Simón Bolívar was meticulous about his personal toilet and that his daily consumption of cologne amounted to a bottle a day. He was right to do so, and I have nothing but praise for his cleanliness. But the fact is that in the four years he stayed in Peru the national treasury had to pay 8,000 pesos—8,000!

—spent on cologne for the use and consumption of His Excellency the Liberator, which compares with this list drawn up by the Great Captain: In axes, pikes, and hoes, three million pesos.

I am not inventing this. Had the archive of the Supreme Court of Accounts not disappeared in 1884 as a consequence of a raging (and perhaps malicious) fire, I could exhibit a certified copy of the objection offered by the member of the court who was entrusted, in 1829, with the examination of the accounts of the Liberator's commissariat.

It was logical, then, to ready good lodging, a good bed, good food, etc., etc., etc. for the sybaritic don Simón.

As fleas were created to infest skinny dogs in particular, so these three etceteras gave the good governor a great deal to think about, for he was one of those men whose mental powers fit in a syringe, and are thicker than bean soup.

His pondering resulted in the summoning, to ask their advice, of don Domingo Guerrero, don Felipe Gastelumendi, don Justino de Milla and don Jacobo Campos, who were, if we may so put it, the dignitaries of the town.

One of those consulted, a young man who boasted of not suffering from a brain stone, said:

"Do you know, don Pablo, what etcetera means in Spanish?"

"I like the question. It's not an impertinent one, a matter of seeing that I'm in a hurry and asking me about my virginity, as a vulgar slattern put it. I haven't forgotten all my Latin yet, and I know well that etcetera means 'and everything else,' señor don Jacobo."

"Well then, you dimwit, why are you wrinkling your brow? It's clearer than spring water. Haven't you noticed that those three etceteras are placed right after the order for a good bed?"

"Of course I've noticed! But it doesn't make sense to me. This chief of the general staff should have written as Christ teaches us: bread meaning bread, and wine, wine, and not wear me out trying to guess his thoughts."

"But in heaven's name, don't tell me you're one of those people who don't buy onions because they have no stem! Can you imagine a good bed without even one etcetera? Don't you realize yet what the Liberator, who's a great devotee of Venus, needs per day?"

"Say no more, comrade," don Felipe Gastelumendi interrupted. "A girl for each et cetera, if my accounting is not in error."

"Well then, go look for three nymphs, señor governor," said don Justino de Milla "so as to obey the order from above, and take no pains to choose them from among young girls wearing shoes with French heels and fancy petticoats, for His Excellency, so I hear, will feel well served if only the girls are as toothsome as supper on Christmas Eve."

According to don Justino, as the possessor of an erotic palate Bolívar was like that drinker of beer whom the servant at an inn asked: "What beer would you like? Black or white?" "Bring me a halfbreed," was the reply.

"And what do you think?" the governor asked don Domingo Guerrero.

"My good man," don Domingo answered, "as far as I'm concerned there's no reverse side of the page, and you're losing time that should have been used in providing etceteras."

II

If don Simón Bolívar had not had the tastes of an Oriental sultan as far as skirts were concerned, he surely would not figure in History as the liberator of five republics. Women always saved his life, for my friend García Tosta,[1] who has every detail of the hero's life at his fingertips, tells of two incidents that in 1824 were already well known in Peru.

Let us note the first one. While Bolívar was in Jamaica in 1810, the fierce Morillo or his lieutenant Morales sent to Kingston an assassin who sank a dagger into the breast of Major Amestoy, who had lain down in the hammock in which the general was in the habit of sleeping. Because of a torrential rain, the latter had spent the night in the arms of Luisa Crober, a beautiful young Dominican girl, to whom there might well have been sung:

> Colored girl of my heart,
> Colored girl, for your love
> I would journey across the sea
> in a paper boat.[2]

---

[1] Francisco García Tosta (1852–1921), a Venezuelan author of traditions and legends, such as *Leyendas patrióticas* (1893–1898).—Ed.

[2] Morena del alma / mía morena, por tu querer / pasaría la mar / en barquito de papel.

Let us speak of the second incident. Almost two years later, the Spaniard Renovales stole into the patriot camp at midnight, entered the officers' field tent, in which there were two hammocks, and killed Colonel Garrido, who was sleeping in one of them. Don Simón's was empty, because he had left for a love-adventure in a nearby town.

And although it doesn't seem the right moment, it is worth recalling that on the night of the 25th of September, in Bogotá, it was again a woman who saved the life of the Liberator, who had been unwilling to flee the conspirators plotting against him, saying to her: "A woman's advice . . ." And she appeared before the would-be murderers, whom she succeeded in stopping as her lover escaped through a window.

III

Bolívar's reputation as a woman chaser, which had preceded him, played a large part in causing the governor to find the deciphering of the meaning of the three etceteras logical and correct, and after mentally passing in review all the pretty girls of the town, he chose three of the ones who seemed to him to be of surpassing beauty. To each of them this song might be sung without qualms:

> of flowers, the violet,
> of emblems, the cross,
> of nations, my homeland,
> and of women, you.[3]

Two hours before Bolívar arrived, the captain of the militia, don Martín Gamero, headed, as ordered, to the house of the girls who had been chosen, and with only a few words in the way of a preamble, declared the three of them prisoner, and as such took them to the house that had been readied to serve as the Liberator's quarters. Their mothers

---

[3] de las flores, la violeta / de los emblemas, la cruz / de las naciones, mi tierra / y de las mujeres, tú.

protested in vain, claiming that their daughters were not royalists but patriots through and through. It is common knowledge that the right to protest is a feminine right, and that protests are reserved for being heard on Judgment Day, at the hour when lamps are lit.

"Why are you taking away my daughter?" a mother cried.

"What would you have me do?" answered the poor captain. "I'm taking her because I have orders from above."

"Well, don't obey such an order," another elderly woman put in.

"Not obey? Are you mad? You seem to want me to oblige you because of your beautiful eyes, only to have the Liberator fry me for disobedience. No, my good woman, I'm not about to enter into any such agreement."

Meanwhile, Governor Guzmán, accompanied by the dignitaries, went out halfway to meet His Excellency. Bolívar asked him if the rations for the troops' mess were ready, if the barracks were comfortable, if the forage was abundant, if the inn in which he was to be lodged was decent; in short, he overwhelmed him with questions. But—and this surprised don Pablo—he didn't say a word that would reveal a curiosity as to the qualities and merits of the captive etceteras.

Luckily for the grieving families, the Liberator entered San Ildefonso de Caraz at two in the afternoon, acquainted himself with what had gone on, and ordered the dove cote opened, without even exercising the prerogative of a glance at them. It is true that Bolívar was free of temptations at the time, for he was bringing along Manolita Madroña from Huaylas (in his baggage, I presume), a young girl of 18, among the prettiest that God had created by way of females in the administrative department of Ancachs.

Don Simón immediately dressed the presumptuous governor down as only he could, and removed him from his post.

IV

When friends made fun of the ex-governor, bringing up his failure in his post, he would answer:

"The fault wasn't mine. It was the fault of the one who didn't express himself with the necessary clarity in his letter.

> Y no me venga un cualquier
> con argumentos al aire;
> pues no he de decir *Volter*
> donde está escrito Voltaire.[4]

Three etceteras listed after a good bed, for anyone in the know, means three girls . . . and I won't back down from that even at pistol point."

---

[4] And let no one come to me / with frivolous arguments; / for I won't say *Volter* / where Voltaire is written. (Voltaire in the last line rhymes with Spanish *aire*.)

Tenth Series

The Incas Who Played Chess

I

Atahualpa
(To Dr. Evaristo P. Duclos, the eminent chess player)

The Moors, who dominated Spain for seven centuries, introduced the love of the game of chess into the conquered country. Once the expulsion of the Moors by the Catholic Sovereign Isabella was ended, it was only natural to presume that all their habits and pastimes would disappear with them. But far from it; among the heroic captains who destroyed the last bastion of Islamism, the liking for the chess board with 64 squares, or checkers as they are called in heraldry, had taken deep root.

Chess soon ceased to be the favorite game only of men of war, for it became widespread among churchmen, abbots, bishops, canons, and eminent friars. Thus when the discovery and conquest of America were a glorious reality for Spain, seeing anyone named to an important post who came to the New World move pieces on the chess board came to be a sort of guarantee or passport attesting to his social background.

The first book on chess to be published in Spain appeared in the first quarter of a century after the Conquest of Peru, with the title: *Invención liberal y arte de axedrez, por Ruy López de Segovia, clérigo, vecino de la villa de Zafra,*[1] printed in Alcalá de Henares in 1561. Ruy

---

[1] *Free invention and the art of chess, by Ruy López of Segovia, a cleric, resident of the town of Zafra.*

López is considered to be the first chess theorist, and shortly after its appearance, the little work was translated into French and Italian.

The little book circulated widely in Lima until the year 1845, more or less, when copies of *Philidor*² appeared. It was the book that it was imperative to consult in those far-distant days of my adolescence, as was the *Cecinarrica*³ for checkers players. Today a copy of either of these two oldest texts cannot be found in Lima, even if one is willing to pay an eyetooth.

Many of the captains who accompanied Pizarro during the conquest, as well as the governors Vaca de Castro and La Gasca, and the first viceroys, among them Núñez de Vela, marquis of Cañete and count of Nieva, whiled away their leisure time absorbed in the changing fortunes of a game of chess. This was not something that attracted notice, since the first archbishop of Lima was such an aggressive chess player that he managed to undermine even the prestige of royal arms, which could not resist paying him tribute. According to Jiménez de la Espada, when the Royal Tribunal entrusted one of its judges and Archbishop Fray Jerónimo de Loayza with the leadership of the royalist campaign against the revolutionary caudillo, Hernández Girón, the popular muse of the royalist camp, reproached the slothfulness of the man with a toga and the fondness for chess of the man with a miter with this bit of song, poor in rhyme, but rich in truth:

> El uno jugar y el otro dormir,
>   ¡oh qué gentil!
> No comer ni apercibir,
>   ¡oh qué gentil!
> Uno ronca y otro juega . . .
>   ¡y así va la brega!⁴

---

²Francoise André Philidor (1726–1795), French opera composer and famous chess player whose *L'analyze des échecs* (1749) was a landmark treatise on the game.—Ed.

³A reference to *Medula eutropelica calculatoria, que enseña jugar a las damas con espada y broquél, dividida en tres tratados* (1718) by Pablo Cecina Rica y Fergel.—Ed.

⁴The one plays chess and the other sleeps, / Oh what a sight! / Neither eating nor noticing anything, / Oh what a sight! / The one snores and the other plays chess . . . / Oh what a sight!

The soldiers, giving in to inertia in camp and neglectful of their supply of provisions, were already beginning to become demoralized, and perhaps fortune would have favored the rebels if the Tribunal had not decided to send elsewhere the judge who slept like a log and the archbishop who was an *ajedrecista,* or chess player.

(Note that I have italicized the word *ajedrecista,* because despite its common use, it is not to be found in the Dictionary of the Academy, nor does the Dictionary show the form *ajedrista,* which I have seen in a book by the eminent don Juan Valera.[5])

*   *   *

TRADITION HAS IT that the captains Hernando de Soto, Juan de Rada, Francisco de Chavez, Blas de Atienza, and the treasurer Riquelme gathered every afternoon in Cajamarca in the room set aside as a prison for the Inca Atahualpa from November 15, 1532, when the monarch was captured, until two days before his unjustifiable execution, which took place on August 29, 1533.

In the room, the five men named and three or four others not mentioned in succinct and curious notes (that we had at hand, set down in an old manuscript preserved in the former Biblioteca Nacional), had the use of two crudely painted chess boards, set on a wooden chess table. The pieces were made of the same clay that the natives used for fashioning little idols and other objects of native pottery, which nowadays are dug up in *huacas.*[6] Until the first years of the Republic the only pieces known in Peru were those made of ivory, sent by Philippine tradesmen for sale here.

The mind of the Inca must have been deeply preoccupied during the first two or three months of his captivity, for even though he seated himself every afternoon alongside Hernando de Soto, his friend and protector, he gave no sign of having realized how the pieces moved or how fortunes changed during a game. But one afternoon, during the end game of a match between Soto and Riquelme, Hernando made a move toward putting the knight into play, and the Inca, touching him lightly on the arm, said to him in a low voice:

[5]Juan Valera (1824–1905), Spanish novelist whose works include *Pepita Jiménez* (1874) and *Morsamor* (1899).—Ed.

[6] See "Friars' Work!," note 4.—Ed.

"No, captain, no . . . the rook!"

Everyone was surprised. After a few brief seconds of reflection, Hernando played the castle, as Atahualpa had advised him, and a few moves later Riquelme experienced the inevitable checkmate.

After that afternoon, and always giving him the white pieces to play as a sign of respect and courtesy, Captain Hernando de Soto invited the Inca to play just one match with him, and after a couple of months the disciple was a credit to his teacher. They played as equals.

The notes that I have mentioned tell how the other Spanish chess players, with the exception of Riquelme, also invited the Inca to play, but he always excused himself for not accepting, telling each of them through the interpreter Felipillo:

"I play very little, and Your Grace plays a great deal."

Popular tradition assures us that the Inca would not have been condemned to death had he remained untutored in chess. The people say that Atahualpa paid with his life for the checkmate that Riquelme suffered because of his advice on that memorable afternoon. In the famous council of 24 judges called together by Pizarro, Atahualpa was sentenced to the death penalty by 13 votes for and 11 against. Riquelme was one of the 13 who signed the death sentence.

II

Manco Inca
(To Jesús Elías y Salas)

After the unjustifiable execution of Atahualpa, don Francisco Pizarro made his way to Cuzco in 1534, and to gain the devotion of the Cuzcans declared that he was not coming to take away from the caciques their lands and properties or to disregard their preeminence. Since the murderous usurper of the throne of the legitimate ruler Inca Huáscar had already been punished by being put to death, Pizarro proposed to hand over the imperial insignia to Inca Manco,[7] a youth 18 years old, the

---

[7]When Francisco Pizarro arrived in Peru in April of 1831, the Inca empire was torn by a civil war between two sons of the Inca Huayna Capac: Atahualpa and Huáscar. Huáscar was executed by Atahualpa in 1532, and Atahualpa by the Spaniards in 1533. That same

legitimate heir of his brother Huáscar. The coronation took place with great solemnity, and following it Pizarro proceeded to the valley of Jauja, and then to the Rimac or Pachacamac valley to found the capital of the future viceroy.

I needn't give an account of the events and causes that occasioned the breaking off of relations between the Inca and the Spaniards headed by Juan Pizarro, and on his death, by his brother Hernando. I need only note that Manco contrived to flee Cuzco and establish his government on the high plateaux of the Andes, where it was always impossible for the conquistadors to defeat him.

In the conflict between the supporters of Pizarro and the partisans of Almagro, Manco lent the latter certain services, and once the ruin and death of Almagro the Younger were an accomplished fact, 12 or 15 of the vanquished, among whose number were the captains Diego Méndez and Gómez Pérez, found refuge with the Inca, who had set up his court in Vilcapampa.

Méndez, Pérez, and four or five other of their companions in misfortune diverted themselves by playing bowls and chess. The Inca easily *hispanified* himself (a verb of that century, equivalent to today's *hispanicized* himself), acquiring a great fondness for and even skill in both games, and becoming an outstanding chess player.

It was written in the stars that, like the Inca Atahualpa, his love of chess was to be fatal for the Inca Manco.

One afternoon Inca Manco and Gómez Pérez were absorbed in a game, with Diego Méndez and three caciques as onlookers.

Manco made a move to castle his king, not allowed at that point by the rules of the game, and Gómez Pérez argued:

"It's too late for you to do that, you cheater."

We do not know whether the Inca realized the insulting implications of the strange Castilian word, but he insisted on defending what he believed to be a correct and valid move. Gómez turned around to his countryman Diego Méndez and said to him:

"Look, captain, at what this swine of an Indian is trying to pull!"

---

year, a third son of Huayna Capac, Manco, was recognized as ruler of the Inca realm by the Spanish conquistadors. Manco rebelled against his Spanish sponsors in 1836.—Ed.

Here I yield the floor to the anonymous chronicler whose manuscript, which goes as far as the era of the viceroy Toledo, is included in Volume VIII of the *Documentos inéditos del Archivo de Indias* : "The Inca then raised his hand and gave the Spaniard a slap in the face. The latter put his hand to his dagger and dealt him two stab wounds, from which he died immediately. The Indians hastened to take vengeance, and hacked to pieces the aforesaid killer and as many Spaniards as were in that province of Vilcapampa."

Several chroniclers say that the quarrel took place during a game of bowls, but others state that the tragic event came about because of a heated disagreement during a game of chess.

Popular tradition among Cuzcans is what I have related, basing myself as well on the authority of the anonymous sixteenth-century writer.

Between Garibaldi . . . and Me

I

Around the year 1865 I was the guest in Le Havre of Luis Cisneros, who held the post of consul of Peru there.

Almost every Sunday we had a visitor, an old man 70 years old, who had lunch with us and entertained us with his talk of America and the war of Independence.

His name was Monsieur Fysquet, and he had a modest post in Le Havre, I don't remember whether it was as a security guard or in the harbor master's office.

When, after the capture of Miranda and the expulsion of his lieutenant general Bolívar,[1] Spanish dominion in Venezuela appeared to be unquestionable, don Simón was forced to wander from one of the Antilles to another, seeking men to revive the revolution.

Petion, the president of Haiti, worked out a secret treaty with Bolívar and secured for him a fleet of brigantines, command of which the latter entrusted to the French naval officer Luis Brion, giving him the title of admiral of the naval forces in Venezuela.

Fysquet shipped out on one of the vessels as chief petty officer, and told us long and amusing tales about his adventures at sea, as well as recounting intimate anecdotes about Bolívar.

[1] Francisco de Miranda (1750–1816), also known as the "Precursor" of Latin American Independence, assumed dictatorial powers during Venezuela's First Republic (1811–1812). When he ceded power to superior Spanish forces, Simón Bolívar arrested him and turned him in to the royalists before going into exile in New Granada.—Ed.

He frequently came out with these phrases: "In the days when I conversed with the Liberator aboard ship" or "In my conversations with Bolívar," but we never managed to find out what the conversations were about.

Finally, one morning I made him down a good many glasses of a magnificent burgundy that had just been given to Cisneros, and I discovered that the conversations that he spoke of in the plural had never gone beyond the singular.

One afternoon off Carúpano, a sail was seen on the horizon, and fearing that it was a Spanish vessel, the admiral notified Bolívar.

The latter came on deck on his way to the bridge, and met Fysquet, leaning over the gunwale and looking through a spyglass at the suspicious ship.

Given Bolívar's impetuousness, it was only to be expected that he did not have the patience to wait the half minute that he would have needed to join Brion on the bridge and use his spyglass.

Without a word, Bolívar took the spyglass from Fysquet, searched the horizon for half a minute, and not trusting his eyesight, gave it back to Fysquet and said to him:

"Does that ship have a flag?"

"No, general, but it is hoisting one this minute."

"Is it a Spanish flag?"

"No, general, it is English."

"Then there is no reason for alarm."

And he headed for the bridge to join Brion.

When he came to lunch with us, Fysquet proudly displayed on his old but well-brushed frock coat the gold medal that Venezuela and Colombia awarded to those who fought for its independence. If the curiosity of some of my readers leads them to want to know more about the chief petty officer who was a contemporary of Bolívar, I recommend that they read a delightful novel by Luis Cisneros entitled *La medalla de un libertador.*

II

Well then, *mutatis mutandis,*[2] my conversation with don José Garibaldi was cut from the same cloth as Fysquet's with don Simón Bolívar.

---

[2] The necessary changes having been made [Latin].

In 1851, the poet Trinidad Fernández and I, a lad of 18 Februaries, were columnists and proofreaders at *El Correo de Lima,* with the hefty salary of 30 pesos a month. What a sinecure!

The print shop did business in a large house on the calle de Aumente.

The editor's office was located in a spacious room off the patio.

The furniture consisted of a desk with a blue baize top for the boss, two extremely rickety little tables, a wooden bench that had probably belonged to some convent, and a dozen more or less broken down chairs.

The get-together of friends began a little after four o'clock in the afternoon. Those who attended regularly were, among others, the members of the Supreme Court, Mariátegui, León y Lazo (the father of the famous painter), Colonel Juan Espinosa (who signed his writings with the pseudonym "The Soldier of the Andes"), and a French merchant, don Carlos Ledos, a sketch of whom I feel obliged to offer my reader.

Ledos, who had come originally from Mexico, had lived for years in Lima. He wanted to set up a farm for growing silkworms, and when his efforts did not meet with success he established a mercantile agency in the calle de las Mantas, an occupation that went quite well for him, and might have gone very well indeed had he not had the wild idea of becoming a journalist and a patriot in a foreign country, for rather than settling bills and doing sums, he busied himself in giving the government of Peru lessons in running the country from the columns of *El Correo,* and all his articles appeared with the initials C. L.

When those in authority did not provide him with good and abundant material to write about, he resorted to a subject that, under his pen, was inexhaustible: religious tolerance. He consumed more ink on the subject that the famous Tostado, bishop of Avila, in all his works put together.

After the revolution of 1848 in France, Mazzini and other apostles of freedom began to gain favor as they spread the idea that he would bring unity to Italy and the disappearance of the temporal power of the Popes. Such grandiose ideals must not have earned the sympathy of don Carlos Ledos, for he published an article in which he treated Mazzini very condescendingly, derided Carlos Alberto and the courage of the Italians, and ended by calling Garibaldi a second-rate hero.

Here begins the story of my relationship with Garibaldi.

It was shortly after two o'clock on the afternoon of December 6, 1851, and I was at my editor's desk scribbling a page of my column, when a gentleman appeared, and without crossing the threshold, said to me:

"Good afternoon. Has the Frenchman Ledos come in yet?"

"No, sir," I answered him.

"What time does he come in?"

"After four."

"Can you tell me where I can find him at present?"

"In the calle de las Mantas, in his office."

With no more than a slight nod of his head, the person who had asked me the three questions strode off.

He was no less than the heroic paladin of the seven-year siege of Montevideo, the great captain who had humiliated the battle-hardened army of the tyrant Rosas, which up until then had always been victorious: It was don José Garibaldi,[3] who had been in Peru for several months; thanks to his renown he was looked upon in Lima with admiration and greeted with respect when people met him on the main streets of the city.

A quarter of an hour had not gone by when there arrived at the print shop the news that something serious was going on near the main square, and this columnist, in fulfillment of his obligation, rushed to the calle de las Mantas.

There was an immense crowd, and the prefect of Lima, on horseback, with a squad of police was doing his best to break it up.

In the doorway of Ledos's office, surrounded by many gentlemen, was Garibaldi, and a few steps away, señor Ledos, with a ruler in his hand and fighting to get loose from Dr. Douglas (a famous doctor in Lima) and others who were holding him down. Both of them had blood on their faces.

What had happened? On saying goodbye to me after I had given him directions to Ledos's office, Garibaldi had rushed to the calle de las Mantas and asked a passerby to point out Ledos's office to him.

---

[3] Guiseppe Garibaldi (1807–1882) lived in Brazil and Uruguay between 1836 and 1848. In Uruguay, he distinguished himself as head of the Italian Legion, and fought against the Argentinian dictator Juan Manuel de Rosas. After his failure to hold Rome against Neapolitan and French forces in 1849, Garibaldi retreated and went into exile in Tangier, Staten Island, and Peru.

He was there, pen in hand, settling a bill, and in the back of the shop a clerk was busy opening a box of merchandise.

Garibaldi had in his left hand an issue of the newspaper and in his right his cane. A counter separated him from his adversary, who was writing in a large portfolio or file.

"Are you the riffraff who has written this slander about Carlos Alberto and Italy?" Garibaldi asked him in correct French.

"Riffraff, no; the one who wrote that, yes," don Carlos answered arrogantly.

The illustrious Italian did not wait to hear more, and dealt the French polemicist two blows with his cane, and the latter, with a nimbleness that belied his age, leapt over the counter with a ruler in his hand.

The caning that Garibaldi gave the irascible journalist to keep him from hitting him in the head with the ruler was not very gentle.

Two merchants of the neighborhood intervened, and succeeded, with no little effort, in separating the adversaries.

Don Antonio Malagrida, a wealthy Italian merchant of the day, in whose house, of recent construction, he had had Garibaldi as a guest when he had just arrived from Callao, appeared on the scene and led his excited companion away by the arm. Malagrida's house was at the corner of Palacio and Polvos Azules, with large shops in the lower part.

III

Fysquet's conversation with Bolívar, while it may be as laconic as mine with Garibaldi, had many fewer consequences. Fysquet's did not end with a naval battle; it was pure alarm or complete nonsense.

Do you believe that if Garibaldi had not spoken with me, and if I had not had the unconscious indiscretion to give him the address of old Ledos, blood would have flowed? Let it be acknowledged that the conversation between Garibaldi and yours truly is destined to go down in history.

Consolación

I

Reader, are you hunchbacked?

If, to your misfortune, the hand of the Creator has placed on your shoulders that bulky sugar loaf known as a hump, throw away this page without reading it, and I swear to you that you will not have lost much.

It has always been said that hunchbacks are sarcastic and evil-minded, and that the protuberance they carry about is a depository of venomous satires and biting blasphemies. God keep me from accepting such an opinion, since I am someone who has known one of these unfortunates who had the heart of an angel buried beneath so rough and deformed an exterior. Andrés was like a beautiful diamond mounted in an iron setting.

II

Andrés was 19. I have never seen a gaze more gently languid than his, in eyes as blue as a cloudless sky. His words had something of the perfume of innocence, and his smile was as tender as a maiden's. We friends of his never hear him voice a complaint about Fate, and when we had a feeling, whether slight or serious, to tell him about, one of those infernal disappointments that break one's heart string by string, the words that came to his lips were always ones of blessing, peace, and consolation. There was in his voice an echo suggestive of a profound melancholy that moved us, and after hearing him our distress disappeared. That is why his friends called him "Consolación."

III

Youth without love is like a fountain without murmurs. Love for that age of life is what aroma is to a flower, what blue is to the sky. Take away from youth that divine fire and you will have robbed it of its illusions, you will have taken away its faith and turned the world into an infinite space where deep shadows reign.

Andrés loved Cesarina in silence. Never did the lad's lips dare to declare the passion that was consuming him, because he feared that his love would become an object of mockery. Can a deformed being not long for the bliss of having another soul that understands his? Perhaps not. A woman's exquisite sensibility sees the sublime as her ideal, paying little attention to what is beautiful.

Cesarina did not understand the treasure of love buried in Andrés's heart.

One afternoon we noted that Andrés's face was paler than usual.

"Are you sick?" we asked him.

"Yes. Heartsick," he answered.

There was such intimate pain in his voice that it startled us.

"Could you be in love?"

Consolación looked at us, trying to make his face register as great an air of indifference as possible, and replied:

"Can a hunchback be in love?"

"Then what's the matter, Andrés?"

The usual thing . . . my friend . . . the usual thing, my hump!"

But we saw that Andrés was so deeply affected that we understood that he had just received one of those wounds to his soul for which there is no balm on earth.

What had happened?

Consolación had just declared his love to Cesarina, who gave a merry, resounding peal of laughter, and addressing three girls who were friends of hers standing in a hallway in her house, she said:

"Shall I let you in on a bit of news?"

Andrés looked at her in terror.

"What is it?" the friends asked as one.

"I can't help laughing . . . you'll never guess . . . Andrés is in love!"

And the happy chorus burst into laughter because it could not imagine that a hunchback had the passions of a man.

As I was coming downstairs from Andrés's rooms I heard a pistol shot.

VI

That night there was a ball at Cesarina's. When I entered her salon she was in the arms of a young gallant who was leading her in the seductive turns of a Polish dance.

I approached her and said in her ear:

"Andrés has just died of love for you."

"How utterly mad of him!" she said with a smile.

And drawn away by her partner, she was lost in the confusion of the ball.

That young woman who was so beautiful had a heart of ice.[1]

[1]This article, in rough draft in 1851, is a faithful reminiscence of this tragic event that took place in my days as a schoolboy. I had forgotten it, but by chance there came to my hand the small periodical in which it had appeared more than half a century ago. I reread it with intimate affection, and for that reason I include it in this book [Author's note].

Appendix
Listing of the Peruvian Traditions by Historical Period

"A Mother's Love"
"The Witches of Ica"
"Saint Thomas's Sandal"
"An Adventure of the Poet-Viceroy"
"A Heretical Viceroy and a Rascally Bell Ringer"
"Drink, Father, It Will Keep You Alive!"
"The Christ in Agony"
"The Countess Who Was Summoned"
"A Viceroy and an Archbishop"
"The Latin of a Young Lady of Lima"
"Santiago the Flier"
"Two Excommunications"
"Everyone the Master in His Own House"
"Margarita's Wedding Dress"
"The Corregidor of Tinta"
"The Black Mass"
"Abascal's Clever Trick"

INDEPENDENCE AND REPUBLICAN PERIODS (NINETEENTH CENTURY)

"The Protectress and the Liberatrix"
"The Major's Calf"
"The Royalist Smells of Death to Me"
"The King of the Camanejos"
"Bolívar's Justice"
"Canterac's Bugler"
"The Liberator's Three Etceteras"
"Between Garibaldi . . . and Me"
"Consolación"

Bibliography

SELECTED WORKS BY RICARDO PALMA

Poesías. Lima: Imprenta de J. M. Masías, 1855.

Corona patriótica. Lima: Colección de apuntes bibliográficos, 1860.

Anales de la Inquisición de Lima. Lima: Tipografía de Aurelio Alfaro, 1863.

Congreso constituyente. Semblanzas de un campanero. Lima: Imprenta J. M. Noriega, 1867.

Tradiciones. Primera Serie. Lima: Imprenta del Estado, 1872.

Tradiciones. Segunda Serie. Lima: Imprenta Liberal de El Correo del Perú, 1874.

Tradiciones. Tercera Serie. Lima: Benito Gil, 1875.

Tradiciones. Cuarta Serie. Lima: Benito Gil, 1877.

Monteagudo y Sánchez Carrión. Lima: missing pub., 1877.

Verbos y gerundios. Lima: Benito Gil, 1877.

Tradiciones. Quinta Serie. Lima: Imprenta del Universo de Carlos Prince, 1883.

Tradiciones. Sexta Serie. Lima: Imprenta del Universo de Carlos Prince, 1883.

Refutación a un compendio de Historia del Perú. Lima: Torres Aguirre, 1886.

Ropa vieja. Lima: Imprenta y Librería del Universo, 1891.

Tradiciones peruanas. (4 vols.) Barcelona: Montaner y Simón, 1893–1896.

Neologismos y americanismos. Lima: Imprenta y Librería de Carlos Prince, 1896.

Recuerdos de España precedido de La Bohemia de mi Tiempo. Lima: Imprenta "La Industria," 1899.

Cachivaches. Lima: Imprenta de Torres Aguirre, 1900.

Papeletas lexicográficas. Dos mil setecientas voces que hacen falta en el Diccionario. Lima: Imprenta "La Industria," 1903.

Mis últimas tradiciones peruanas. Barcelona: Casa editorial Maucci, 1906.

Apéndice a mis últimas tradiciones peruanas y cachivachería. Barcelona: Editorial Maucci, 1910.
Epistolario. (2 vols.) Lima: Editorial Cultura Antártica S.A., 1949.

SELECTED EDITIONS OF THE *PERUVIAN TRADITIONS*

Las mejores tradiciones peruanas. Barcelona: Editorial Maucci, 1917.
Tradiciones peruanas. Madrid: Calpe, 1924–1925.
Traditions peruviennes. Trans. Matilde Pomés. Paris: Imprimerie Floch, 1938.
Flor de tradiciones. Ed. George W. Umphrey and Carlos García Prada. México: Ed. Cultura, 1943.
The Knights of the Cape and Thirty-Seven Other Selections from the Tradiciones Peruanas of Ricardo Palma. Ed. and trans. Harriet de Onís. New York: Alfred Knopf, 1945.
Tradiciones peruanas completas. Ed. Edith Palma. Madrid: Aguilar S.A., 1952.
Cien tradiciones peruanas. Ed. José Miguel Oviedo. Barcelona: Biblioteca Ayacucho, 1977.
Tradiciones peruanas. Ed. Julio Ortega. España: Archivos, CSIC, 1993.

SELECTED SECONDARY WORKS

Andreu, Alicia. "Una nueva aproximación al lenguaje en las *Tradiciones peruanas* de Ricardo Palma," *Revista de Estudios Hispánicos,* no. 2 (May 1989): 21–36.
Arora, Shirley. *Proverbial Comparisons in Ricardo Palma's Tradiciones peruanas.* Los Angeles: University of California Press, 1966.
Compton, Merlin D. *Ricardo Palma.* Boston: Twayne Publishers, 1982.
Cornejo Polar, Antonio. *La formación de la tradición literaria en el Perú.* Lima: Centro de Estudios y Publicaciones, 1989.
Durán Luzio, Juan. "Ricardo Palma, cronista de una sociedad barroca." *Revista Iberoamericana* vol. 53, no. 140 (July–September 1987): 581–93.
Escobar, Alberto. "Tensión, lenguaje y estructura: las *Tradiciones peruanas.*" *Tradiciones peruanas,* 1993: 539–90.
———. "Comentario a 'Don Dimas de la Tijereta.'" Flores: 96–102.
———. "Comentario a 'Los ratones de Fray Martín.'" Flores: 123–27.
Feliu-Cruz, Guillermo. *En torno de Ricardo Palma.* Santiago: Prensas de la Universidad de Chile, 1933.
Flores, Angel, ed. *Orígenes del cuento hispanoamericano (Ricardo Palma y sus tradiciones).* Mexico: Premia Editoria, 1982.
González, Aníbal. "Las tradiciones entre la historia y el periodismo." *Tradiciones peruanas,* 1993: 459–77.

Loayza, Luis. "Palma y el pasado." *Tradiciones peruanas,* 1993: 523‒33.

Mariátegui, José Carlos. *Seven Interpretive Essays on Peruvian Reality.* Trans. Marjory Urquidi. Austin: University of Texas Press, 1971.

Miró, César. *Don Ricardo Palma; el patriarca de las Tradiciones.* Buenos Aires: Editorial Losada, 1953.

Monguió, Luis. "Comentario a 'Los ratones de Fray Martín.'" Flores: 127‒31.

Nuñez, Estuardo. *Ricardo Palma escritor continental: las huellas de Palma en los tradicionistas hispanoamericanos.* Lima: Fondo Editorial, 1998.

Ortega, Julio. "Las *Tradiciones peruanas* y el proceso cultural del siglo XIX hispanoamericano," *Tradiciones peruanas,* 1993: 409‒38.

Oviedo, José Miguel. *Genio y Figura de Ricardo Palma.* Buenos Aires: Editorial Universitaria de Buenos Aires, 1965.

―――. "Palma entre ayer y hoy." *Cien tradiciones peruanas:* ix‒xli.

Palma, Angelica. *Ricardo Palma.* Buenos Aires: Editorial Tor, 1933.

Rodríguez Arenas, Flor María. "Las Tradiciones y el proceso de su recepción." *Tradiciones peruanas,* 1993: 490‒502.

―――. "Historia editorial y literaria." *Tradiciones peruanas,* 1993: 381‒409.

Rodríguez Peralta, Phyllis. "Liberal undercurrents in Palma's *Tradiciones peruanas.*" *Revista de estudios hispánicos,* vol. 15, no. 2 (May 1981): 283‒97.

Salazar Bondi, Sebastián. *Lima la horrible.* Mexico: Ediciones Era, 1964.

Salomón, Noel. "Comentario a 'Las orejas del Alcalde.'" Flores: 107‒19.

Sociedad Amigos de Palma. *Ricardo Palma, 1833‒1933.* Lima: Sociedad Amigos de Palma, 1933.

Tanner, Roy. *The Humor of Irony and Satire in the Tradiciones peruanas.* Columbia: University of Missouri Press, 1986.

―――. "Las anotaciones marginales de Ricardo Palma en la Biblioteca Nacional." *Romance Quarterly,* vol 37, no. 1 (Feb. 1990): 83‒93.

Unzueta, Fernando. "Las Tradiciones peruanas y la cuestión nacional." *Tradiciones peruanas,* 1993: 503‒19.